the series on school reform

Patricia A. Wasley
Coalition of
Essential Schools

Ann Lieberman
NCREST

Joseph P. McDonald
Annenberg Institute
for School Reform

SERIES EDITORS

This series also incorporates earlier titles in the
Professional Development and Practice Series

REACHING

FOR A

BETTER STANDARD

ENGLISH SCHOOL INSPECTION AND
THE DILEMMA OF ACCOUNTABILITY FOR AMERICAN SCHOOLS

Thomas A. Wilson

TEACHERS
COLLEGE
PRESS

Teachers College, Columbia University
New York and London

Published by Teachers College Press, 1234 Amsterdam Avenue, New York, N.Y. 10027

Library of Congress Cataloging-in-Publication Data

Wilson, Thomas A., 1938–
    Reaching for a better standard: English school inspection and the
dilemma of accountability for American schools / Thomas A. Wilson
        p.   cm.
    Includes bibliographical references (p.   ) and index.
    ISBN 0-8077-3497-7. — ISBN 0-8077-3496-9 (pbk.)
    1. Educational evaluation—United States.   2. School management
and organization—Great Britain—Case studies.   3. School management
and organization—United States.   4. Educational change—United
States.   5. Education—Standards—United States.   I. Title.
LB2822. 75.W55   1996
379. 1 '54' 0973—dc20   95-37947

ISBN 0-8077-3496-9 (paper)
ISBN 0-8077-3497-7 (cloth)

Printed on acid-free paper
Manufactured in the United States of America
03 02 01 00 99 98 97 96   8 7 6 5 4 3 2 1

For my mother and father
with love and memories of what's past;

For my wife, Leslie Oh
with love;

For our children: Rachel, Thomas, John, Debby, Mark, and Peter
with love and anticipation of what's ahead.

CONTENTS

FOREWORD

In a democracy, how does the public come to know, judge, and improve its schools? In the U.S., especially in the last thirty years, Americans have come to know their schools by the numbers: test scores, dropout rates, costs of vandalism, and incidents of violence. These numbers, derived from social science concepts and the quest for quantifiable precision under the mantle of scientific objectivity, have led to a harsh judgment: Schools have failed. They don't prepare our children to be workers and citizens and they are increasingly unsafe. Based upon such social science knowledge and judgments, the recipe for American school reform in these decades has solidified state authority by mandating higher academic standards in order to improve the numbers. States deliver reform after reform to districts and their schools in new academic standards, curricula, tests, extended school years, site-based management and shared decision making. But, as time passes, they turn into little more than slogans that fit nicely upon car bumpers. Why?

There are, of course, many reasons for the life and death of school reforms but a few deserve more attention than they have received in the current surge of school reform delivered by national and state policy makers, foundation officials, academic entrepreneurs, and corporate executives. Because most Americans come to know their schools through the numbers and, in the light of those numbers, have come to judge schools as failing, social-science driven reforms have seldom concentrated upon the central task of schooling—teaching and learning. Yes, there have been obligatory references to teaching and learning but the talk often disappears as the reform is implemented. Over time, what actually happens in schools and classrooms between adults and children gets disconnected from reformers' best intentions.

The foot soldiers of reform—teachers and school administrators—soon recognize that once the reform talk disappears, the new policy or program has little to do with the daily realities that they face in schools. Moreover, it becomes increasingly clear that the practitioner–knowledge that they have gained over the years working in classrooms is dismissed or given only token attention by those who make policy. So the very people who are crucial for any improvement in teaching and learning steadily become disengaged from the hard work of improving schools because others outside their workplace decide what the reform is to be and how they are to do it. Thus, over the last thirty years, how Americans have come to know, judge, and improve their schools has largely ignored the central tasks of teaching and learning and a sizable body of practitioner–knowledge resting within the very people who are responsible for schooling.

Now along comes Tom Wilson with a powerful tale of how another country has come to know, judge, and improve its schools. Wilson's story of how Britain established the tradition of Inspection, how the system has worked for a century-and-a-half, and what is now happening to it in the 1990s is a mirror held up to American eyes about the importance of teaching and learning and the strengths of practitioner wisdom in judging and improving schools. But it is a cautionary, if not an ironic, tale because recent changes in Britain have altered substantially Her Majesty's Inspectorate (HMI). It has become more closely aligned with the American tradition of social science concepts, quantifiable evaluations of school progress, and externally-imposed standards.

In a fresh and vivid style of writing about schools, Wilson will provoke readers to re-examine how expert knowledge, not practitioner know-how, has come to dominate how Americans judge and improve schools. His tracing of the 150-year history of inspection in England, with its twists and turns, locates the central premise of inspection as practitioners knowing what happens in classrooms and schools and then judging their value. That trust in experienced teachers and heads of schools, he argues, is the rock upon which worthy school reform is built in a democracy; everything else is wordplay. His description of how individual Inspectors' opinions are seasoned and expanded through repeated group discussions—moderation as it is called—to become a team judgment when Inspectors visit a school will be an eye-opener for American readers.

The process of "moderation" will be familiar to academics who make tenure and promotion decisions and other guilds of practitioners where group discussions both elaborate and broaden strong individual opinions about what is the best group decision. It will be unfamiliar, however, to most American teachers and principals who can only make weak comparisons to preparations for accreditation reviews. What will also become clear to readers after reading chapters 3 and 4 is that the tradition of Inspection has been built upon trust in gifted veteran teachers and principals using their practical experience to figure out what actual standards are at work in a school and how a group of Inspectors spending a week at a school can help that school improve what a faculty does for its students.

Tom Wilson is wise in not providing us with a final chapter that neatly shows how inspection could be transplanted to the U.S. He resists that temptation because he respects us as readers and wants us to reflect upon British–U.S. differences. He provokes us to consider what about it is useful in an American context. He raises difficult questions for American readers, especially the linkage between making policy and being informed about what actually happens in schools.

A cardinal purpose of HMI reports is to inform policy. Wilson's recording of the history of HMI points out that the reports and actions of inspectors have had some influence. In the American experience however, what has informed educational policy, most clearly in the last half-century, has been economic, social, political, and demographic changes impinging on schools with the use of social science evidence getting dragged in to support policy mandates. The notion of experienced and thoughtful teachers and principals writing reports, forming commissions, and working to inform educational policy has yet to take root in American soil. A reliance upon practitioner knowledge as a basis for judging what happens in schools and those judgments as a basis for school improvement remains foreign to American policy makers and educators. Such thoughts came to me as a gift from the author's reluctance to provide readers with easy answers.

And that is the way Tom is. I have known him for over thirty years as a gifted and irreverent teacher (we team taught an American Studies class at Cardozo High School in Washington, D.C. decades ago). Tom's dedication to improving schooling and his passionate commitment to the centrality of better schooling to a democracy that works for all its citizens is well captured in this study of the English system of inspecting schools.

Larry Cuban
Stanford University

Preface

This book is an exploration of the way Americans come to know and judge schools. It is clear that how we know schools permeates not only how we think about them, talk about them, and make policy for them, but also directly affects what teachers and students do in them.

Often, when we consider what schools do and how well they do it, we must stretch to understand new jargon, consider weak and irrelevant information, and be guided by ideas that confuse what we thought we valued. We end up learning more about the difficulties in how we know schools than we learn about schools.

In August 1991, after spending most of the preceding 30 years working to reform public schools, my musings brought me to that conclusion. Most of my work was part of major national reform efforts and a great deal of it was focused on school assessment and accountability. I had spent 2 years in the Philippines, 9 years in Washington, D.C., Cambridge, and Boston, 15 years in Chicago, and most recently 6 years in Providence, Rhode Island, with the Coalition of Essential Schools at Brown University. Like most reformers, I believed I could overcome the difficulties of reform with conviction and energy.

In August 1991 I found my energy depleted for the second time in those 30 years. Looking back at what had happened, pondering my accomplishments and the difficulties I had faced, I realized that some of the difficulties were mine, but not all.

The intensifying national discussion about poor school results and reform made it even more important to think about how we know and judge schools. Plans for new standards, new assessments, and the philosophical critiques of the existing approaches revealed that our tradition for knowing and judging school could not meet these demands. Our ingenious habit of skirting, knowing, and making judgements about the quality of what actually happens in schools had become a major flaw.

Upon hearing about the English tradition of school inspection in the 1970s, I was intrigued. In this different national tradition of knowing schools the work of inspectors is to visit them. I decided to learn about inspection and to see what it might offer American education. In April 1992 my wife, Leslie Oh, and I embarked for England, where I would plunge myself into the world of English school inspectors for 10 months.

Interesting challenges arose immediately. The English school reform, begun by the Education Reform Act of 1988, was having a definite impact on every English school I visited. My American experience had not prepared me for this. My amazement was soon pushed aside by questions about whether these changes were good or whether they were making schools worse. In addition to the noticeable reform of schools, the Government had serious plans to change inspection. In February 1992 Parliament passed the Education (Schools) Act, targeted to recast both the organization and method of inspection. What I found in England confirmed my earlier judgement that my task required an eclectic approach.

To garner the requisite understanding of the practice of inspection, I spent most of my time in England shadowing 39 local and national inspectors while they worked. I visited 14 elementary schools and five high schools, spending 2 days to a week at seven schools and 2 or more weeks at two others. In a number of ongoing conversations inspectors carefully reviewed early drafts of my attempts to describe the method. Although there is scant material available that is appropriate to the study, I found a good sample of historical documents.

During the course of the study, I concluded that the methods and organizational structures of inspection are clearly a national tradition for knowing and judging schools, that the ideas of inspection challenge the basic assumptions of the American tradition, and that inspection provokes us to invent interesting possibilities for American education.

§

Many people supported my work and aroused my thinking and writing by sharing their ideas, their curiosity, and their experiences. Without their support, skills, and thoughtful probes, this book would not have been possible.

IBM, The Pew Charitable Trusts, the Carnegie Corporation of New York, The Pew Forum on Educational Reform, the Joyce Foundation, the Lilly Endowment, and the Rockefeller Foundation provided the requisite financial support.

A number of staff from these funding organizations and others provided encouragement and advice: Janet Carter, Warren Chapman, Jamie Beck Jensen, Joan Lipsitz, Sam Matsa, Milbrey McLaughlin, Lallie O'Brien, Hugh Price, Robert Schwartz, and Vivien Stewart.

The Project Senior Advisors (from both sides of the Atlantic) offered counsel on many matters related to funding, design, and presentation: Michael Alexander, David K. Cohen, Lawrence Cuban, Linda Darling-Hammond, Robert V. Dumont, Jr., Frederick Erickson, David Green, Thomas James, James Learmonth, George F. Madaus, Samuel M. Matsa, Barbara MacGilchrist, Neil McClelland, Joseph McDonald, Deborah Meier, Lauren Resnick, Arnold Shore, and Theodore R. Sizer.

Boston College, Brown University, and the University of London provided the necessary institutional bases. The following were key in arranging and providing that support: George Madaus and Suzanne Hanson, Center for Study of Testing, Evaluation and Educational Policy at Boston College; Thomas James, Reginald Archambault, Yvette Nachmias-Beau, Ann D'Abrosca, and Patricia Balsofiore, Education Department at Brown University; and Barbara MacGilchrist, the Institute of Education at the University of London.

A number of people contributed directly to the completion of the research tasks: John Abbott, Charlene Franklin, Alan Ginet, David Green, Walter Haney, Clive Hopes, James Learmonth, Brendan Rapple, Ann Jones, Michelle Riconscente, P. Singh, and Arabella Wood.

Those who made valuable comments and suggestions on drafts of the manuscript include Michael Alexander, John Bartholomew, Larry Cuban, Linda Darling-Hammond, Robert Dumont, Frederick Erickson, Norma Empringham, David Green, Steven Groak, Harold Howe II, Thomas James, Denise Jenkins, James Learmonth, George Madaus, Colin McCall, Joseph McDonald, Deborah Meier, Mary Helen Miller, Lallie O'Brien, Debby Pattiz, Judith Pelchat, Steven Perkins, Lauren Resnick, Caroline St. John-Brooks, Dorothy Shipps, Arnold Shore, Steven Seidel, P. Singh, Theodore R. Sizer, Maggie Szabo, Brian Wilcox, John P. Wilson, and Peter N. Wilson.

Teachers College Press and my editor, Brian Ellerbeck, furnished unusual care and skill in both the editing and publishing of the book.

This book would not exist without the cooperation of 61 British colleagues, as well as many teachers, students, principals, and LEA staff. Except for those few who have explicitly given me permission to list their names, I have honored the English tradition of confidentiality, which applies particularly to British civil servants. Several people, whom I cannot name, offered useful critiques of the manuscript drafts. Even though I cannot acknowledge everyone individually, my English colleagues made a vital contribution to my work.

It was my intent from the beginning that this book would be helpful to American school practitioners, who are working at all levels to make schools better. Toward that end a host of people contributed to discussions about research questions, presentation, and implications, including Jacqueline Ancess, Doris Anselmo, Anthony Bryk, Ann Cook, Louis DelPapa, Diane

Devine, Pasquale DeVito, Nancy Dunbar, Chester Finn, Kenneth Fish, Thomas Fitzpatrick, Wendy Harris, Sam Husk, Martin Leggott, Heather Lewis, Leonard Lubinsky, Gene Maeroff, Peter McWalters, Vito Perrone, Susan Rotblat-Walker, the faculty of School One, Thomas Sobel, and Beverly Vileno.

While it is impossible to pinpoint all special contributors, it is appropriate to mention two. Many years ago Bob Dumont at NAES College, Wolf Point, Montana, taught me the value of considering the particular in educational matters. Leslie Oh, a writer and also my wife, has given me her unstinting support on both good and bad days during the 3 years of this work. As my first editor, she cleared away many of the cobwebs in my thinking and writing.

This varied legion of talented supporters and critics makes it easy for me to acknowledge that the final responsibility for what follows rests with me.

ℵ

While I come to this book as an educator, I also come to it as a writer who seeks connections in metaphor, allusion, or anecdote, as well as in argument. The crafting of this book has been important to me.

I wrote *Reaching for a Better Standard* to raise questions on both sides of the Atlantic about how we know and judge the value of our schools. I hope it will be of help to those who are engaged at some level with the important, confusing, and exciting daily life of schools and who are struggling to make learning happen in a better way.

Thomas A. Wilson
Providence, Rhode Island
April 10, 1995

The flow of life, which is always taking us by surprise,
is the only permanent challenge to the human spirit
to strive for new achievements.

—Václav Havel (1992)

Chapter 1

Prelude: Ghosts in the School Yard

In 1961 I became a Peace Corps volunteer in the small town of Radam, Philippines. As our assignment was "to improve Filipino education," my colleague and I proposed that we use our home, specially built for us in the large school yard, as an evening library for the town children. For several weeks officials spoke at great length with us and with each other about the merits, deficiencies, and potential of our plan before finally approving the proposal. Many town and school officials came to the library open house.

No one ever spoke about what became the most important influence on the actual use of the library: most townspeople, certainly the children, believed that in the evening the school yard was haunted by ghosts.

—*1962 Journal Entry[1]*

It is time to consider the possibility that the disappointing results of our 10-year effort to reform American schools is more the result of how we think about schools and reform than with how we carry out reform. This book explores the possibility that we are stymied more by a failure to make good use of our democratic and moral imagination than by a failure in our planning, our implementation of reform, or our politics. At some basic level our ability to reform schools is closely connected to how we think about them. Consider some of the puzzles we stumble over again and again:

- It is conventional wisdom that, although political leaders give lip service to education when the polls suggest they should, their interest is only superficial. Why is that? Education generates high-flown rhetoric, commands significant public outlay, and touches most of a politician's constituents. Why isn't it as important as defense, crime, or the economy?

- With the nation boosting the importance of education, why are its institutions, teachers, and administrators held in such low regard? Why do most citizens find educational discourse banal, even if it is occasionally emotional? Is this because the public has a short attention span, because the ideas are trivial, or because important ideas are hidden in boring language?

- People talk and write eloquently about their visions for education with a remarkable, and sometimes monotonous, consistency. Yet, the talk about the nuts and bolts of learning is confused, ill at ease, and argumentative. Since we seem to agree about the purpose of education, why do we fight about how to do it?

- Most people find test scores uninteresting, considering them neither valuable nor accurate as a measure of educational progress. What creates the widespread fascination with comparing test scores of individual children or schools? Why do test scores become the focus when we ask the hard questions about the success of schooling?

- Finding costly government bureaucracies complex and bewildering, people are wary of national and state governments intruding into local school issues. Why do most people accept the assessments of student progress prepared by government agencies as being more objective than a teacher's report of a child's progress to that child's parent?

- It is common wisdom that schools must be better managed and that good management will improve the quality of education. Why do wave after wave of management visions, management approaches, and costly management workshops move through the schools without creating real, sustained change in what goes on in classrooms?

- Believing we have certain knowledge about how to teach and how to do school well, many people believe the problem is the result of political will, union intransigence, or the public's resistance to change. How can we be sure about how to keep schools when knowledge itself is changing at an unprecedented rate? If it were only a matter of implementing the right knowledge, why wouldn't "knowledgeable" reforms have dramatically better results than "dumb" ones?

- It is in vogue to believe that more effective, centralized measurement of student performance against precise standards will force schools to change. Lacking historical support, this notion is inconsistent with Americans' ideas about the best relationship between their government and its schools. Why is this belief given such credence at this time?

- People argue that schools are important because a society determines its future through the future of its children. Yet, it is not prudent to try to secure the future through programming lives not yet lived. Why do we think this is the way to secure the future?

We need more than new solutions; we need more than to restructure our system. We need to consider how we think and talk about both the problems and the solutions.

WHY SCHOOLS NEED TO CHANGE

Why should schools change? Americans, and the English as well, have defined a number of unprecedented challenges for schools that cry for reform.

Competition in the New World Order

Many believe American schools must improve to ensure the skilled work force necessary for our national survival in the global marketplace. Advocates for English school reform make the same claim.

To meet the international economic challenge, we must raise the level of student performance in the basic skills of reading, math, science, and writing and in the new skills of critical thinking, problem solving, and working as a member of a team. This is so important to the national welfare that some have said, "If the schools can't provide these skills, another way must be found." Some believe the new information technologies will replace schools, leaving them behind as costly, outmoded artifacts of older technologies.

Falling Student Performance

The heightened importance of educating for survival has been coupled with our concern that the current generation's performance in school is declining, as evidenced by falling test scores, whether current student performance is compared to the performance of other countries or past generations. English and American experts make similar points: young people are not well prepared for work; they cannot read, compute, or think on their feet; test standards are lower; educational institutions have lowered their standards; teachers require less rigor; curriculum has gone soft; students have no desire to excel—they are lazy, indulgent, or despondent.

The despair that the whole society is in decline exacerbates our sense that youth are in decline. When we argue that work is no longer valued, excellence is not appreciated, our political systems are not working, and our moral fiber as a nation is unraveling, we are often talking about young people. Having a strong need to protect their children from the sloth and decay they see around them, or wanting to ensure that the institutions that influence their children will have a positive, not a negative, influence, some people have formed alliances to save the schools and to boost the teaching of moral codes.

Disconnection of Youth from the Adult World

In both England and the United States there is widespread agreement that our young people are becoming more violent, suicidal, disconnected, alone, and poor. They have lost the sense that their lives matter in the destiny of the world. In addition, their sense of traditional right and wrong and their knowledge of their heritage is in a disastrous disarray, and growing worse.

In the United States, more often than in England, we look to schools as the social agency of last resort, expecting them to replace many functions families once served, from providing good nutrition to giving children a sense of values.

Changing Knowledge

Many think the rapid changes in knowledge are profoundly challenging our schools: the explosion of new information, the changing definitions of the academic disciplines, the changing notions of what skills are necessary to produce knowledge, and even new definitions of what constitutes knowledge. Changes in our conception of the nature of thinking and learning fundamentally challenge how schools carry out their central function. These new concepts, based on the most current research, are making bold appearances in the proposals for school reform.

While the force for school change emanating from changing knowledge has been dramatic, it is reasonable to expect that it will increase significantly in the years ahead. Thus, schools are challenged both by the new ideas about knowledge and learning and by the need to find a balanced way to handle this accelerating challenge.

Inadequate Teachers

The history of public education in both England and the United States is permeated by the notion that something must be done for schoolteachers to make them equal to their task. English inspection began because of the concern about the lack of education of the young women who were the first elementary school teachers. The Conservative Government began its 1988 reform by blaming teachers for the collapse of British education. While Americans have not blamed their teachers so stringently, they perceive teachers as having many inadequacies: insufficient knowledge of their disciplines; low performance in the basic skills of reading, writing, and computing; ignorance about the most recent advances in technology or knowledge; insensitivity to the needs of students different from them; membership in the wrong social class; inability to change; and a lack of management skills.

A number of reform efforts are based on the premise that teachers are inadequate. The current focus on teaching and learning has called for major changes in the professional development of teachers. A new literature is growing on teacher change.

Equity

The American system upholds the ideal that public resources should be distributed equitably to all citizens. Equity is not as prevalent a concern for the English.

Analyses of statewide public spending on American education have shown profound inequities. Several states have used the equity requirements of their constitutions as the springboard for reform. Kentucky, for example, launched an ambitious effort to restructure the total state school system in response to the mandate that school funding must be equitable for all students.

The Government's Reaction: Regulation

Responding predictably to these challenges, governments mandate more regulations to make the schools work, mount more intervention programs to change the schools, and create more reporting forms for schools to complete. In English and American schools many believe their biggest challenge is coping with the responses of their government funding agencies that not only distract the schools from meeting the challenges directly, but also become new problems.

Democracy in the New World

A democracy forges an ideal covenant between its schools and its youth—schools provide the skills for the individual student to pursue personal goals and the student takes care to use those skills to strengthen, stretch, or re-create a workable democracy that is true to its ideals and germane to an ever-changing world.

Advocates of this covenant believe that in order to meet the changes in how the world defines, orders, and carries out its affairs in the post–Cold War, we must continually renew democracy. In addition to providing strengths, knowledge, and skills, schools must root children in their democratic heritage so they can draw on the resources of our history.

HOW WE CHANGE SCHOOLS

By the mid-1980s it was clear in both the United States and England that something drastic had to be done. The failure of the schools to produce satisfactory test score results was symptomatic of an underlying issue: Modern democracies are confused about how to educate their children.

Restricting their focus to the failure of schools, funding agencies began to demand that schools improve. They required schools to meet new standards and absorb program interventions in many areas: curriculum, management, governance, expectations for students, and school culture. While some saw schools as institutions with integrity that could not be bullied into doing better, others voiced the more common claim, "We know what needs to be done. The schools should get off their duffs and do it."

Heavy reliance on measurable results was an integral part of the outside intervention strategy. Specific reform programs were pushed forward by the argument that they would improve test results. Some reformers based their arguments for deregulating the schools on a *quid pro quo*—the state would get off the school's back and the school would increase student performance. The intonation, "The public wants demonstrable results," became constant.

This approach to change is not new. American reform for the most part has intensified old concepts about schools and reform. From 1862 to 1898 the English used these ideas as the basis for Payment by Results, probably the first example of national school reform in a democracy. There is little evidence that outside intervention is effective. Payment by Results (discussed in some detail in Chapter 5) fizzled out with almost universal agreement that it had failed.

A new wave of discontent and disillusion about the prospects of changing schools is already under way. Cracks have begun to appear in the public's confidence about the value of public schooling. Parents, both rich and poor, do not assume as readily as they once did that their children should be in public school. The movement to educate children at home is spreading beyond homes in which parents hold specific religious beliefs. Rather than improving schools, we may simply move on to other issues. Such a shift may already be apparent as the federal government moves away from its strategy of setting standards.

THE ARGUMENT OF THIS BOOK

If our efforts to improve schools are to work well, we must move beyond looking at them as the simple cause of the problem. The challenges schools face and how they respond to them are part and parcel of the larger issues we face in making a modern democracy work.

How we talk about schools will shape our ability to improve them. The national discourse not only supports what is possible in terms of the practical politics of change, but it also provides the crucible for working out better and inventive ways to make schools work well. That discussion takes place in the workplaces of policy experts, the chambers of our legislators, the boardrooms of our school districts, the meeting rooms of our state and district systems, the staff rooms of our schools, and the homes of our children. It is not only reflected in the well-argued presentation of school reform advocates, but in the opinion polls, the evening news, and the talk shows.

Our analysis of the problems, our plans for reform, our ideals about what is possible, and our assessment of progress all hinge on our knowledge of schools. This book explores the notion that the way we know and judge schools hinders our ability to reform them and trivializes our national discussion.

By studiously avoiding knowledge about teaching and learning in schools, our traditional approach has avoided the particulars of schools. What happens between a particular teacher and a particular child is what determines if and what that child learns that day. This knowledge is the crucial ingredient missing in our discussion.

This book depicts the tradition of English inspection to provoke us to invent better possibilities for how we know and judge schools. Neither a theoretical nor a philosophical discussion, it is based on the practical reality of a 155-year-old national tradition. Markedly different from our tradition of testing and measuring specified objectives, inspection focuses first on knowing what goes on in actual classrooms.

The freshness of how inspectors think about schools is much different from how a researcher tries to draw generalizations about school life. It is different from how an American curriculum developer tries to figure out what teachers want. It is different from how an American administrator approaches schools—different from "hands-on management." It is different from making sure a school is "in compliance" with this or that regulation. The inspector is a person of practice, who, using judgement as a tool, works to make sense of a particular school.

This comprehensive description of inspection sets the stage for the concluding sections of the book that explore the implications of inspection for the American way of knowing schools.

THE STRUCTURE OF THIS BOOK

The value of English inspection for us is its potential to provoke thoughtful discussion. I believe we need that discussion more than we need new programs of reform. Recommendations about what we should do in American schools should be built on a solid analysis of the American experience, not the English. That is the task for the next book, not this one.

This book does not proceed down the usual path of stating a problem, presenting evidence, making an argument, and offering a set of conclusions and recommendations. It takes a more winding path. Its speed is more like the saunter of someone asking questions, rather than the fast walk of the solution bearer. It is an exploration.

This book is organized in three parts. They are:

I — *The English Tradition of School Inspection*   In this lengthy, careful consideration of the English tradition of school inspection, each chapter provides the reader with different aspects of inspection: its practice, elements, history, tensions, and contributions.

II — *Six Provocations*   The ideas from inspection that challenge common American assumptions about knowing and judging schools are "being there," judgement, the practitioner's way of knowing, helping schools, standards, and the nature of government accountability. As provocations, these ideas are intended to provoke the reader, not to be prescriptive, comprehensive, or exhaustive.

III — *New Possibilities*   The book concludes by considering if and how these ideas could make a difference to American education.

Hopefully this book will generate new ideas about how to know and judge schools. I hope it will enlarge our imagination of what is possible.

PART ONE

■ ■ ■ ■ ■

The English Tradition of School Inspection

The knowledge you gain from inspection is like seeing ripples in the water instead of seeing only your reflection or the stone that you threw. That knowledge transforms a muddy puddle into a clear pool.

—An English Inspector

■ ■ ■ ■ ■ Chapter 2

Preliminaries

When the English want to know whether a school is good or not, they send an inspector to visit it, as they have done for more than 150 years. We will consider the methodology of inspection—what inspectors do—and the structures of inspection—the ways inspection organizations support and respond to the work of inspectors.

Knowledge about how teaching and learning actually happen at a school is at the heart of the inspection method.[1] The only sensible way to gain that knowledge is to visit a school. Inspectors will visit a school, learn what is happening there, and make judgements about its value. This is not a casual dropping by, but a rigorous exercise to know a school. The knowledge garnered from inspection has value to policy makers, to those who seek ways to help the school, and, most important, to those at the school itself.

Inspection methodology is based on a practitioner's way of seeing, thinking about, and discussing school value. Since 1900 most of England's inspectors have been veteran teachers. Inspection has evolved as a methodology of practitioners, not as a social science methodology. What inspectors consider important, how they decide what is true, how they value goodness and excellence, and how they carry out their day-to-day work—all vary in interesting ways from the usual American approach to evaluating schools.

The long history of inspection and the numerous situations in which the English have used inspection provide a rich array of organizational structures to support the process and to use the knowledge gained. This wealth of experience offers important insights as well. This section will give the reader a thorough sense of the methods and structures of inspection.

Before beginning, it will be helpful to consider two points about the history and structure of inspection. First, it is important to note the difference between local and national inspection. Before 1992, an HM inspector, hired by the Government as a civil servant, became a member of Her Majesty's Inspectorate (HMI). HMI is headed by Her Majesty's Chief Inspector of Schools (HMCI), who reports to the Secretary of Education. Until the 1992 reform, HMI was an integral part of the Department of Education. The inspectors comprised their own group within that Department—and a tight, elite group at that. Their working relationship with the politicians and bureaucrats, who make up the rest of the Department, was built on a tortuous and changing set of definitions, permitting them to advise the Department, on the one hand, and to be independent from it on the other. HMI has exerted major influence on national education over the years, including defining the tradition of school inspection.

However, up to five times as many school inspectors have worked at the local level than at the national level. Since 1902, England has had over 100 Local Education Authorities (LEAs) that have had administrative control of the public schools in their geographic districts. The local school district is the American analogue of the LEA. The tussle between local and national control of schools has been an important theme in English educational history. Before the current reform, the LEAs had great autonomy in defining and managing their functions. LEAs over time found a myriad of ways to inspect, some more effective than others.

Second, at the time of this study the English school reform, dating from the Education Reform Act (ERA) of 1988, was having significant impact on the daily lives of schools. ERA established the National Curriculum that specified what students should know in 12 subject areas at four "key stages" of their school careers. ERA also mandated a new system of assessment based on testing student performance. Since ERA, three other Acts have been passed mandating change for almost every aspect of school governance and practice. The English school reform is the most comprehensive national effort to reform schools undertaken by a democracy.

As the major school accountability system for the English, inspection also is undergoing radical change. The Education (Schools) Act of 1992 required a major reorganization of inspection, making HMI a part of the Office for Standards in Education (OFSTED), which relates to the Department of Education on a fee-for-service basis. OFSTED contracts with private inspection teams to inspect all schools that receive public funds every 4 years. This is a tenfold increase in the volume of inspection. The Act and its implementation have significantly changed the core of the inspection method. Influenced by modern ideas about school evaluation, OFSTED inspection is more regimented.

THE CHAPTERS

The following chapters consider the methods of inspection and the history and organizational issues that have been part of the English experience.

Chapter 3 describes the practice of inspection in a composite journal that takes the reader on a 5-day inspection visit. *Discovery* is the lodestone for this section, and indeed for the rest of the book.

I have carefully constructed this visit, rather than describe actual events, for good reason. It both honors my promise of confidentiality (which is even more of an issue in England than in the United States) and has allowed me to describe a typical visit more thoughtfully. To increase its authenticity within the limits of fiction, I asked several HM and local inspectors to review it. I have accepted their corrections and many of their suggestions. Endnotes provide further detail about the authenticity of events.

Keep in mind that this composite visit took place when the organization and methods of inspection were undergoing radical change. While I was in England, most changes the Education (Schools) Act of 1992 set in motion had not yet appeared in practice; they were apparent only in planning documents, workshops, and inspector anxiety. What I saw and what I will report here is the practice of traditional inspection.

This composite visit was built on the HMI full school inspection that came to HMI from the Secondary School Inspectorate at the beginning of the century. In 1992 full school inspection was more important than its low-frequency use suggested. It is the archetype usually present when inspectors and people in the schools talk about the purpose and methods of inspection. You have not really inspected and you have not really been inspected unless it was a full school visit.

Interestingly enough, the new inspections called for in the current reform by the Education (Schools) Act of 1992 are closer to this archetype than the inspections of the last 15 years.[2] The HMI full school inspection reveals more amply the differences between English and American views about how to judge the value of schools. This full school visit does *not* well represent the more varied, less formal LEA inspections before 1992.

The defining elements (Chapter 4) of the method of inspection have been tugged from its history and practice. Begun without a blueprint, inspection has become so tangled that it resisted being pulled apart in this way. After reviewing early drafts, several LEA and HM inspectors adjusted these elements and, finally, confirmed them.

Chapter 5—History—provides a context for understanding some of the structural issues. The English tradition not only offers a different methodology for knowing schools, but different organizational structures that support and use inspection.

It surprises American scholars to find that the written history of inspection is scant (Taylor, 1989, pp. 59–60). The handful of available books and articles focuses on the organization of inspection, not on the history of the ideas behind this approach. Because HM inspectors are required to subscribe to the Official Secrets Act, source documents aren't readily available. This Act prohibits civil servants from revealing any document associated with their Government service or, for that matter, from even discussing it.

Though scant, the historic documents that came to my attention, including different sets of instructions to inspectors and internal memos on problems encountered in the field, indicate a wealth of experience and thoughtful reflection that will deepen our understanding of how inspection works and what its history has been. I found these texts more useful than the better preserved formal school inspection reports. Hopefully, the changes in HMI's functioning won't result in loss of more material or the access to it.

Chapter 6 sharpens the picture of the organizational structures that have surrounded inspection. The major tensions analyzed here will be familiar to the American reader.

Chapter 7 describes the contributions of inspection to English education and raises several implications for American education.

A NECESSARY DIGRESSION ABOUT TERMS AND SPELLING

Before proceeding, we must be sure that English terms do not cause unnecessary confusion, so that we can save our confusion for more important issues. Since many Americans think the English call their public schools "private" and their private schools "public," it is important to make several key terms clear.

In fact, the English no longer use either public or private in this sense when they refer to schools. What we call private schools, the English call *independent* schools. What we call public schools, they call *maintained* schools. I will use *public* in the American sense to refer to English schools that are supported at any level by taxes, thus avoiding the English term *maintained*.

How the English use *provision* is crucial for understanding the assumptions that underlie inspection. Americans find this use peculiar. *Provision* is the total of what a school provides for the education of its students. The term includes more than the physical objects of the school plant and equipment—those are *accommodations*. Teaching and learning are at the center of what a school provides. *Provision* is tangible; an inspector can see and comment on it. He or she does not need to infer its presence from a component of the school, such as school climate, curriculum, or the number of books in the school library.

The English usage is similar to what Americans mean when they say, "A good parent provides well for her child." The American usage includes not only the physical accommodations, but a great deal more.

When the English think about how well a school provides for its students, they think less in terms of inputs and outputs and more about all that happens at a school. Provision does not separate student performance from what a school provides. How students perform and how a school adjusts its provision in light of that performance are integral parts of provision. I will use *provision* as the English do, adding comments about its meaning when appropriate.[3]

The English refer to those having current national political control as the *Government* (always with the initial letter capitalized). Americans use *the administration*. The English don't use *government* (with a small "g") as we do. These differences are, in fact, quite profound. They are embedded in our individual histories. For example, the English Government includes what we would label legislative and executive functions. I will stick with *Government* when the reference is English or British.

I call the national Government office responsible for English education *the Department of Education*. Although it has had six different names throughout its history, this office has never been called that. In April 1992, shortly after I arrived in England, the Government suddenly announced that this office, which had for several years been called the Department of Education and Science (DES), would henceforth be known as *the Department For Education*—with a capital "F" for emphasis. (The capital "F" was later dropped.) There appears to be little value in being exact about this name. Although my approach loses some interesting subtleties about English educational history and the English organizational mind, those are not integral to the substance of the book. I will use the Department of Education for ease, consistency, and clarity.

Likewise, the head of the Department of Education has had many titles. Indeed, one of the Prime Minister's explicit powers is making up titles. The consistent use of *Secretary of Education* will make it easier for the reader to follow, even though some subtleties will admittedly be lost.

HMI is another problem. It probably first referred to the inspectors themselves. During 102 of HMI's 153 years, England had a queen, so the inspectors were known as Her Majesty's Inspectors. Queen Victoria, who began her reign in 1837, was the first *Her Majesty* of HMI. The librarian at the University of London didn't find it funny when I suggested we check both *Her* and *His* to find all references to HMI over time. Her disdain over my attempted humor was not because she is a woman and I am a man, but because she is English and I am American.

As more people tried to explain inspection, and as the inspectorate took on more importance, it became convention to use HMI to refer to the national inspection agency—Her Majesty's Inspectorate—and to refer to the inspectors as HM inspectors. I never knew an HM inspector who called himself an "HM inspector" with any feeling. It did mean something when someone declared, "I am an HMI."

This quest for simplicity was made complicated when in 1992 HMI was absorbed into OFSTED. Bowing to prevailing convention, I will use HMI to refer to the national inspectorate prior to 1992, and OFSTED after that. I will use HM inspector to refer to national inspectors.

I have made one important exception to American spelling by spelling *judgement* with an "e", as the English do. How inspectors use the word has other than American connotations. The ideas of the inspector's individual judgement and the corporate judgement of the inspection team are vital to understanding the differences between how inspection works and how Americans decide if schools have value.

■ ■ ■ ■ ■ Chapter 3

Discovery:
What Inspectors Do

The only way to learn the methodology of inspection is to watch what inspectors do. Seeking to capture the way I discovered inspection and serving as a lodestone for the more analytical treatments that follow, this chapter takes the reader on a fictional visit.

This is a composite visit built from my journals during the 10 months I watched both local and national inspectors at work. It blends events that took place on both LEA and HMI inspections. The distinctions that have been lost will be more important to an English audience than to those viewing inspection as a different template for American concerns. What is gained is a more general view of the inspection method than most inspectors hold. I think this view will be the most helpful to those considering the possibilities of inspection.

This visit is fictional in a specific way. I have woven particular events and conversations recorded in my field notes into a visit that did *not* happen. All the inspectors and teachers are composites of more than one person. OFSTED did not test its *Framework for Inspection* in this way. Rosewood School is a composite of four schools I visited in three different cities. British civil servants must not allow their private remarks to enter the public record, particularly those critical of the Government in power. Thus, the inspectors' private remarks are fictional. I take full responsibility for them. Any effort to attribute them to an actual person, living or dead, will be mired in the swamp between truth and fiction.

TUESDAY, JULY 14, 1992—THE FIRST INSPECTION

King's Cross and The Queen Mother

Inside the train shed at King's Cross Station, London, I waited for Sue Nicolson to meet me by the track leading to Woolseyeford. Two tracks away, a wonderful, modern steam engine slowly came to the end of its morning journey. Images of the last steam engines I had seen as a boy in New Hampshire were quickly pushed aside when I saw the black and white sign on the engine boldly proclaiming it was "The Queen Mother." My mind leapt from remembering my mother's warm affection for the Queen Mother, to imagining an argument with a feminist friend about whether a steam engine could be a mother, and then to picturing a place I know on Chicago's South Side where a rap group is performing its new hit, "The Queen Mother." Sue abruptly brought me back to London and King's Cross.

Sue Nicolson is a local inspector for the London borough where I had been attached for 3 months. Her inspection expertise is special education. Over 6 feet tall, she's thin. Her light brown hair was cut with precise bangs on her forehead, revealing her classic features, before falling to her shoulders. She said, "It's easy to spot you through the rush-hour crowd because I'm so tall."

We laughed, rushing to board our second-class coach and recalling the last time I had waited for her. I had passed the time drinking coffee with several teachers in the staff room at Harpsbow School when Sue had rushed in and abruptly asked me, "Why are Americans so big? Last night I met with Nicole (the English inspector) and 20 American teachers to talk about how our English teachers teach English. Those Americans were all big."

Straining to look up at her, I said, "I don't know. Why are you English so tall?"

As her eyes filled with mock wonder, she said, "I don't know; maybe it's because we're so crowded here."

When I had mentioned that I was looking for a number of different schools across England to visit during the autumn term, Sue had invited me to accompany her to Woolseyeford where she had professional business with Helene Beaumont, a local inspector there. She had asked Helene to arrange a quick visit to Rosewood School for me and to discuss with me afterward the possibility of a longer visit in the autumn. Sue had high regard for Helene. As the LEA inspector most closely assigned to Rosewood School, Helene was most knowledgeable about the school. Sue said Helene had described Rosewood as an interesting school that had gone through some difficult times. She thought it sounded like a school I would like to visit.

The train had reached the outskirts of London before we were settled into our seats. More or less taking over the conversation, Sue explained:

I hope you won't find me rude, but I must finish a project while we are on the train. You know how short staffed we've been with the cuts at the LEA. The work seems to grow and grow with the reform. Also, it's near the end of summer term.[1] My work load is always worse then.

Let me brief you quickly. Then I'll have to work on my inspection report on Harpsbow School. It's almost done. The team members have been over it three times and I think we're close to a final agreement on the wording.

I asked her about the city of Woolseyeford, Rosewood School, and our schedule for the day. Sue always does well when the focus is clear.

As you know, Woolseyeford is almost 100 miles north of London. It began in the 13th century as a wool marketing town. In the 18th century, during the Industrial Revolution, it became one of England's iron and steel cities. In the late 18th and early 19th centuries the Industrial Revolution moved much faster in England than in America, you know. It reached its zenith during the war. During that time, many Pakistani immigrated there. The language and religious differences and the prejudices of the whites created problems in the school. Like most of England, Woolseyeford is now in a deep recession. I think the unemployment rate is over 50%.

Rosewood is a comprehensive secondary school situated where a middle-class neighborhood abuts two estates (public housing projects). When the Pakistani moved into one of the estates after the school was built, it found itself serving a more mixed population than before.

The school had a particularly difficult time during the early eighties. There have been two Heads (principals) in the last 2 years. Rosewood has suffered through considerable internal strife and difficulty as it has tried to adjust to the new student population. Because she has worked closely to help the school during this time, Helene will be able to tell you more.

Helene is highly respected for her work as a local inspector in English. Her reputation has been built on her outstanding 12-year career as an English teacher and on her experience as Head of Department for English in a school in a nearby LEA.

She will be meeting us at the station. She and I must meet to discuss our business at hand—the difficulties teachers are having with how the Government will pilot the new tests in English next May. Helene thought that while she and I talk, you might like to visit a class to gain a sense of the school.

Then Helene has arranged for you to meet with Jane Edwards, the current Head. Helene says Jane is brilliant and she has turned Rosewood around in the 2 years she's been Head. Is this plan all right with you?

It sounded fine. While Sue edited her report, I watched the country-side north of London slip by, wondering if the electric-powered engine on our train had a name.

The First Inspection

Helene was older than Sue. Her blond hair circled her round face. Although shorter and slighter than Sue, she carried more weight. Driving quickly past the Ibis Hotel to Rosewood, she complained about the rain that had start-ed early that morning, making it difficult to see the city. A relatively new comprehensive school, Rosewood was built in the sixties. The two-storied rectangular modules had been built around a courtyard. The monotony of the modern building had fortunately been broken by incorporating into the school plant the Victorian primary school that had first occupied the site. In 1978 a new wing was added.

When we entered Rosewood, students were passing between classes with the same bustling orderliness as in other English secondary schools I had visited. Although prepared to find the mixed student population, I was surprised by how the students dressed. While many wore uniforms, many did not. It was more usual for all to wear them or none. In English sec-ondary schools uniforms were definitely coming back.

The Government requires all schools that receive public funds to teach religious education. Thinking an American would be interested in seeing how religious instruction is handled, particularly in a school with a 55% Muslim population, Helene had arranged for me to visit a religious education class.

Sitting in rows of movable desk-chairs, the 28 students were quiet, attentive, and distant when Helene introduced me to Mr. Fisher. His ner-vousness seemed to be pre-performance jitters. His meticulously combed thick brown hair, his dark wool suit, his precise manner—all suggested he had prepared carefully for this meeting. He began by telling his students, "Today our class will be visited by an American inspector." Smiling, I sat in the seat he designated at the back of the room. The sun burst from the clouds, flooding the room with a soft glow.

Beginning with the common preamble teachers use when inspectors are present, Mr. Fisher told the class they would continue with the creation stories. He listed myths from countries they had previously discussed, end-ing with Pakistan. He said the final myth in the unit would be the creation of the universe, as described in Genesis.

After an eloquent reading and explication, he asked, "What's the importance of this story?" He glanced toward me, pausing almost deliberately before answering his own question.

> Well, you could say this was the first inspection. God worked on important tasks. He stopped, looked over His work, and made a judgement. "God saw that it was good." Pleased, He went back to His work of creation with renewed confidence.

I think I was the only one taking notes. As if intrigued by my note taking, Mr. Fisher continued, "God was a planner. He had management objectives and He evaluated His results." I stopped writing.

When the bell rang, the students quickly left for lunch, except for one who stopped to ask if I had ever seen Elvis Presley. When I thanked Mr. Fisher for allowing me to observe, I didn't ask him why God needed management objectives.

Lunch

Sue and Helene were amused when I told them about the class. Sue pointed out the irony of the sun's coming out after days of gloomy rain. Impishly serious, Helene said:

> It's interesting Mr. Fisher was able to cover Genesis today. He likes it better than the other creation stories he's required to teach. I suspect the students had heard that lesson before, but that's only speculation. Did you ask them?

I suddenly realized I hadn't moved around the class like an English inspector would. I had behaved like an American observer.

Helene had arranged for me to meet with Jane Edwards, Rosewood's new Head, after lunch.

Meeting with Jane

Jane ushered me into her bright office, where the midday sun hit the coffee table in front of the comfortable, but not too comfortable, chairs arranged around the corner opposite the door. Several school scenes painted by students hung behind us. A tray holding a coffee thermos, a teapot, and a plate of biscuits (cookies) waited on the table. Jane clearly wasn't going to waste time asking her assistant to bring tea or coffee later.

Jane's constrained, intelligent energy was obvious from the start. Her short dark hair sculpted her face, much as her well-tailored suit outlined her small frame. Her eyes sparkled while she tried to figure out how to respond to the next scene in front of her—my being there.

> I understand you're here to learn about inspection. That really surprises me. I thought Americans were interested only in testing. Helene says you must be an archeologist—inspection is really changing, you know.

Declining her offer of tea or coffee, I said it would be most helpful to learn about the educational issues the school faced. She looked pleased:

> I'm glad you asked about the educational issues. As you undoubtedly know, an important part of Rosewood's context has been its recent history with Woolseyeford. Helene Beaumont is a much better person to brief you on that because she has been around longer than I. I trust you know I've been here only 2 years?

Jane thought it would be most helpful to describe the major problems the school faced. I agreed. Her remarks seemed rehearsed, but still fresh. She pointed out three problems facing the school:

- The most important issue is for teachers to learn how to teach children who have different backgrounds than theirs.
- The National Curriculum often interferes with teaching a diverse student population.
- Several chronically weak departments seem unable to learn anything new.

Then she began the story:

> It's best to start in 1986 when Rosewood's well-respected faculty representative to the teachers' union resigned. He was a strong, but quiet, spokesperson for teachers' concerns. He was maliciously attacked by the press for being too soft. Many here were appalled by the Government's public attacks on London teachers because we faced problems quite similar to theirs. The personal attack on Lewis made it all the more difficult, because the faculty knew the public accusations were false and malicious.
>
> Before 1988, when the national reform began, a group of younger teachers and LEA teacher advisors were making progress in developing an interdisciplinary approach to writing that not only had rigor, but that honored cultural differences and accepted individual stu-

dent skill levels. This was an excellent approach for our diverse student population.

This group hoped to use the National Curriculum to extend this approach to all subjects taught at Rosewood and to make their approach available to other schools.

The National Curriculum brought their hopes to an end. First they were overrun by trying to understand the concepts of the Curriculum. Then it became clear the Curriculum couldn't support their efforts, because it was too strongly subject based. They were overwhelmed by the work required to change all instruction to fit within the Curriculum.

The older teachers, who had originally supported the National Curriculum, thinking it would return us to the golden days, soon felt their professional integrity was being undermined by the precision of the attainment targets and the programs of study. It was worse when they realized the Government wasn't listening to what teachers had to say about revising the Curriculum. The revisions were even more restrictive than the original schemes.

The faculty had supported the early plans for the National Curriculum and for more thorough methods to assess student progress. They liked the idea that the new assessment would be built on Standard Achievement Tasks (SATs) that would be closely tied to the Curriculum.

They were disappointed and exhausted by the early pilots of the SATs. The tests simply were not worth the inordinate amount of time they required or the continual conceptual and statistical confusion they created. The Government responded to these difficulties by moving to traditional standardized tests, which made it worse.

I told Jane I had been surprised by how England's teachers had complied with the new regulations, by how earnestly they had tried to make the Curriculum work, even though many had little confidence in its value. I noted how American teachers simply ignored edicts from offices on high, particularly those that implored them to teach in a way that contradicted their convictions or past practice. An intensity drowned the sparkle in Jane's eyes, as she went on:

National law requires us to implement the National Curriculum. In spite of our griping, we believe we have that public responsibility. That's what has made it so difficult. We know we need to do better. National law requires us to implement the Curriculum in order to do better. But that seems to have made matters worse. The early strategists of the reform knew that the only way to force England's querulous teachers into harness was to make the reform and the Curriculum a matter of law. We may be querulous, but at heart we are good subjects.

When Jane grew quiet, I felt she was perhaps afraid she had been too outspoken with a foreigner. Finally breaking the silence, she said she would gladly agree to my visiting Rosewood, if I could work it out with Helene.

Classes had begun to change, making my transition to the busy school corridor abrupt.

Helene's Briefing

At the Rosewood staff lounge I learned Helene and Sue had had a productive work session. Jane's approval of my visiting Rosewood had already reached Helene. After helping me find tea, she said:

Well, it's time for me to brief you. Shall we call it "Helene's Briefing"? Sue told me what questions she thought you would ask and I have the answers. But first I must stop briefly by the LEA office; then we can go to a pub near the BR station and talk until your train leaves.

Helene had worked with Rosewood for 5 years and she was proud to show Sue and me what she knew. She wanted me to understand the complexities:

In the mid-sixties Rosewood began as a new comprehensive school that served a primarily middle-class neighborhood and two working-class estates. In the early eighties the school entered a bad period. Parents were unhappy, teacher morale was low, and there was considerable tension between the older whites and the Muslims who were moving into one of the estates. Some said the school's decline was part of the overall national decline in standards and education. But most blamed the Muslims. After listening and observing, I decided the decline had begun well before the large increase in minority students and that it had resulted from the poor leadership of the former Head, Harry Osler.

As you know, the Education Reform Act of 1988 gave the school's Governing Body greater power and authority. Ruth Thornton, a strong advocate for comprehensive schools when her children were in school, became chair of the Rosewood Governors. For generations her family has lived in Ramlot, the good neighborhood in Woolseyeford. Neither Tory nor Labour, she is a Liberal Democrat.

The LEA director asked her to be chair because she was concerned Rosewood was going downhill. Ruth thought the 1988 reform would give her a new opportunity to do something about it.

In 1989, after much behind-the-scenes discussion, Ruth convinced Harry Osler to step down as Rosewood Head to take a position in the LEA. Brian Woodcliffe would stay on as Deputy Head. The Governors supported her in the appointment of Michael Franklin as the new Head. Because he was a specialist in multicultural education, they had high hopes his leadership would improve the school.

In fact, matters quickly became worse. Increasing unemployment heightened frustrations in the community. While Michael tried hard to articulate the needs of the Muslim community, he never actually gained their respect. Because they felt he'd been hired to appease the minority community, the white community never had much faith in him.

After being forced to call the police to quell a racial disturbance on the school grounds, Michael was never the same. The teachers had little confidence in his knowledge of subject content or teaching practice. Unhappy as Deputy Head in the new regime, Brian Woodcliffe effectively manipulated a vocal minority of the school's Governors to ensure that Michael would have neither their full support nor peace of mind. Fully aware of what was happening, Ruth was dismayed that she couldn't do anything about it. Meetings of the Governors were contentious and unproductive.

The Woolseyeford LEA was concerned about what was happening. When the Chief Inspector of the LEA informed the Director of the LEA about this in some detail, he was asked to pay close attention to Rosewood. As link inspector to Rosewood in 1989, I was asked to make the school my first priority during summer term. That's when I became heavily involved.

In February 1990, after a series of intense meetings between Michael Franklin and the LEA Chief Inspector, Michael gave notice that he was leaving the headship. The LEA publicly announced it had given Michael a year's sabbatical to study intercultural education in the United States. Explaining that he was an educator, not a manager, Michael told people he was leaving because the reforms had turned the headship into a management role. Both Michael and the LEA Chief Inspector kept their private meetings in confidence.

The reform had already heightened the LEA Director's concern about the welfare of our schools. We are profoundly worried schools will choose to opt out of the LEA and become funded directly by the national Government. Each school that decides to opt out will mean fewer resources for the LEA. A school's decision to opt out rests with its parents. The Governing Body decides whether to put the vote to the parents. We've seen how, when a school's Governors are frustrated with how a school is going, they turn to opting out as the easiest solution. If enough schools opt out, the Government can close us down. One good result of the reform is that it has forced the LEAs to work even harder to be responsive to the needs of their schools.

With great difficulty we persuaded Ruth to remain as chair of the Governing Body. I took advantage of the opportunity provided by Michael's resignation to meet frequently with her. We agreed that appointing a new Head would be a pivotal opportunity for the school. Striving to heal old wounds and build a new base for progress, we proceeded carefully through the selection process.

We successfully involved the teachers, the school staff (including Brian Woodcliffe), the LEA and the two communities served by the school. We presented Jane Edwards for consideration. Her leadership was strong. After the school Governors selected Jane as the new Head, Ruth and I considered how best to set the stage for her.

Thanks to Sue, we knew about the "contract" inspections her LEA had conducted in London. Sue told us how her inspectorate worked closely with a school's Governing Body to design an inspection with the primary purpose of meeting the school's needs, as defined by its Governors. The report of a contracted inspection was available only to the school Governors and the new Head. It wasn't made public. The Governors could decide to include staff and faculty in feedback.

My LEA inspectorate thought such an inspection would finish some old business at Rosewood, establish a baseline for Jane, and provide a productive focus for all of us to move forward. Although we hoped to do the inspection before Jane came on board, it was put off time and again because of the uncertainty about LEA resources. You realize that, as inspectors, we could all be gone in about 6 months. It's already happening in a number of LEAs. Our Chief Inspector plans to ask the LEA Director for his final decision about us by the end of next week. I'm not overly optimistic.

If this inspection comes to pass, I'd be glad to propose to our Chief Inspector that you be attached to it. If not, you'd be welcome to visit Rosewood in the autumn anyway.

I told Helene I would be pleased to be attached to the inspection, if it took place, and that I'd like to come back in any case. I then asked, "Is HMI involved in this?" This question usually provoked an answer of little consequence.

Helene stopped short and looked at me with new intensity. "Have you been talking with HMI?" she asked. When I confessed I had, she replied, "It figures. Do you know John Turner, the HM inspector assigned to Woolseyeford?"

"I know who he is," I said.

"Have you talked with him recently?" When I said I'd never actually talked with him, I only knew who he was, she sighed. "Well, I'm being cautious because of the strange circumstances we all find ourselves in. I'll tell you something, if you promise to keep it in strict confidence."

She told me how, when she was a teacher, she'd considered applying for HMI at about the same time the LEA had begun to recruit her for the local inspectorate. Although a position with HMI was considered the crowning achievement of a teacher's career, she felt that was out of her reach.

She had been an LEA inspector for 7 years before she met John Turner. They attended several official LEA meetings and teacher workshops together. He'd asked her to lunch, saying he was curious about whether or not she would ever consider becoming an HM inspector. She'd been pleased. She met him several times after that, describing her work at Rosewood in some detail. To her surprise, he had been intrigued by the notion of the contract inspection, even though it was well outside the HMI approach. She had been impressed with his knowledge and wisdom about schools.

At their last meeting in autumn 1991, Helene directly asked him about HMI, having heard its future was uncertain. Admitting this was true, John finally agreed that it wasn't a good time to pursue an HMI position. She had been sad to learn that an HMI career was now fraught with anxiety.

Helene was aware that Jane had met John at a district workshop on the National Curriculum. Jane had also been impressed by his belief in the importance of good education and by his knowledge of how change occurs.

On our drive to the train station, Helene and I agreed that I would ring her in early September to set dates to visit Rosewood.

MONDAY, SEPTEMBER 7, 1992—THE RING

As it turned out, Sue rang to say that Helene had rung to tell her that the LEA had decided against a contract inspection for Rosewood. But Jane Edwards had received a letter from OFSTED (formerly HMI) saying Rosewood would receive a full school inspection during the week of November 9, 1992, that there would be eight members on the inspection team, and that Reporting Inspector (RI or team leader) John Turner would be in touch with her to make the arrangements. Helene told Sue that OFSTED's letter had had the same formal and sparse tone as old HMI letters. Since national law required schools to accept inspection, there was no need for OFSTED to explain why Rosewood had been selected. The letter indicated this inspection would not

be part of the new round of inspections that OFSTED was required to manage by the 1992 Act. Those inspections would not take place for another
year. Jane was nevertheless surprised, because over the last 2 years the number of full school inspections had greatly decreased as HMI's future had
become increasingly uncertain.

To meet the requirements of the Education (Schools) Act of 1992, OFST-
ED had prepared a draft *Framework for Inspection* (HMCI, 1992).:2 Quite sure
that John Turner had been heavily involved in preparing that, Helene suspected he had been asked to select a school to test out the *Framework* and
he had somehow been able to influence HMI to choose Rosewood.

Later, Helene suggested I ring my HMI (now OFSTED) contacts to see
if I could observe that inspection. She said she would talk with John. In
addition to agreeing to seek approval for my observing that inspection,
Helene and I worked out that I would spend September 21–22 and October 15–16 in Woolseyeford to see the preliminaries for the inspection visit
at Rosewood School.

MONDAY, SEPTEMBER 21, 1992—THE FIRST MEETINGS

John Turner

I am a defender of BR (British Rail), England's nationwide train system.
But on my trip to meet John Turner in Barringham, BR was a full hour late
and so was I.

As soon as he learned I was "at reception," John came down, his coat in
hand, to say we would depart immediately and that he would have to brief
me during the drive to Woolseyeford to meet with Jane at Rosewood School.

In his late fifties, John was solid, neither too tall nor too portly. His
thick brown hair almost covered the ear pieces of his glasses. Immediately coveting his overcoat, I decided to splurge on an English trench coat.
John wore his magnificent coat with rugged ease. While dashing to his car,
a new Vauxhall, I asked him where his HMI briefcase was. "I don't use it
anymore," he said.

As he began to point out landmarks during the drive, I reminded him
I'd been to Woolseyeford before. I didn't mention it had been raining hard.

He wanted to go over a few details with me. Although he understood
I knew the importance of confidentiality, he asked several questions to be
sure. I gave the appropriate pledges before he seemed satisfied I would
behave. Then he discussed the meeting:

> The circumstances of the Rosewood inspection are unusual. I believe
> you know HMI, I mean OFSTED, has published the new *Framework*

for Inspection that will govern all new inspections. This *Framework* includes four areas of attention specified in the 1992 Act: quality of education provided by the school, educational standards achieved, efficient use of resources, and the spiritual and moral development of students.

OFSTED asked me to lead a pilot inspection to test this *Framework*. Rosewood was chosen because it's an interesting school and it's near my office.

About 2 weeks ago, after Jane received the formal letter from OFSTED about the inspection, I rang her to set up this appointment. Although she has agreed to your presence at this meeting, I want to emphasize again that either of us may ask you to leave at any time.

We'll meet with her for about an hour, then I'll take you to your hotel where we can talk further. Jane expects you to attend the meeting with her senior management team tomorrow. This is a very busy time.

He was clearly tense. He drove with unusual concentration and focus for either a Brit or an American. Taking advantage of a complicated traffic jam at a roundabout (rotary) that interrupted his thought, I expressed how much I appreciated his providing me this rare access to an HMI/OFSTED inspection. I also mentioned I'd met Jane on a previous trip. But it wasn't until I cursed BR for being late that he visibly relaxed.

Chocolate Biscuits

Greeting us when we entered the school, Jane quickly ushered us to the meeting room. John presented himself formally. Following HMI procedures carefully, he explained the purpose of the inspection, how the school was expected to prepare for it, what the rough outline schedule of the week looked like, what the nature of the feedback would be, and what the final report would be about (HMI, 1988). He then explained that the inspection would be conducted using the new *Framework* as much as possible. He thought this might make the inspection even more intense than usual. In keeping with the traditional procedures, he offered to meet with the Rosewood faculty beforehand to talk about the purpose and procedure of the inspection.

Jane thought that was an important step, so they scheduled such a meeting for October 16, 1992. Jane planned to meet with her senior management team and the whole faculty several times before that. She confirmed that I would attend the first meeting of the senior management team the next day.

John asked if she had received the 44-page OFSTED form for secondary schools that the school Head was expected to complete. This specimen form, constructed in August as part of the new *Framework*, was still being

revised. Noting the length and detail of the form, John said it was unlikely all the necessary information would be easily obtained from current
school records. If Jane found sections of it extremely difficult to complete,
he would add a note so it wouldn't reflect poorly on her. He needed the
completed form by October 13.

John had been encouraged to use the form so he could comment on all
aspects of the new approach. Knowing that it had been drawn up by the technicians who were designing OFSTED's new computerized information system, he told me he had little hope that it would be modified, regardless of
how badly it worked in a school. The technicians believed information was
concrete and that ambiguity was the result only of confusion in communi-
cation or sloppy thinking, while he believed ambiguity was inherent in the
collection of information. Although OFSTED officials understood his objec-
tions, John thought they went along with the technicians because they were
afraid to appear dumb about the new methodologies.

After John finished his presentation, Jane asked about my welfare,
expressing her enjoyment of our last conversation. After being offered tea
and biscuits, John relaxed. Jane asked if, given the unusual nature of the
inspection, it would it be all right if they had a "chat."

Allowing that it would, John looked toward me to make sure I understood this would be off the record. I stopped taking notes.

Jane characterized the upcoming inspection as a critical event in their
efforts to put Rosewood on its feet. She felt it held risk both for her and the
school. She admitted that the school had serious weaknesses that needed
to be addressed. But she was afraid, if those became the central message
of the report, it would greatly weaken the school. Her concern was magnified
because none of the schools that competed with Rosewood for students
was being inspected.

John listened intently, while Jane plunged ahead:

Rosewood has about 70 surplus places. The school's budget is based on
70 more students being in attendance than in fact there are. The LEA
has protected us from the Department's campaign to eliminate them.

The loss of that money would have a devastating effect on our
efforts here. What position will you take on this? What's your relationship to the Department of Education these days?

John immediately assured her that the inspection wouldn't investigate
such issues. He reminded her he was an HM inspector and that it wasn't
going to be an investigation, but an inspection, and that there is a difference.
Admittedly, the new *Framework* contained a focus on "the efficiency of the
school" that directed attention to how the school used its financial resources.

One of the inspectors would be asking about the school's sources of money and the school's accounting in light of the new LSM (the Local School Management system that was part of the national reform). He would make judgements about the school's efficiency in those matters.

Later John confessed to me that he thought some designers of the new *Framework* saw inspection as investigation. He thought, if that distinction weren't kept clear, the goodwill of Heads and teachers, which was absolutely necessary for good inspection, would be lost.

Lightening up, John told Jane that, even if inspectors were supposed to investigate bureaucratic constructions, such as surplus places, they wouldn't be terribly good at it. Realizing she no longer needed to worry about this, she turned to her second concern: "How can the inspection help our efforts to move Rosewood forward?"

Mentioning her involvement in several LEA and HMI inspections over the years, she confessed she had never found any particular magic in inspection. In some cases it had worked well; in others it had created confusion and silliness.

I still remember my first inspection by an HMI when I was a beginning teacher. I knew my class had been included on the visit schedule. But, because the inspectors had complained about working under a tight schedule, I was surprised when the inspector stayed through two of my classes.

I knew he knew what he was doing by how he walked around the room, which students he chose to question, what questions I overheard him asking about the text we were reading, which examples of student work he asked to see, and how students responded to him. He showed me that he not only understood teaching, but that he was also well versed in the vicissitudes of teaching English.

When he asked if he could talk with me after the second class, I was quite anxious.

That half-hour conversation was the most important professional development experience I had in my entire teaching career. At first I was properly polite. I resisted his critical judgements, considering him arrogant. But, while he talked, I began to realize he was extremely accurate about what had happened during my class. He was making greater sense of it and using a wider range of experience than I had. He knew the latest ideas about how to teach writing and could critically relate them to my class.

That conversation changed the way I taught, even how I taught my class the next day. It changed how I thought about my teaching. I was more able to learn from my own work as a teacher.

John responded:

> You were lucky. That HM inspector knew you were going to be good.
> It was easier for us to do that kind of thing before all this reform.

Pouring John a second cup of tea, Jane offered him another chocolate
biscuit. Then she asked, "May I tell you what the best possible result of the
November inspection for Rosewood would be?"

When John said nothing, she continued with remarkable clarity and
confidence:

> First, we need official confirmation that we are providing quality
> education for all of our students, even while the school program con-
> tinues to change to meet the requirements of the National Curricu-
> lum and even though our students are a diverse lot.
>
> Our survival depends on attracting more students. Parents aren't
> sure about us. The difficulties we've had in the past have become
> excuses for the faculty and explanations for the community about
> what we're trying to do now. The past is looped around our necks.
> Many of the changes we're making are proactive and will make posi-
> tive contributions to the education of our children.
>
> Most people will see your report as an HMI report, because they
> don't understand yet what OFSTED is. While I've heard community
> leaders and some parents scoff at the value of HMI, almost every-
> body respects the legitimacy of HMI's overall judgements about
> school quality. Both Muslim and white parents want assurance that
> Rosewood is the best school they can choose for their children. They
> want to know that we know what we are doing. They want to be
> sure their children will be safe and well treated here. Muslim parents
> want to know that we know their children are Muslim and that we
> respect them for that. White parents want to know the school hasn't
> turned bad because Muslim children now come here.

John took a sip of tea; Jane went on:

> Second, I hope your judgements will suggest how I can unravel a diffi-
> cult faculty problem. Some of our younger teachers are committed to
> interdisciplinary units they had developed before the advent of the
> National Curriculum. Having been reorganized into the subject
> departments, as specified by the Curriculum, they are now in the Eng-
> lish, history, and math departments. Forming a cabal among them-
> selves, they're causing difficulties for the older Heads of Department.
>
> In working through the organizational tensions this has caused, I
> find I'm not sure about the quality of their interdisciplinary

approach. In my heart I agree with much of what they are saying about good curriculum. There's no question in my mind that the loss of their enthusiasm and commitment would be a big loss for the school. But their struggles have worn them down; one left teaching last year and another is seriously considering leaving at the end of this year. They're liked by many students.

The problem is that, when I have watched some of them teach, their classes seemed sloppy and lacking in rigor. So at the heart of my dilemma, I question the value of their work. HMI's view about that could be very helpful.

John and I sat attentively, waiting for Jane to continue:

The third point is the most difficult. I'm concerned about the quality of our technology department. The Head of Department is a male chauvinist. I've learned he has close ties to the group of school Governors who supported my predecessor. I've avoided the technology classes as much as possible, so I have no real basis for judging the quality of the department. The Head of Department has gone out of his way to assure me that he knows what he's doing. But he has shown me trivial examples of student work. My instinct is to suspect he has been trying to pull the wool over my eyes. I lack the expertise to know for sure and I don't know how to evaluate what he's doing.

Setting his tea cup down, John said kindly:

You are expecting a lot from an inspection, Jane. You know I can't respond directly to the points you've made. That wouldn't be professional. But, you've made some very good points.

By the way, did you know the scholars working on the OED *[Oxford English Dictionary]* think it's possible the expression "Don't let them pull the wool over your eyes" comes from America? That it may be based on an old meaning of wool, which is "eyebrows"! If that's true, then "Don't let them pull the wool over your eyes" would mean something more like, "Don't submit to their meanness," rather than "Don't let them trick you." I like it when they discover that even our clichés aren't as simple as we would like to think.

Glancing quickly at his watch, John announced:

Well, Jane, we must go. Thank you very much for the tea and chocolate biscuits. I'm glad we had this chat. I'll see you at the faculty meeting on the 16th of October.

Before leaving Jane's office, John asked me if I'd heard about chocolate biscuits. He said it was a common story about inspection:

> The Head of one school, who had been through an inspection, advised the Head of another school that was going to be inspected for the first time, "Serve the inspectors good tea and chocolate biscuits just like their mothers used to make."

Then turning to Jane, who was smiling, he said, "Those are good biscuits."

Back to the Hotel

John drove me back to the Ibis Hotel, where he joined me for a pint of bitter in the lobby. He asked what I thought about the meeting. I said I'd been impressed by the school, as well as by his meeting with Jane. I asked how he saw it. Was this any different from other pre-inspection meetings? Why had Rosewood been chosen? What difference would my presence make? Later, sitting side-by-side at the bar, John answered my questions, but mostly he thought out loud into his glass:

> Jane is unusual. I've known her a little while. She's "brilliant."[3] I've worked with a number of extraordinary Heads, and she's among the top. She has neither asked hundreds of anxious questions nor has she built tense walls of protection against the real and imaginary threats of inspection. Instead, she's thinking hard. I like that. So few people in schools seem to think anymore. They're caught up in attainment targets for the National Curriculum or tangled up with the management objectives of the required school development plans. Approaching schools with all these concepts about how they should manage themselves may seem easier, but it discourages thinking about how to teach children.
>   For example, that bloody form she's required to fill out. I guess none of the information it requires is worthless, but it doesn't help the school think about its most important task: teaching its particular students.

John seemed fully absorbed by the bubbles rising through his bitter:

> Even if they might be helpful, those questions aren't eloquent. How can something that isn't eloquent be helpful to teaching?

He looked at me and returned to his earlier conversation:

Jane has accepted the proper role for a Head that makes inspections work. Because she has taken responsibility for the school and for its response to the inspection, we'll be more able to focus on the inspection without always having to consider how the school will take what we say "on board." That's still important, but we won't have to worry so much about it.

The Rosewood inspection has begun to take over my thoughts. That's good because I've spent so much time doing silly things these last few months.

As I think you know, this inspection will test the new *Framework for Inspection*. I worked with the team of inspectors that pulled the *Framework* together. Since I've had many concerns about it, OFSTED asked me to be Reporting Inspector for this pilot. Mostly to quiet me down, I suspect.

As I understand the reasoning behind it, we have no choice but to have the new *Framework*. Yet, I'm not at all sure about its value. I'm afraid we may become like the Government bureaucrats we're trying to advise. These strange times and dramatic changes sometimes make me think I'm being watched.

Inspectors hope that inspection will help the school. This meeting has reminded me again of the enormous difference between talking about a school and actually being in one. Rosewood is a real and important school. My first concern is to make sure the inspection will work well for the school. That doesn't mean, you understand, that we end up saying nice things. That isn't what I mean.

I don't think your presence will make much difference. I hope we have some time to talk so I can explain what's happening as we go along. In fact, talks like this are helpful, and I enjoy them.

I don't pretend to understand why an American is interested in inspection, particularly now. I was glad to learn you are going to be here for 9 months. Two years ago I spent 2 weeks visiting schools in California, as part of a teacher-exchange program. I don't think it's possible to learn anything important about schools in another country in the short time I had.

Turning to me, he smiled:

I was surprised by how many pills Americans take. Last week I read an article in the *Independent* about American visitors fussing about how unhealthy our sweets and clotted cream are. Well, I guess I'm a true Brit. I much prefer our clotted cream and chocolate biscuits to your pills.

I've enjoyed this. I hope you won't take offense. I am beginning
to discover how tired I am. All the work in London the last few
months has kept me away from home. The next few weeks won't be
any better. We don't have control of our time anymore. I'd like to go
home and spend the evening with my wife. Is that all right?

I knew he wasn't asking my permission, but inquiring if I would be all
right alone. I assured him I'd be delighted to have time to write and to prepare for the school management team meeting the next day. I planned to
return to London after that, so I wouldn't see him again until next month
when I would come for the first meeting of the inspection team.

TUESDAY, SEPTEMBER 22, 1992— ROSEWOOD'S SENIOR MANAGEMENT TEAM MEETS

While all English schools have a senior management team, the team membership and structure vary in each school. As long as the school's tradi-
tions of power are reasonably respected, the Head can construct a team
however makes the most sense for her particular school.

Like many secondary schools, Rosewood had organized the faculty
into two overlapping administrative structures. Academic issues were the
responsibility of the Heads of Departments (HODs), who met monthly. The
pastoral (guidance) functions were the responsibility of the Heads of Years
(HOYs), who met every 2 weeks to consider student life issues.

Rosewood's senior management team consisted of the three Deputy
Heads (assistant principals) and the four senior teachers. Of the four senior
teachers, two were HOYs and two were HODs for math and English. Jane
had also instituted two revolving positions on the team for younger faculty.

After introducing me, Jane briskly briefed the team on the events to
date. In conclusion she entreated them not to see the inspection as a hur-
dle that fate had thrown in their path, but as an event that could help them
improve Rosewood.

She then presented her plan for accomplishing this. Brian Woodcliffe,
Deputy Head, would be responsible for scheduling. His assigned tasks
included providing a copy of the school's schedule to each inspector, along
with a brief written explanation of how it worked; briefing all HODs and
other managers on scheduling requests that inspectors made when they
arrived; and tracking actual events in detail during inspection week. This
involved knowing where each inspector was at all times and knowing when
and what was happening throughout the school, including unexpected
events, such as a student meeting or an absent teacher. Jane reminded Brian
that inspectors determined their own schedules and could change them as

they wished; his job wasn't to constrain them, but to help them.

She asked Tina Foster, another Deputy Head, to monitor all feedback the faculty and staff received during the visit. Jane expected her to know what had happened in every class that had been visited and at every interview that had been conducted, to know what questions had been asked, and to identify the issues and concerns that had emerged for the staff.

Jane asked the senior teachers to be sure that all departments and all those in the student support structure, including tutors, were fully prepared, and that they understood that Brian must know everything related to scheduling and that Tina must be given a brief summary of each inspection event.

Jane asked Fred Jenkins, the Deputy Head for management, to help her complete the 44-page OFSTED form that had to be submitted by October 13; to compile all the school's extant handbooks, policy statements, forms, and marketing materials; and to set up a briefing paper for the faculty about the new inspection *Framework*. He should also be sure the budget and management information of the school was ready for inspection. To prepare for that he should study both the 44-page form and the *Framework*. She asked him also to tell Jennifer Cooper, the office assistant, that work on the inspection should be her first priority, and to make sure all clerical staff understood that. It shouldn't be their sole priority—they should keep as much on track as possible—but it should be their first.

During inspection week, she expected Tina and Brian to stay in contact with her throughout the day. They were to alert the staff about the importance of attending the regular daily staff meetings in case there was need to communicate to the full staff. Jane would meet briefly each morning with John Turner, the Reporting Inspector. During inspection week, the school management team would meet at its regular time to conduct business as usual. An inspector would more than likely attend. In addition, the school management team would meet for 15 minutes during the lunch hour each day. The inspectors shouldn't be told about these meetings. Finally, there would be a faculty and staff party at the close of school on Friday after the inspectors had gone. She would quickly sum up the feedback and they'd celebrate the end of the week.

Jane then spoke eloquently, as she had spoken to John, about the importance of the inspection for the school, telling the team that their working well together under pressure would be crucial for a positive outcome. She asked them to allow an extra half hour for their weekly meetings. While she hoped they wouldn't need to use this extra time, she wanted no one to have an excuse for leaving early, if the extra time should be necessary.

The team listened attentively. Understanding the importance of the inspection, they quickly agreed to the plan. There was a new electricity in the air as they began to respond to the challenge. Nevertheless, by the time they left the room, they were already sharing old jokes about inspectors.

THURSDAY, OCTOBER 15, 1992—
"A CUPPA TEA": THE INSPECTORS MEET

John and I met briefly at the Barringham division office of OFSTED before his first meeting with the Rosewood inspection team. He explained it was unusual for HM inspectors to meet before an inspection. Since the purpose of this inspection was to try out the new OFSTED *Framework*, he had called this preliminary meeting. It was also unusual that he had been allowed to choose his team.[4] It would be a smaller team than normal for a full inspection of a secondary school this size.

He planned to brief me more fully about the team members but time was short. BR had been late again. The meeting had been scheduled to begin in 5 minutes and he always began meetings with his HMI colleagues on time.

John gave me a copy of the printed agenda, which is shown in Figure 3.1. My notes that follow are keyed to the agenda items.

The Meeting's Agenda

1.1 *Introduction of Our American Observer and Team Members.*   After first introducing Roger MacPherson from the Scottish HMI as a team member, John introduced me, asking me to say why I was there. I didn't catch everyone's name.

1.2. *The School—Rosewood.*   John's brief introduction of the school covered points I already knew. He concluded:

> I haven't told you much about the school because I know you'll want to find it out for yourselves. Jane Edwards has included an excellent two-page overview of Rosewood with the pre-inspection form that you'll see later.

1.3 *The OFSTED Framework and the Organization of the Inspection.*

1.3.1 *What the Pilot Means.*   John continued:

> Everyone knows why they asked me to be the RI for this pilot inspection. I think the *Framework* is somewhat better than it was when we started. The two most troublesome issues for me now are how standards are defined and used and how the new forms will affect how we carry out inspection.
>
> We shouldn't expect what we say about the *Framework* after this

Figure 3.1 Agenda for Rosewood Inspection Team Meeting

---

1. Briefing 11:00–1:30
    1.1 Introduction of Our American Observer and Team Members
    1.2 The School—Rosewood
    1.3 The OFSTED Framework and the Organization of the Inspection
        1.3.1 What the Pilot Means
        1.3.2 Standards
        1.3.3 Forms and the Report

2. Lunch 1:30–2:30

3. Individual Review of Preinspection Information 2:30–3:30

4. Summary and Logistics 3:30–4:30
    4.1 Team Member Responsibilities
    4.2 Issues from Pre-inspection Evidence
    4.3 Inspection Schedule

---

inspection to make much difference. OFSTED feels it must prove to the Government that it knows what it's doing. Now that the *Framework* draft has been released for comment, OFSTED won't be interested in making significant changes—particularly if the changes come from within OFSTED.

We should remember that OFSTED doesn't see our task as questioning the *Framework*, but as piloting it and finding out how to make it work. I understand Americans are always piloting things. [He didn't look at me!] OFSTED will carefully consider our final report as an example of what the new *Framework* will produce. We should give it an honest go.

1.3.2 *Standards.* John continued:

As you know, I think the *Framework* sets in place a different definition of standards. While you work, please pay particular attention to the "Standards and Quality Achieved" section. To help us think about this further, I've asked Roger to lead an informal discussion on standards on Tuesday night after we've reviewed student work.

1.3.3 *Forms and the Report.* John continued:

We'll use the outline of the *Framework* for our report and report our work on its forms. Many of us have fussed a great deal about these forms, which so limit our professional judgement. I think OFSTED is right that we should try the forms before we criticize them further. If we give the forms an honest trial, then our comments about them later won't seem self-indulgent.

We'll report our observations of each class on the "Pro Forma for Lesson Observation." We'll use the "Subject Summary Sheet" to summarize our judgements for all the lessons in a subject area. I've asked Maggie, who has agreed to be Assistant Reporting Inspector (ARI), to collect these forms from you and to build the Record of Evidence (ROE) that we're required to submit with our report. I'll be responsible for the ROE with Maggie's help. We'll talk more about our responsibilities when we meet later this afternoon.

Finally, Rosewood has completed the *Framework*'s pre-inspection form. There's a copy for each of you. I'd like you to review this carefully after lunch to identify any concerns or questions in your area. We'll discuss these later this afternoon when we review the visit and the visit schedule.

2. *Lunch 1:30–2:30.* After we broke for lunch, George Myers introduced himself as the inspector for art and music. He was the only team member wearing a brown suit. When he asked, "Would you like a 'cuppa'?" I told him, "Yes, thank you very much."

"Oh, you know what a 'cuppa' is?" he asked, surprised.

"Yes. I learned that the first time I visited a school staff room during break."

After bringing me a cup of tea, George seemed unsure about what to say next.

3. *Individual Review of Pre-inspection Information.* John suggested that, while his colleagues spent the next hour working on the pre-inspection information, he and I talk further in his office.

He began by reminding me that it was extremely rare for an HMI inspection to be observed. Members of the team were nervous about my presence. The uncertainties that inspection was facing created additional pressures for caution. He again explained the importance of confidentiality. When I said I understood, he went on to say he was pleased with how I had handled myself in the school and during this first meeting in particular:

British educators have learned to expect American visitors to share a videotape of some wonderful school program in America. In fact, some HMI officers recently had to watch a video brought over by an American undersecretary of education. I'm glad you didn't do that.

He was intrigued by the written explanation of my study that I had given him when we last met. He said, "You know, it's difficult for us to believe that an American educator like yourself is interested in inspection. It goes so much against what we know about the American system."

He reminded me that, because I could shadow only one inspector at a time, I would see only a small part of the total inspection. He asked how I'd like to arrange my time. I suggested I spend time watching and talking with each inspector while he or she moved about the school and that I attend all team meetings and as many other meetings as possible and appropriate between him and Jane.

He told me each inspector would have to agree to my going along. I'd be welcomed at all team meetings, as long as I understood that he might exclude me at any time. He didn't want me to meet with him and Jane on the first day. If it didn't seem to interfere with the inspection, he'd confer with her and see if she would agree to my presence at later meetings.

Noting that I'd already observed several meetings between inspectors and Heads, and that I understood their delicate nature, I assured him his response seemed realistic and proper.

When I confessed I was having trouble assimilating the details about the team members, he gave me the document he planned to pass out that afternoon, listing the specific responsibility for each inspector in six areas:

- Inspection of *subject* disciplines. Each inspector had one or two subject area specialties. Providing coverage of the subjects was the most important and difficult aspect of team selection.
- Inspection of *themes* (such as curriculum management, school as a community, equal opportunities). Themes were tailored to the design of a particular inspection, given the school and the purpose of the inspection. Inspectors were also known for their expertise in different theme areas.
- Inspection of the school's student *support* system. Assignments to each class year were usually made last because they were spread among the team members, depending on each member's overall work load.
- Each inspector was responsible for preparing evidence for the Record of Inspection Evidence (ROIE). The assistant reporting inspector was usually responsible for collecting all the pieces of evidence from the individual team members and for putting the final record in order.
- John held the overall responsibility for writing the *final report*. Each inspector had a writing assignment for the first draft and all team members would review the draft several times before it was final.

- The *tasks* that had to be performed during inspection week involved logistics, such as arranging for photocopying and lunch money.

John suggested we go through the assignment for the team, Figure 3.2, so he could tell me a bit about team members. I have noted John's comments on each team member.

Maggie Alexander, Assistant Reporting Inspector, physical education.— Like me, Maggie was a founding Head of a comprehensive. She has a national reputation for her work on racial and intercultural issues. She should be helpful as the assistant reporting inspector.

Judith Barnes, technology.—I tried to get Olive Learmonth on the team because she is one of the country's leading experts on technology. Olive recommended Judith, who had served as a member of a recent task force on revising technology guidelines in the National Curriculum. She's tough like Olive. Judith says what she thinks.

Figure 3.2   *Rosewood Inspection Allocation of Team Responsiblities*

John Turner, HMI. Reporting Inspector. SUBJECT: English. YEAR: 8–9. THEMES: Curriculum. ROIE: Basic information about the school and main findings. REPORT: Overall coordination, final drafting, first draft of: introduction, main findings, record of evidence base. TASKS: Overall coordination and liaison with the school Head.

Maggie Alexander, HMI. Assistant Reporting Inspector. SUBJECT: PE. THEMES: Equal Opportunities. ROIE: Oversee collection of lesson proformas and summary sheets. REPORT: Assist the RI. TASKS: Liaison with school on administrative arrangements.

Judith Barnes, HMI. SUBJECT: Technology. YEARS: 8–9. THEMES: Equal opportunity.

George Myers, HMI. SUBJECT: Music, art.

Lynn Hubert, HMI. SUBJECT: History, economics. YEARS: 12–13. THEMES: School as a community, student support and guidance. ROIE: School as community. REPORT: Quality of the school as a community. TASKS: Meet with community leaders.

Roger MacPherson, HMI (Scotland). SUBJECT: Business, religion.

Mike Nettles, HMI. SUBJECT: Maths. YEARS: 8–9. THEMES: Standards of achievement, assessment recording and reporting. ROIE: Standards of achievement. REPORT: Standards of achievement and assessment. TASKS: Consider standards and the *Framework*.

George Myers, music and art.—George is a pianist. He's an old friend of mine. We joined HMI the same year. He shares my concerns about the new *Framework*, particularly about its impact on art education. He thinks well and contributes well in moderation discussions.

Lynn Hubert, history and economics.—Lynn previously taught in a difficult comprehensive school. As the youngest team member, she's a good representative of younger HM inspectors, whom I consider important in view of testing the Framework. I don't know her well. She seems quieter than I remember.

Roger MacPherson, Scottish HMI, business, religion.—I don't know Roger. HMI sometimes tries to find ways to cooperate with the Scottish, Welsh, and Northern Irish inspectorates. They suggested I include Roger.

Mike Nettles, math.—Mike and I have worked together several times. We have disagreed often. Most recently we served together on the Framework task force. He is not only an excellent math inspector, but he also has a deep understanding of standards.

John ended by accepting my invitation to dinner to talk about his career as an inspector. He'd already found a good restaurant. We returned to the meeting.

4.1 *Team Member Responsibilities.* While the team reviewed the list John had given me, there was considerable in-house teasing, most of which I didn't understand. John accepted their few suggested changes.

4.2 *Issues from Pre-inspection Evidence.* The discussion was direct, familiar, and spirited. Even though these inspectors had never been on the same team, their personal jabs and undercurrents were typical of a group that has worked well together for a long time. They didn't take long to establish a manner of working together that reflected the meshing of style, purpose, and power relationships of an effective and established group. They worked from a common understanding of the ground rules for their meetings.

The meeting focused on each inspector's reading of Rosewood's pre-inspection report, supplemented occasionally by John's quiet observations, based on his knowledge of Rosewood and his meeting with Jane. The team agreed that the following strategy would shape the inspection:

○ Greater reliance on following students.

 GEORGE MYERS, MUSIC AND ART: As you all know, I think we should follow individual students more. If, at the end of the day, our main objective is to determine whether the school is giving our children a good deal, we must see it as the students see it.

While that point has a long way to go within HMI—I mean OFSTED—there has been more general agreement that shadowing students is particularly useful in difficult urban schools that serve students from different communities. It's more important to see student perspectives, which may possibly conflict in these schools. Since how well teachers meet individual student needs is more important, the focus on an individual student is valuable. From my reading of the pre-inspection documents, I think we must include more student tracking than usual in the Rosewood inspection.

The other team members agreed.

- o Consider the "value added" by the school.

  MIKE NETTLES, MATH INSPECTOR: From what I can tell, the test scores for Rosewood are near the national average, but there are strange blips. Some Years appear to do better in technology than others. Given Rosewood's difficult past, it's important to see if we can judge how much the school has contributed to these results and how much can be explained by student intake (what the students bring to the school when they come).

  As you know, HMI hasn't fully embraced the value-added approach that some researchers hotly advocate as a way to think about what the school contributes that's independent from the students it serves. But we've found the idea particularly useful for urban schools or schools where parents or others are actively wondering whether or not the school is providing quality education.

The team agreed, making several asides that Mike must lead the way since they weren't sure how to differentiate between what a school contributes and what a student brings.

The final strategic issue was in response to Jane's unusual emphasis on the challenges facing the technology department. Judith was sure that John's silence did not meat that he thought they should ignore it. She proposed the third issue:

- o Observe every teacher in technology.

  JUDITH BARNES, TECHNOLOGY: John, I think I'm beginning to understand why you asked me to join this team, other than to demonstrate how sweet you are to include a woman for technology. From the comment the Head has made in response to the question on technology, I infer that she thinks the Head of Department isn't up to standard. [John's quiet nod was the only confirmation Judith needed.]

In this situation, the best strategy would be for me to focus more attention on that department. I'll interview and observe the head and observe each teacher.

John, it would be good if you could observe some of the class work independently from me so we can have two views on some classes. Also, if you could attend the interview and the feedback session, it would strengthen whatever we have to say. If we decide in the early going that Jane is wrong, we might lighten up a little. But, regardless of what we say, we want to be sure of our judgements and be able to offer strong evidence to support them.

There was virtual agreement. Judith wryly noted that everyone was being unusually agreeable. Roger asked, "What do you expect with both a Scot and an American here?"

○ Observe the teachers in the interdisciplinary group, but consider them only within their department structures.

LYNN HUBERT, HISTORY: In her answers to questions about the school's implementation of the National Curriculum, Jane has indicated there is a group of teachers who want to continue their work on interdisciplinary curriculum. This is not unusual. Last year I inspected a school where this was an issue. We concentrated on it because we believed it was a question of national significance, as schools were beginning to grapple with the new subject-based Curriculum.

I'm afraid we contributed to the tensions in that school. No matter what a Head believes about the value of intersubject work, or for that matter what we inspectors believe, the new statutes and circulars require the Head to support, and the teachers to teach, the subject-based Curriculum. While the Curriculum guidelines say the school can add any subject it wants, its responsibilities for the National Curriculum will not change. The heavy load of making the new Curriculum work and the focus of the new assessments on the mandated basics of that Curriculum have prevented that from happening.

We should observe some of the interdisciplinary classes, but we shouldn't isolate the group even more by how we proceed. We should consider each teacher as a member of his or her department and make our judgements within our subject summaries for each subject.

Two or three members commented about how HMI had advocated establishing the National Curriculum and how no one had foreseen how it would evolve and what it would mean for the schools. They agreed to see the interdisciplinary classes from the perspective of individual subjects.

4.3 *Inspection Schedule.*   Noting that they would begin inspecting when the school opened at 8:30 A.M. every morning, John passed out the schedule for their meetings, which is Figure 3.3.

It was HMI practice for inspectors to arrive at the school as early as each person could on Monday, the first day of an inspection. While this protected weekends for inspectors who were often away from home, it created raggedy inspection beginnings.

John urged everyone to check into the Ibis Hotel in Woolseyeford on Sunday night, so they could begin promptly on Monday morning. As rationale, he cited that they were a small team and they were testing the *Framework.* This spurred a spirited discussion, much that I didn't understand, about time off and legitimate reimbursable expenses. Everyone finally agreed, reminding John that they would do it for him but that he would owe them one.

John reminded them that Maggie was responsible for the forms. All subject summaries were to be completed in draft form in time for the Wednesday afternoon meeting so the team could use them to prepare for the reporting back to departments. The Thursday night meeting would

---

Figure 3.3   *Schedule of Team Meetings for Rosewood Inspection*

NOVEMBER 8, SUNDAY
   Register at the Ibis Hotel in Woolseyeford

NOVEMBER 9, MONDAY
   4:30   Team Meeting
   7:30   Dinner

NOVEMBER 10, TUESDAY
   3:30   Review Student Work
           Discuss Standards
   8:00   Dinner

NOVEMBER 11, WEDNESDAY (REMEMBRANCE AND RECONCILIATION DAY)
   7:00   Dinner—Moderation Discussion I

NOVEMBER 12, THURSDAY
   Reporting Back to Departments
   4:00   Moderation Discussion II
   7:30   Dinner

NOVEMBER 13, FRIDAY
   Reporting Back to the Senior Management Team

---

have the usual purpose: they would come to agreement on the main find-ings for the final report. These findings would be outlined in the report-ing-back session on Friday.

After making several disgruntled comments about how it seemed inspection was becoming all paperwork and no thought, John called the meeting to an end.

> While I don't know when the first inspection occurred, I suppose it's possible, with all the changes taking place, that we may come to see this as the last inspection for us as HMI.
>
> Let's end on that cheery note. I will look forward to seeing you on Sunday, November 8, 1992, in Woolseyeford.

Dinner with John

John had selected the Distaff Wine Bar for dinner. It was old, dark, and dank in the cellar of Barringham's best wine store. The wine store had originally been a wool merchants' pub. Someone had discovered its nat-ural temperature was perfect for a wine cellar, but it was too big. The owner, who often traveled to France to buy wine, had become an aficionado of French cooking. He finally provoked a chef-friend into opening this small restaurant. A cheery fire burned in the grate. It was a place for a long conversation.

After we settled into the rhythms of the dinner, John began the story of how he became an HM inspector:

> Before I joined HMI, I was the Head of a large urban comprehensive school in Liverpool. It was like Rosewood in many ways. As you know, Liverpool is a port city, not at all like Woolseyeford.

The waiter gently interrupted us to see if my lamb and John's roast beef were satisfactory. Turning back to John, I asked if he'd be willing to start at the beginning. He looked surprised, but was glad to oblige.

> I was born just before World War II to a working-class family in Southampton. Not long after that my dad was killed by a bombing raid on the Southampton docks. My mum, an extraordinary woman, raised three of us. I'm the youngest. She still lives in Southampton.
>
> I don't remember much about the war, except for one time when my mum and I were in a bomb shelter. I can still hear the noise and feel the fear that enveloped us when a bomb exploded nearby. I have

absorbed many stories about the war, including several wonderful stories about American soldiers. Even though America was rather slow in joining the war, what you did for us and for civilization created a deep bond between your country and English people my age and older.

My aunt loved to go to the dance halls when the big dance bands came to town. I remember a story she used to tell about Glenn Miller's band playing when the air-raid sirens sounded. Glenn announced they would not retreat to the shelters. When they heard a plane diving to drop its bomb, the trombone player aimed his slide at it and "shot" it with several loud blasts.

My two older brothers still live in Southampton. Both are tradesmen. I had a different destiny. As the youngest, I was the right age to benefit from an Act that authorized LEAs to pay for students to attend independent schools. This was part of the new national policy to do better by the children of the working class. In 1948 I found myself at Bullfield Hall Academy. As you probably know, Bullfield Hall, which was founded in 1492, is one of the most prestigious independent schools in southwestern England.

I relished the opportunity from the beginning. I had no interest in following my wealthy classmates, destined to join the ranks of the national Civil Service. I decided I would become a teacher.

In 1960, after finishing my national service, I began teaching at Arnold Secondary Modern in Liverpool. Arnold students were from the worst working-class neighborhoods of the city. I was rather quickly promoted to head of the English department. I was proud of my reputation as a teacher who demanded good work from my students and who paid attention to each of them.

In 1965 the Labour Government issued its 10/65 Circular declaring that it was Government policy to end academic selection in secondary education. Selective examinations for secondary schools, primarily the grammar schools, were eliminated. Challenged to develop new comprehensive systems for secondary education, the LEAs started the comprehensive secondary schools. I became a strong advocate of the comprehensives. In 1972 the Liverpool LEA asked me to be the founding Head of a new comprehensive.

Churchill School was sited to make sure students from all classes in the eastern section of the city were included. I thought the most important issue was to build a school that met the diverging student needs with a constant demand for challenge and rigor. Whether or not to define curriculum by subjects had not been the important issue; that doesn't determine rigor. Curiosity, challenge, and push do that.

I also worked hard on supporting the faculty. Churchill School was considered a good place to teach. Everyone thought I would spend the rest of my career there. I loved that school.

In 1974 Sheila Browne was appointed Chief Inspector at HMI. I think it was in 1979 when a Bullfield Hall classmate of mine, who had become an HM inspector, told me HMI was strengthening its ranks. I was surprised when Tony said HMI was looking for people from working-class backgrounds. I guess, once again, the old boys weren't enough. Earlier they'd stepped aside to make way for teachers, then for women. Now it was the working class.

I thought the pinnacle of a teacher's career was to become a school Head, not a self-important HM inspector. More important, I didn't believe HMI was actually independent of the national Government. HM inspectors always insisted they were independent, as if somehow being in Her Majesty's service made them immune to the pressures of mere mortals in Government service. Loving my school and my work, I saw no reason to leave. I resisted the idea.

Tony persisted. Soon we were meeting almost once a week. I learned from other colleagues that HMI was serious about seeking new blood. I knew the development and nurture of good comprehensive schools would be a delicate enterprise and that it was particularly vulnerable to changes in national policy.

My wife, Lisa, is from the Lake District. While she had adapted to life in Liverpool with spirit and enterprise, she'd begun to wonder if the change might allow us to move to a more peaceful place, one more in tune with her childhood memories.

It was John's intrigue with inspection that finally made the difference. He was excited about the idea of visiting many schools across the nation to observe what was happening and to discuss each one, making judgements about quality, discussing those judgements in depth with fellow inspectors, and then writing about what they had decided in a way that would be helpful to the school and that would also meet the requirements of a public document.

You know, at heart I guess I'm a bit of a romantic—rather out of place in this modern world. When I think about it now, I had to camouflage my real reason. Most HM inspectors are proud of our old adage, "Do good as you go." That is why I decided to join. I believed I could do more good as an inspector than by staying on as Head of Churchill School.

While not all HM inspectors will agree, I believe the only rationale for inspection is that it helps schools become better. All my fussing about the *Framework* and the reform has stemmed from my fear that the Government is trying to change its purpose from making schools effective to keeping them in line. That's abhorrent. You can't have a democracy if it's government policy to control what is taught.

I'm not so romantic that I think doing good becomes my traveling companion simply because I have declared myself a do-gooder. You have to do it. An inspector can do good when he or she has acquired a working knowledge of the school. That knowledge comes only from hard, precise, repetitive work. That is what makes good inspection.

The crucial starting place is being there—observing at the school, seeing how students are or aren't learning, and coming to an understanding about what each school is all about. Each school is different. As you will see, the team spends a lot of time talking in order to come to corporate judgements about its quality. We tie our judgements closely to evidence that has been an integral part of that process.

Personally, the most important and satisfying part of inspection for me has been how we finally make sense out of all the details, how we create a snapshot that has meaning for other people. That's the heart of the process. I imagine it's similar to what a composer must feel when he finally says, "That's it. This piece is complete."

I'll be curious to hear what you think about it after this inspection is over.

John didn't confess until the meal was over that he had brought me to this restaurant because it had the best sweets (desserts) in Barringham. He insisted I have the fresh strawberries with Devonshire clotted cream. It was better than pills! When I proposed we meet for another evening during the inspection, he readily agreed. I told him I'd like to learn more about what happened after he joined HMI.

FRIDAY, OCTOBER 16, 1992—THE INSPECTOR MEETS THE FACULTY

The next morning John and I drove to Woolseyeford to meet briefly with Jane before meeting with the full Rosewood faculty.

John approached the faculty with the same businesslike manner as Jane had introduced him. He explained the purpose of the inspection and the use of the new *Framework* before making some specific points about how the team would go about its work:

We will judge the quality of teaching and learning at the school based on the work we see; we won't evaluate the work of individual teachers.

We will collect evidence by observing classes; talking with you; analyzing documents; and examining student work, both in class and at a special team session on Tuesday evening.

When we visit a class, we will look at the content of what the students are learning, the pace of the lesson to see if students are being challenged, and the standards of achievement in light of the National Curriculum.

We'll visit everything going on in the school: assemblies, the playground, homeroom. We'll try to talk with every teacher, but we are a small team and that may be impossible. We'll hold our own meetings after school and in the evenings.

We'll work out with Jane and the department heads how we will report back to departments. We'll want to do as much as we can, but, as you know, our schedule is demanding. We'll hold an informal reporting-back session with the senior management team on Friday. I'll return the following week for the formal feedback to the Governing Body. It's normally 6 months after that before the final report is published.

The inspection week will be a tense time for you, as well as for us. We intend to be straightforward and honest. We don't intend to try to catch you up or find you out.

The staff was alert but quiet. They asked a few questions, mostly about logistics. Jane was attentive. Her confidence suggested she was ready, that she felt her school was ready.

SUNDAY, NOVEMBER 8, 1992—SUNDAY NIGHT AT THE IBIS

Meeting with John

When I registered at the Ibis Hotel in Woolseyeford at 8:00 P.M., the clerk gave me John's note. Meeting in the lobby a short time later for a drink, we again considered the vicissitudes of British Rail. John was his more formal self.

I told him how, while reviewing the notes from my last visit, I'd been struck by the great care both he and Jane had taken with the many details of the inspection logistics. I noted that an inspection visit wasn't a casual dropping by.

He said LEA link inspectors were more informal than HM inspectors, but that attention to detail was part of the inspection tradition. "When an inspection is less than satisfactory for either the school or the inspectorate," he said, "it is usually the result of missing details. Inspection is a live event—

almost a performance—and much can easily go wrong if care isn't taken. When an inspection has been weakened because the RI has been sloppy or lazy, I am infuriated." Still, he reminded me that Rosewood wasn't a usual inspection. He felt the unorthodox preliminary meeting had been helpful in this regard. He went on:

> Speaking of details, I had time on the train to think about your presence. I think we should go over some details before tomorrow. As you know, I am expecting you to follow the procedures the team will follow in regard to these matters.
>
> THE INSPECTION TEAM'S BASE ROOM. We have asked the school to assign a room for our base of operations. It should be large enough for each inspector to have work space and for the whole team to meet. The most delicate understanding is that the room must be private—solely for team use while we are there. We will expect the school staff to honor the confidentiality of our work and, during the week, to enter the room only with our permission.
>
> THE STAFF ROOM. Most English schools have a faculty–staff room that's used for meetings, tea and coffee breaks, and as a retreat for individual faculty. We will honor the faculty's right to privacy and need for space away from us. We seldom visit a school staff room unless specifically invited.
>
> TEA, LUNCH, AND COPYING COSTS. We will make clear arrangements with the school to pay for our lunches, tea, and office services, such as phone and copying. I was told that you would cover your own costs. Maggie will coordinate this with the school staff.
>
> CONFIDENTIALITY. We will take great care to maintain the confidentiality of our notes, working documents, and the content of our internal discussions. The school will not be privy to the internal workings of the team. Ensuring this confidentiality is part of our professional responsibility.
>
> COORDINATION WITH THE HEAD. As Reporting Inspector, I will maintain contact with the Head [Jane] during the week to deal with logistical problems and any other problems that may arise, such as an individual teacher taking umbrage either that she has been visited too often or not enough. One pattern of contact is a brief meeting each morning. That's what Jane and I have agreed to do. The RI must not discuss any team judgement with the Head before the reporting-back session.
>
> FORMALITY AND PROFESSIONALISM. I suspect you may find all this a bit formal. At least it will be consistent with your observation about the importance of paying attention to detail.

Formality is important because it conveys a message to the school that we are there to complete serious work, but that the teachers' work is the most important of all. Our formality will acknowledge that, while our presence will create difficulties for the school, we'll proceed with decorum and not intrude into their lives any more than is necessary for us to do our job.

I think it would be good if you followed each of us for more than one class. Would you be content to begin with Judith tomorrow? She's agreed to that and the others would prefer to wait.

Having finished his business, John asked if it would be all right if he returned to his room to finish preparing for the next day.

I think we'll eat dinner together as a team. I've found that helps the team immeasurably. Would you join me for a night cap on Tuesday after dinner?

A short while after John left, I returned to the bar for another cider, my preferred drink. The bartender predictably acknowledged I was American. His age was the forecast for another World War II story. I hadn't counted on Ian, the raggedy-looking fellow sitting at the end of the bar, who drove a mini-cab. Ian had been to America. "Where?" I asked, bracing myself for the usual answer, "Orlando."

He had visited his brother in Atlanta. For 2 weeks they had traveled through the Appalachian states—Tennessee, Arkansas, and North Carolina. They had avoided the interstate and the Civil War battlefields. They had camped out. He loved it. He understood what I meant when I told him how Les (my wife) and I had found that the best way to learn about a town was to ask the tourist bureau what to see and then to go in the opposite direction. When I asked about Woolseyeford, he and the bartender told me a great deal, some I already knew.

Presently Britain's eighth largest city, Woolseyeford began as a sheep town in the 13th century and became a steel town in the 19th century.

Figuring he was telling me more than I understood, Ian explained that ancient sheep towns grew where roads crossed. They had a stronger middle class and more culture than steel towns where there were sharper class distinctions between workers and owners. At least 20 years ago the jobs in the mills attracted large groups of immigrants, such as the Pakistanis. In a typical steel town the working class settled on the east side of the mills, the upper classes on the west—because the wind blows from west to east. That was always a prime consideration in the layout of steel towns.

Woolseyeford was more mixed up than the typical steel town. When steel took over, the older merchant middle class had unhappily merged with the mill owners on the west side of town. Although most of the city's estates (public housing) were on the east side of the river, two on the west bank touched middle- and upper-class neighborhoods. The large Muslim settlement was in one of the two estates at the edge of the west side. Woolseyeford University, on the west side, was highly rated and had a good engineering course.

Woolseyeford was the most southern of the steel towns. Considered marginal, it always suffered most when steel went down. The city was suffering badly in the current recession. The steel industry was almost dead. It looked like it was finished. Unemployment topped 50%. Many of the steel plants had been torn down, leaving empty lots. This recession was different from others in another important way. In the mid-1980s many people purchased their estate homes under Margaret Thatcher's much touted privatization program. Due to the recession there was no market now for these homes. Those with their money tied up in homes they couldn't sell couldn't leave Woolseyeford. "They are Thatcher trapped," Ian said. This created considerable tension between the white and Muslim communities.

Ian and the bartender knew little about Rosewood School. Two years ago there had been a race riot at the school. They thought it had originated in the racial tensions in the town.

When I paid my check, I asked the bartender, "How did Woolseyeford get its name?" He had no idea. Ian explained with wonderful animation how many years ago, when Woolseyeford was a small sheep town, a commoner had tricked the son of the local Lord out of most of his father's sheep. Dismayed, the Lord had told his son, "Never let them pull the wool over your eyes." From then on it had been known as Woolseyeford.

When I left, the bartender was smiling, still shaking his head.

MONDAY, NOVEMBER 9, 1992—THE FIRST DAY

8:15 A.M.—The First Encounter

The team traveled together in a van from the Ibis to Rosewood School. Brian, a Deputy Head, met us at the school door to alert John that in an half-hour Jane would like him to make a brief comment at the start of the regular daily faculty meeting.

Brian led us to the room designated as our base, where each inspector found desk space for his folders and binders. He offered to answer any questions and to take us on a quick tour of the school before the students arrived at 9:10 A.M. Giving Maggie the key to the room, he was exact in informing her that all staff, including the custodians, had been told not to enter the room during that week. Maggie asked about lunch arrangements and copying. Brian said he would introduce her to Jennifer Cooper, the office manager.

8:30 A.M.—The Curtain Rises

The staff room was already bustling with activity by the time John, Maggie, and I entered. Jane met us with graceful efficiency. In what seemed like no time at all she was addressing the faculty and staff:

> The curtain is about to go up on Rosewood's inspection. I would like officially to welcome the inspection team to our school. They are represented here by John Turner, HMI, who is the Reporting Inspector, and Maggie Alexander, HMI, who is the assistant reporting inspector. Mr. Turner, would you please say a few words before we begin?

Visibly relaxed, John began: "I would have thought the curtain had already gone up."

Even, or particularly, at this early hour the teachers appreciated his wit. John briefly conveyed the team's pleasure at being there and shared his anticipation that it would be a productive week for both the school and the team. Maggie then told the faculty more about what they should expect:

> I was a teacher before I became an inspector. I was inspected three times during my teaching career. I know that's rather frequent and I won't bore you with why it happened. But I understand some of what you are thinking, as you look toward the week ahead.
>
> There are two practical suggestions I wished someone had made to me before I was inspected.
>
> First, don't feel you *have* to introduce us when we come into your class. It's your classroom. Do what *you* think is right.
>
> Second, don't be afraid to show us the context of your lesson— what happened in the class before. Be forthcoming and show us what we should see.

After the meeting John went with Jane to her office, while Maggie and I returned to base.

9:10 A.M.—The Titanic Hits Ice

I planned to join Judith for the day. While fixing ourselves a cup of coffee before first period, Judith explained that, because of the concerns about the technology department, she had planned to start gently but to cover more classes than normal. After visiting her first class the next period, she planned to interview the Head of Department.

John arrived on the run, wanting to talk briefly with us. Jane had told him about an exceptional drama class that met first period. Because of his other commitments, it was impossible for him to see it later. Jane had suggested that "The American would find it interesting." He wondered if I would go with him. Judith suggested I go with John and catch up with her later, when she was interviewing the Head of Department. She didn't think that would be a problem, even if I hadn't seen the class.

John and I rushed off to the auditorium. Revealing no frustration with our late arrival, the teacher told us her Year 8 students had been working for 3 weeks on the dramatic implications of the wreck of the *Titanic*. The first week they had improvised a meeting of the builders, deciding what kind of ship to build. The second week they had improvised the first night on board the ship. Today they would improvise hitting the iceberg. The class had been divided into four self-selected groups. Each group would construct a 10-minute enactment of the collision, using one of four assigned dramatic styles: mime, documentary, exaggerated humor, or social criticism. They had worked on the definition of each of these in prior classes. I decided to sit with the group using exaggerated humor.

I was amazed at the quality of thought, independence, and collaboration demonstrated by the eight students. After deciding to set their scene on the *Titanic*'s bridge, they quickly assigned parts. In 40 minutes they managed to run through their skit three times. After each trial they expunged "bits" they didn't like, created new ideas, and adjusted their relationships. They were critical of one another in a supportive way, witty in thinking up new parts, and independent of adult input.

The best moment came during the third attempt. The impact of the ship had sent the whole cast sprawling to the floor in ridiculous positions. Breaking the pause, the captain rose on his elbow bellowing, "I need a drink." Staggering to his feet, his steward picked up a glass, started toward the front of the boat, then turned to the captain and said, "I'll get you some ice."

Meeting briefly afterward with the beaming teacher, John said:

That was indeed good. I was impressed by your insistence at the beginning that they start with an understanding of what happened. They worked it through well and with verve. You are to be commended for the high standards your class demonstrates.

Later he told me why Jane had asked him to visit the class. The teacher was thinking about leaving teaching because she deplored the National Curriculum.

I think Jane hopes that our seeing her teach might encourage her to stay. Some HM inspectors believe we must never be directed by the school. I'm glad to accommodate a school, providing it doesn't interfere with the integrity of the inspection. We would all be losers if that teacher left.

10:20 A.M.—Judith Interviews the Head of Technology

Beginning in a businesslike manner, Judith asked Mr. A. F. Watson about the technology class schedule and whom she should see when. She wanted to set her observation schedule.

I thought his short answers were hostile. Judith became even more formal, as if wanting to emphasize that her professionalism, as an inspector, and her expertise in technology were beyond reproach. She asked him to describe the department's policies, the department plan, the types of problems the department faced in working with the diversity of students at Rosewood, and how the department related to the design and business curriculums. Many of her questions directly referred to the pre-inspection materials she'd been given and that she had carefully reviewed. Assuring Mr. Watson that he had been helpful, she thanked him, saying she would see him when she visited his class later in the week.

Afterward she told me she had indeed shifted her tone because she felt he had been defensive. She thought he knew technology was a particular target for the inspection. She also thought that his obvious arrogance had been partly because she was a woman.

In spite of that, Judith found him more forthcoming than she'd expected. His policies and plans were about standard for technology. She explained that technology had been a difficult area in recent years. The changes it had undergone had indeed caused confusion. She had participated on several national work groups to help solve the difficulties of introducing technology into the National Curriculum. While she knew it was difficult, she wouldn't tolerate teachers using the National Curriculum as an excuse for poor teaching. Judith said, "A teacher must not allow the reform to distract him from his prime job, which is to teach."

Having modified her schedule as a result of the interview with Mr. Watson, Judith planned to return to base to write up her notes and to review the more detailed test score data and the policy materials he had given her. Meeting John at the base, Judith told him she would visit two technology classes after lunch. When John invited me to go to another English class with him, I accepted.

11:50 A.M.—"The More I Think ..."

John told me we would be visiting Timothy Merrill, a first-year teacher. He would be teaching poetry and tying it closely to writing. A writer himself,

Mr. Merrill had had one or two poems published.

After introducing ourselves to Timothy, John told him we would sit in the back of the class. He asked where the student folders were, so he could look through them at some point. He said we'd talk individually with the students at appropriate times during the class.

Timothy looked thoughtful, sensitive, and scared. Students entered noisily, more interested in lunch (which would come the next period) than poetry. They quieted down when they saw the two of us sitting in the back. I could hear them whispering, "They are inspectors."

Introducing us, Timothy told the class we were there to inspect him:

> Will you please behave yourselves during this lesson and remember what I told you yesterday. Give them a good show and I'll do well.

The students laughed and the class seemed to come together. John showed no emotion. Timothy continued:

> Today will be like last Friday's class. First, we'll finish reading the poem we started. Then you'll redraft the paragraph you wrote on what a simile is. Everyone should have a copy of the poem.

Everyone had a copy, except for three students who quietly worked out an agreement with a neighbor to look on.

They worked quickly through the second half of the poem, discussing what each line meant. The line, "Kissing the leaves of trees," created some prurient interest. One student suggested it meant, "running through the bushes." Capping the conversation by declaring that the line was an image, Timothy ended the excitement. He then asked the students to call out examples of similes from the poem.

The pause was broken by a girl who entered the class with great flair. Slamming the door behind her, she walked as loudly as she could toward Timothy, announcing, "I'm late and here's my note." I suspected it was the unexpected silence of her classmates that led her to look around and see John and me. Showing little surprise, she was only a bit more subdued when she took her seat next to me. Beyond accepting her note, Timothy completely ignored her. After explaining that a simile is a comparison using the words *like* or *as*, he asked the class if they had any questions.

A boy in the front row asked, "Sir, last night I tried to think about what *like* means like you asked us to do. It isn't very easy."

This caught something in Timothy. His face lit up and he began talking about the meaning of words and images. I imagined this was how he talked with his fellow poets after school. Restless noises abruptly stopped and the class listened. I wasn't sure they understood a great deal of what he said about the ambiguity in language and the importance of images, but they knew what he was saying was important to him. He ended with, "The more you think about it, the more complex it becomes. At least at first. If it isn't hard, then you aren't learning."

The fact that the class had become quite attentive seemed to unnerve him. He stopped, then regaining his composure, said, "*Like* has three meanings. We are concerned only with how it is used to make a comparison."

The noise level in the class returned to normal.

Timothy asked a student to pass back the papers from the day before that he had marked. He asked each student to read his comments, to read the poem again, and then to rewrite the paragraph. He would walk around the room and they could ask him for help.

John had been taking notes in a small pocket notebook. Looking through student work, he eventually put their folders down to go to each table to question the students directly. He most frequently asked:

> May I see your work?
> What's the purpose of this exercise?
> Do you think you've done it well?
> What do you need to do to improve your writing?
> I see Mr. Merrill [Timothy] has made a note in the margin of your
>   paper. What does it mean? What are you going to do about it?

Gossip and frustration appeared to accompany Alexandria, the girl who had come in late. When Timothy arrived at her desk, she demanded to know how many words he required in the paragraph. He gave her a vague answer and moved on. He gave her no reason to believe this exercise was any more important than all the others she had rejected over the years.

While the students rushed to turn in their new drafts before the lunch bell rang, John asked Timothy if he had plans for lunch. Since he didn't, John invited him to join us in the student cafeteria.

1:00 P.M.—Cafeteria Feedback

While walking to the cafeteria and while waiting for our food, John asked Timothy about what we were seeing:

> Who is responsible for the artwork displayed in corridors?
> Who were the groups of students who had assembled in the playground
>   during the morning break?
> Were students better behaved because the inspectors were here?
> What parameters define the groupings we see in the cafeteria?

Who had lunchroom duty and how did it work?

After finding a table, John asked about the Rosewood football team, about Timothy's career and why he had become a teacher. John then asked what support Timothy received from the school Head and his department head and what in-service experiences he had had and anticipated having during the next year. Finally, John paused, then smiled and turned his full attention to Timothy:

> I suspect you're wondering why I haven't said anything about your class. The official reason is that HM inspectors don't always give feedback to teachers in the same way as LEA inspectors. The unofficial reason is that I always like a little time to think about and digest a class I've seen. You talked about complexity that comes from ambiguity. I find what goes on in a class is very complex.
>
> Anything I say here is in confidence. We don't comment on the work of individual teachers in our formal reporting-back sessions or in the final report. So what I tell you now won't be made public. It will be much more specific than what you'll hear later.

Nodding, Timothy seemed distracted by a worry about what might come. John continued:

> Even though that wasn't a good class, you demonstrated potential to increase your teaching skills. You missed too many opportunities. I know you were nervous because we were there. I know you are a beginning teacher. We're supposed to talk with you about the National Curriculum. But, the most important thing I can say to you now has nothing to do with that. It has to do with you. You'll become a powerful teacher when you learn how to connect your real intellectual life with your teaching. I can't tell you how to do that, but that's what you need to do.

Timothy fished for easier advice. John didn't offer any.

After leaving Timothy, I asked John why he hadn't commented on how Timothy had handled Alexandria. "Oh, he did that perfectly!" John said. "He ignored her."

I noted in the reflection section of my journal: "Ideas about what makes good teaching practice are not universal."

2:00 P.M.—"Systems, Artifacts, and Environment"

After meeting at base, Judith and I hurried to a senior class in design technology. Judith had been puzzled because the test scores she had examined earlier had been better for the lower years than for the upper. We were going to a class that was taught by Jeffrey Snow, whom Judith had learned was a close friend of Mr. Watson, the department head.

When we followed the students into his class, Jeffrey looked flustered. He had expected us the next day. Explaining that a conflict had developed in her schedule, Judith apologized that she could see him only today. She suggested, since he was an experienced teacher, it shouldn't matter to him. Jeffrey knew she was fully within both her legal and professional rights.

On a recently drawn mural on the side wall of the room there was a question: "What is technology?" The answer lay in three interlocking, Olympian-like rings, each circling one of the concepts from the Technology Curriculum of the National Curriculum: Systems, Artifacts, and Environment. The mural explained each term:

1. Artifacts are "an article that someone has made," with coloring-book illustrations of a teddy bear, a key, and a shoe as examples.
2. The Environment is "our surroundings," with a house, a beach, and the recycling area as examples.
3. Systems are "objects working together to complete a task," with a computer, a refrigerator, and an old radio as examples.

I knew better than to ask, "Why not a new radio?"

The questions Jeffrey asked the students about a demonstration he had conducted the day before on using different metals for making bonds, such as soldering with lead, demanded simple, play-back descriptions:

What did we do first?
What did we do next?
What did it look like?
What's the special name for dilute sulfuric acid?

Although they tried to please him by being correct, the students failed to give good answers. Jeffrey answered his own questions half the time. Then, as if panicked for time, he announced, "We'll have one of our special quickie tests." Students looked at each other, apparently to see if anyone knew what he was talking about. "Take out a piece of paper and we'll begin." While asking 10 questions, such as, "What's the name of cutters for copper?" he wrote the answers on the back of an envelope. The bell rang.

Alert, but expressionless, Judith approached Jeffrey. She said, "I realize you weren't expecting me. But you missed many opportunities. Your students were well behaved, but I don't think they learned much."

Jeffrey carried on for 3 minutes about how his students were poorly motivated compared to those he had when he first came to Rosewood. His students now had no basic skills; they neither spoke, nor wanted to speak, proper English; they were not as motivated as he and his friends from working-class families had been. They didn't seem to care whether they were getting a good education or not.

Letting his rationalizations pass, Judith told him clearly that technology had been included in the National Curriculum to ensure that all students were well prepared in it. Jeffrey lashed out at the National Curriculum, how impossible it was, particularly in technology. He ended with, "If they don't know what we should teach in technology, why do they expect me to know?"

Judith ended the session, telling him, "Mr. Snow, I hope you'll continue to consider why you teach, as well as what."

On the way back to base, I filled Judith's ear with comments about how awful the class had been. She listened as she had listened to Jeffrey. I concluded with, "I guess, as an observer, I'm not supposed to make judgements."

Smiling, she told me, "Those aren't judgements. They are what I believe you Americans would call opinions." I, too, became quiet.

3:30 P.M.—The End of the First Day

John had a little trouble entreating the inspectors to leave their forms, notebooks, and portable computers, when he called them together to gain a sense of where things stood. After catching up with schedule changes and filling in pieces of the informal patterns of how both students and adults were organized, the conversation switched to bigger issues. Judith said:

> That was the worst class I've seen in years. But they haven't all been bad. Tomorrow I plan to go to a class that the students at lunch today described as excellent. I've already seen two reasonable classes. You learn, when you're inspecting technology, that the students are frequently ahead of the adults in understanding what needs to happen.
>
> I'm puzzled by how uneven the technology classes seem to be. Even the test score patterns seem uneven. The lower grades are doing better than the Sixth Form.

Other team members commented on the unevenness they had seen. Most felt the school was unusually uneven as a whole. John agreed. He noted that this might be normal first-day vicissitudes. He pushed them to name the explanations they were considering, allowing that they were tentative. Somewhat reluctantly, the inspectors began to consider possible explanations for the unevenness:

The diversity of the students
The old staff fighting the new mission
The old staff fighting the new staff
The poor introduction of the National Curriculum in the upper levels

The inspectors said they would consider this puzzle while they continued their work the next day.

They agreed it had been a good day and that they had made a great deal of progress. After prodding them to keep up with their notes, John reminded them that they would meet for dinner at 8:00 P.M. at Corridors, a well-known restaurant nearby.

8:00 P.M.—Dinner at Corridors

We were halfway through the main entree when Judith began:

> Mike, I heard you started out in music, not math, and that you had played in one of the Liverpool rock bands, occasionally playing with Paul McCartney before the Beatles.

The inspectors, all in their fifties, turned toward Mike. Even though he was badly out of shape and beginning to bald, they expected him to rise with brilliance and wit to this provocation from a colleague, particularly a woman colleague.

Caught with his glass of bitter halfway to his mouth, he exploded with surprise, "Who told you?" Having no choice but to admit it was true, he faced question after question about what it had been like.

Becoming caught up in their own reminiscences of being young in those particular times, the inspectors grew remorseful about their current situation.

After sweets and coffee were ordered, someone asked Mike how he happened to join HMI. This brought other stories to the fore, which George abruptly ended, reminding them, "And now they want to get rid of the whole lot of us."

In May 1992 all HM inspectors received a letter informing them they could "take voluntary redundancy" (early retirement) in July. They had known the changes required by the Education (Schools) Act of 1992 would drastically reshape their functions in OFSTED. They had known that OFSTED would be smaller than HMI and that their jobs would change from doing inspection themselves to managing inspections and training others to inspect.

But they talked less about what OFSTED might become and more about their despair, betrayal, and frustration over the loss of their corporate life together. Certainly some of it was their loss of colleagueship, but there was something more.

They hadn't been prepared for that letter, which they knew was coming but which nevertheless felt like a bolt out of the blue. No one seemed to care that the changes had rashly forced each of them to make the most agonizing decision of his or her career. The inspectors talked about others they knew who, seeing it as an entrepreneurial opportunity, had sought voluntary redundancy in order to begin private inspection organizations that would respond to the new bids. If any of them had such plans, they were quiet about them now in this venue of solidarity and colleagueship.

Everyone had stories about colleagues who had had their requests for redundancy denied. The inspectors felt individual circumstances were no longer being considered. OFSTED wasn't going to be like the special HMI club they had come to appreciate and that had supported them to do work they believed in. They grieved for the institution they had come to value and for the skills they had developed as inspectors, which seemed suddenly useless in the new world.

Maggie asked if I knew HMI had actually been a special club. She recounted the intensity of the mentoring induction and the concern for an inspector when assigning a job. She emphasized the importance of HMI's corporate view—the names of individual inspectors are never used on the public reports, which are written with an HMI corporate voice. She described the bonds and walls of a tight in-group cemented by tradition, ritual, and exclusivity. HM inspectors had discarded their titles and degrees when they joined, proud to be known simply as HMI. Several years ago it would have been unheard of for an observer such as myself to be present for a school inspection.

Walking slowly back to the hotel, we were a quiet lot. I'd heard inspectors talk like this before. Their talk was born of crisis. They felt compelled to talk with each other about the demise of their profession, about their innermost thoughts while they tried to work them and rework them in order to grasp what was happening. I suspect that, if these had been more ordinary times, I would have heard a great deal more about soccer games and the future of the Monarchy.

I wasn't sure how to place what I was seeing and hearing in an American school context. Going to sleep that night, I wondered what American experience would be most like what I had seen. An American had suggested earlier that our Supreme Court might be the institution most like HMI. I imagined what it would be like to take the Supreme Court justices out for a drink after they learned a national constitutional convention had decided to restructure the Court to make it a technical assistance organization. The new organization would establish a much larger federal court system with many courts throughout the country. The current justices would train and certify the new judges, one out of ten who would not have any prior legal experience. The closeness and secrecy that had evolved over the years to protect the justices in carrying out their original functions would make it difficult for them to navigate in such new waters.

TUESDAY, NOVEMBER 10, 1992—THE SECOND DAY

8:30 A.M.—John Sees the Head

Enroute to Rosewood in the van, John told me Mike Nettles was willing to have me accompany him. I said that was fine, but first I wanted to go to a technology class with Judith Barnes.

I explained how, when I had gone on other inspections, I had found it helpful to see the inspection from the point of view of the school, as well as the team. When I asked if I could accompany him to his early-morning chat with Jane Edwards, he said, "No."

Before arriving at the school, he reminded the team that we would meet at half-past three that afternoon to review student work. After that Mike would lead the discussion on standards and the new *Framework*. While we drove through the dreary November rain, the inspectors mostly discussed how they would come to know the school better.

9:10 A.M.—Technology Design with Judith

Judith explained that we would see a class built on students using technology to solve design problems, such as building a new house or creating a new product. Two young members of the interdisciplinary group would teach the class.

While we introduced ourselves to the teachers, Mr. Josiah Morris and Mr. Bradford Sawyer, students took protractors, compasses, and T-squares from well-marked cabinets and gathered their personal work folders from the class file drawers. One drawer was marked "Lost drawer."

"Students are responsible for taking care of their work," Bradford told us. "But, if they leave anything behind, we put it here in the 'Lost Drawer.'"

The teachers apologized for the crowded classroom, explaining that many students had pleaded to be admitted. While there were two boys for every girl, the minority/white ratio was nearly fifty–fifty.

Continuing its work on isometric cubes, the class discussion stimulated wide and lively participation. The teachers maintained an interesting tension between the concept of the cubes and the practical problems of drawing them. Students quickly went to work on their drawings. Roaming

the room and coaching, each teacher played from his strengths, passing
questions to the other that he could handle better. Taking a close-up view
of the students' work, Judith asked them:

Why did you choose to draw a sphere and not a square?
What was the most difficult bit about drawing the shape?
What will you do next?
How did Mr. Sawyer and Mr. Morris help you?
May I see the drawings in your folder?
Why did you decide to take this class?

After talking with a student, she would pull back, write a few brief
notes, and then approach another.

After class Judith had only a few moments to tell the teachers she
thought their class was excellent. She asked if they were familiar with what
other teachers around the country were doing, whose work she considered
outstanding. Although both teachers knew about teachers who were doing
comparable work, they were glad to learn about other teachers who weren't
familiar. Judith was relaxed. The discussion with Mr. Sawyer and Mr. Morris was much more collegial than the discussion yesterday morning with
Mr. Watson, the Head of Department.

Sharing her observation that the class had succeeded for a diversity of
students, Judith asked why it had worked so well. Both Mr. Morris and Mr.
Sawyer believed it was because they expected high-quality work from each
student and because they worked carefully with each individual student.
Working one-on-one with students had been a major concern when they
structured their class. They said it had been helpful to work as a team.

Although they hinted there were differences between them and Mr.
Watson, the department head, they weren't forthcoming about what these
were. They said the HOD had left them alone in spite of these differences.
Judith did not push them hard on this.

Judith's primary intent clearly was not to give feedback, as it is usually construed, but to gather further evidence.

10:20 A.M.—Math with Mike

When I met Mike Nettles outside the math classroom, he told me he wanted first to go back to talk with a few of the students in a math class he had
inspected yesterday that had been taught by Ms. Amarjit Singh, a probationary teacher. It would not be a problem if we were a little late to the second class taught by Jack Duff, a senior member of the math department,
because he would be giving a test the first 15 minutes of class.

When we entered Ms. Singh's classroom, the students already had begun to work in their workbooks on number chains, an exercise in the basic processes of adding, subtracting, multiplying, and dividing. They were working on multiplication when we arrived.

Because she had expected us, Ms. Singh paid no formal attention when we arrived. Mike seemed clear about which students he wanted to approach. He asked one student if he could see his workbook, then worked with him a few minutes, helping him mostly by asking questions. He then approached another student:

MIKE: Do you know your tables?
STUDENT: Not perfectly, Sir, but better than before.
MIKE: Does your teacher know if you know your tables?
STUDENT: No, Sir, she doesn't know.

Examining another student's workbook, Mike wrote down three numbers and asked her to multiply them. She didn't know what to do. Mike asked if Ms. Singh had told them what order to use when they were multiplying more than two numbers. She looked blank.

After examining the workbook of a fourth student, Mike wrote down the four function signs and asked him which was the multiplication sign. The student pointed correctly. Mike then asked what other mathematical process was like multiplication. The student answered, "Subtraction." He asked the student to read the workbook section comparing multiplication to addition, and explain what it meant. Concentrating hard, the student exclaimed, "Oh, it isn't subtraction. It's addition." Smiling, Mike said, "That's right. Good job." He then asked if Ms. Singh had explained this section. The student said, "I don't think so."

When Mike was ready to leave, he waved for me to follow. He said it was always interesting to observe a beginning teacher, because he could see how well the school was supporting its teachers. He had not been impressed.

We arrived in the next class as the students were finishing their test. When Mr. Duff began to describe the process of squaring a number, the students began dutifully to take notes. When they turned to their worksheets, Mr. Duff admonished them, "Use your brain, not your calculator." Each student either had a calculator or shared one. After watching a while, Mike asked a student to square "39" with her calculator. The student entered "39" and then the times sign and then "39" again.

When Mike asked if she knew about the x^2 key, she said she didn't. Mike showed her. Another student, who had been watching, began to experiment with his calculator. The discovery spread like wildfire through the back of the room. When Mr. Duff realized what was happening, he reminded the class, "Remember, I want you to use your heads, not your calculators." Approaching a student at the back of the room, he lowered his voice, asking, "How did you know about the x^2 button?" The student pointed at Mike, who appeared oblivious.

Shortly afterward I saw Mr. Duff studying the three-ring National Curriculum binder that described the Math Curriculum. He interrupted the class to ask if everyone had an x^2 calculator button. When he explained how to use it, the students became more interested. Several asked him about the other function keys.

Mike watched. Later he asked the student, who had wanted to know about the other function keys, if he liked math. His answer was ambiguous. When Mike asked if he liked the new workbook better than the old one, he said he did because he understood it better. The student told Mike that Mr. Duff used the new book only for exercises.

Afterward Mike told Mr. Duff it had been a good class. Neither mentioned the x^2 key. Mike asked how he divided students in his class and how the department divided students between classes.

While walking back to base, where I was to meet Maggie Alexander to attend an assembly, I asked Mike how he had selected the students to question:

> First, I find those who are having the most difficulty. That's easy. In talking with them, I can usually see whether their problem is the result of a poor math aptitude or poor teaching. The good students are easy to spot. They'll give you clues about how hard the teacher has been working to challenge them. I always include students who represent the class. I learn how well the teacher does on the basic elements of teaching, such as giving and marking assignments, explaining clearly, following through, correcting student work, etc.
>
> I like to talk with students. I'm a teacher at heart. I value the brief moments I have with them. That's good, because in some fundamental sense all inspectors must stay in touch with students. They are the whole point of all this.

11:15 A.M.—Assembly: Drugs and Beyond

Maggie suggested I go with her to a Viewpoint Assembly for Year 11. Assemblies give her a good sense of the school context. Besides, the student she was following was required to attend.

Mr. Travis Davis, the Head of Year 11, told the students the assembly would have two parts: first, Ms. Ruth Elroy of Woolseyeford's Youth Service Bureau would explain the work-apprenticeship programs of the Youth Training Scheme (YTS). Then Sergeant Sanders, from a local police department, would speak about the dangers of drugs.

Ms. Elroy explained how the Youth Training Scheme combined work and education for students who chose to drop out of school. YTS students were paid a small stipend and placed in businesses that offered specially designed jobs. "We offer hair dressing now and soon we'll be approved for child welfare," she told them. She showed slides of former Rosewood students at their job placements. The pictures were dark, fuzzy, and boring. She concluded by asking any interested student to come to her office:

> First, we would interview you to see what you want to do; then we would arrange a placement interview for you with the business. After that, a training coordinator from our office would work with you for a day to train you for the job and, finally, one of our counselors would visit you on the job once a month to assist you and monitor your progress.

The quiet audience had no questions.

Sergeant Sanders first established that he was the police officer responsible for drug control in a nearby town. Showing slides, he pressed his argument that students shouldn't even consider using drugs:

> Young people use drugs because of peer pressure. You are better than that.
> There's no such thing as a soft drug. Once you try a drug, you are inevitably on the road to heroin.
> A drug addict has a miserable life. [He documented this point with pictures of miserable-looking people with ugly scabs on their arms.]
> It's illegal. You could end up in prison.
> History shows that American life has deplorably deteriorated because they rely on drugs. We don't want that to happen to Britain.

Finally the sergeant showed them several artifacts from his job, including handcuffs, and bags of heroin and marijuana that had been seized. The students buzzed when he told them the street value of each bag. In conclusion he showed a movie about a dog sniffing out drugs in airport luggage. When the dog caught his head in a suitcase, everyone laughed. But, when various officials, trying to help the dog, made the situation worse, the laughter escalated.

The sergeant asked for questions. One girl near me boldly asked, "What are the limits of your authority as a policeman? Can you arrest people who you suspect are carrying drugs? Can you arrest someone in another town?"

The sergeant drew himself up with the full weight of his authority and told her: "Don't you worry. If you buy drugs, we will know all about it and you'll soon be on your way to jail."

As there were no further questions, Mr. Davis thanked the two speakers and the students began to file out to their next classes.

Shrugging, Maggie suggested I go with her to a tutorial meeting (similar to homeroom) the next morning where a group of Year 11 students were expected to discuss the assembly, before we talked about it.

1:00 P.M.—Lunch

Sandwiches were brought to our base room. The inspectors began quickly to catch each other up on a variety of information about the day, but there was not as much discussion as the day before. They were absorbed with completing the reporting forms for what they'd seen in each class.

2:00 P.M.—"A Clear Mind for Base Two"

Mr. David Douglas, HOD for math, told the Year 10 class that they would finish their work with whole numbers today. After clearly explaining how to do calculations that involved both multiplication and addition, he asked them to turn to their workbooks.

Mike went to a student working on the optional advanced problems. The problem was to determine what combination of adding, subtracting, multiplying, and dividing five "2"s would equal "1," then determine what combination would equal "2," and so on up to "15." The student was stuck at "13."

MIKE: What do you need to do these problems?
STUDENT: A clear mind.
MIKE (smiling): Yes, but what do you need to know?
STUDENT: How to multiply, add, subtract, and divide. And how to get an odd number from even numbers.
MIKE: Good. You seem confident about how to do that. Why?
STUDENT: We've been working on it a while. I did well on my tests. Look at the early pages of my workbook.
MIKE: Fine. You've done well up to number 13. It might help to figure out what question you need to ask to understand why 13 is giving you trouble.
STUDENT: Why is 13 so different?
MIKE: That's a good question. Keep at it and I'll be back.

By the time Mike went back, the student had figured it out. Congratulating him, Mike asked:

MIKE: What is 10% of 90?
STUDENT: 9.
MIKE: What is 12% of 90?
STUDENT: I don't know.
MIKE: When you finished the last problem, what did you think about? Did you think about math or were you more concerned about going on to the next exercise in the workbook?
STUDENT: Going on to the next exercise.

Mike had visited Mr. Douglas's class before. After the class they discussed how the class and the workbook fit into the 16 strands, the four levels, and the five attainment targets that defined math as a core subject in the National Curriculum.

3:15 P.M.—I Bump into the School Head

On my way back to base, Jane Edwards stopped and asked how my visit was proceeding. John had told me she was becoming more anxious about how the inspection was going. I told her it was fascinating. She seemed to wait for me to say more. I said I had been struck by how competent the inspectors were.

She said she was surprised the team had not interviewed either her or the deputy heads about the management of the school. She said reporting back would be the key part of inspection and she wasn't sure how much this team would provide.

3:30 P.M.—Student Work Reviewed: Standards and Traditions

Promptly calling them together after the school day ended, John reminded the inspectors of two important tasks they had to accomplish: reviewing student work and discussing the new *Framework* and standards. He suggested they spend the first hour examining the student work that had been collected.

Each inspector had requested a sample of student work from the department head for his subject. It was common strategy for the inspectors to select classes randomly within the subject and for the teacher of those classes to select current work of two able students, two average students, and two less able students for them to examine. The sample work of each student was to comprise all written work, including drafts, regular notes, and

tests. Students had been knocking on the door of the base room throughout the day to drop off piles of student folders from each department head.

Taking the appropriate subject pile of these folders, each inspector
began carefully to peruse them. Although concentrating on the task at hand,
their quiet banter indicated they were judging the quality of work against
their long experience of having looked at much student work in a great
variety of contexts. Teachers' comments on student work were always noted.

Reconvening the group, John asked if they had had enough time for
their review. Then, after each inspector summarized what their work showed,
the inspectors began their comments:

> Satisfactory progression in German during Year 9, but not enough free
> writing.
> Nothing notable in the sciences.
> Writing often seems purposeless, writing merely for the sake of writ-
> ing. Not enough redrafting.
> Lack of a consistent school practice in marking papers.
> The teachers aren't challenging the students enough.
> This teacher writes "smashing" on the first draft of a poorly written
> year 10 paper. He talked with me at length about the importance
> of self-esteem, especially for minority students. Several students
> told me he was too easy on them, that they weren't learning much
> about writing.
> "Smashing" is good for student self-esteem only when the work *is*
> "smashing." Otherwise it's patronizing.
> Some teachers give an "A" for effort, not accomplishment.

John asked anyone who had new observations or questions about Rosewood to add them to those they shared the day before. Although the formal moderation session wouldn't be until Thursday, he reminded them
that it was helpful to share reflections as they went along.

Judith mentioned that several classes today were better than classes
she had seen the day before. After she talked further with several teachers
about the quality of teaching, she wondered if she had gone too far in thinking that the schoolwide policy structure was responsible for the overall
unevenness of student performance. She didn't think poor teaching was
merely idiosyncratic. Something was going on. It was her hunch that it
somehow related to the diversity of students.

They agreed to keep working on this issue to increase their certainty
about what was happening, knowing they would come back to it in their
moderation discussion. John deliberately avoided forcing a clear team consensus. Several suggested they would learn much more the next day from

their scheduled interviews with the heads of departments.

After 2 hours John suggested they break briefly for tea and coffee before talking about the *Framework* and standards.

The next day I asked each inspector how useful the review of student work had been. I felt they had attacked that task with much less rigor than I had seen in an LEA inspection. They said it was a useful check that sometimes raised new questions. But everyone felt it was more useful to see student work in the class context, where they had control of selecting it and where they could talk about it on the spot with both the teacher and the student.

Roger McPherson, whose subjects were business and religion, found reviewing student work was helpful when his time was limited. He thought it was useful training for new inspectors. Summing up his main point, he said:

> Because you're there in the class, you know the context for the work. Systematic ways of collecting information are efficient and sometimes necessary. But I find the most useful knowledge comes from information I have collected myself, without the interference of some procedure.

Mike began the discussion on standards:

MIKE: As HM inspectors, we've always been concerned with standards. But now it has become a rage. The Government's *Citizens' Charter* requires all public services to set standards and to measure and report on accomplishment. The rationale for the National Curriculum seems to follow more from that than from good ideas about what a curriculum structure should provide. If standards are set and progress is measured, improvement will happen. It's a simple idea in a complex world.

LYNN: What makes them think it will work? It doesn't make any sense.

MIKE: Well, that's no longer an issue for us to discuss. As OFSTED, we're now concerned with standards in education. So it's at least consistent that the new *Framework for Inspection* has been built around "standards of achievement."

Most of us see the two most important changes as problems. First, we must separate what students achieve from the quality of learning the school provides. The new report outline makes this division quite clear by providing two separate reporting sections. Second, instead of using the provision of education as the focus (or, as expressed by the new terminology, the unit of analysis), we're expected to consider the achievement of the individual student. The last time inspectors were asked to do this was during Payment by Results.

MAGGIE: Somehow, when they made standards explicit, they made their meaning less clear. Even if we agreed with the new definition of standards and with how to measure them, wouldn't we still lose what has been our most important focus, which is to try to figure out how we can help schools improve?

ROGER: I remember how impressed I was on my first day as an inspector, when my mentor Jim Thornbury told me, "Roger, HM inspectors are professional. We have responsibility for a great public trust. We must decide if our schools are doing what they should be doing to provide a good deal for our children." Because the *Framework* specifically takes away our professional judgement, our work is no longer based on public trust but on a limited document. Much has been lost.

GEORGE: While I know not all of you will agree, I firmly believe the standards a school sets for itself must be honored. If standards are going to make any sense, the school must be engaged. That's difficult work, because the standards that actually shape what happens in the classrooms aren't necessarily the same as those a school has written down. They certainly aren't what some distant task force has put down. Standards that a school actually puts in practice have always been central to our task of knowing schools. These are the ones that make sense and that we should comment about. To understand what they are, we have to know the school.

JOHN: Well, we have no choice but to write the report making the separation the *Framework* requires. Right now we're talking from the luxurious position of not having tried it before. I think we should think critically about it while we work with it. Then our comments might make more difference.

7:30 P.M.—Dinner at Corridors

Before dinner I told John about my conversation with Jane Edwards, mentioning her concern about the amount of reporting back the team would give. He thanked me for that information. Pausing thoughtfully, he added, "I think I can arrange for you to interview Jane on Thursday, if you would like." He and Judith were scheduled to interview her about school management during lunch that day, but he thought possibly I could meet with her before that. Almost as an afterthought, he said:

You're always asking what inspectors look for when we make our judgements—what we *don't* write about. Well, one thing I look for is how well the Head has managed the inspectors. Jane Edwards does that very well.

During dinner I sat next to Maggie Alexander, who was responsible for the community aspects of Rosewood. I asked about the major departure of the 1992 *Framework* in regard to parents. HMI had never really considered the role and opinions of parents. Community and parental involvement isn't the same good but elusive theme in English schools that it is in the United States, where it is a slogan no one will refute. The new *Framework* requires the Registered Inspector to solicit parents' questions and views about the school at a parents' meeting called for that purpose. The school is required to send the final published inspection report to all parents. I asked Maggie how they were going to consider parents in this inspection.

> We have given that some thought. Because no one has had relevant experience meeting with parents and because we are reluctant to do anything that might in any way stir what we believe are volatile racial tensions at Rosewood, we have decided not to call a parents' meeting. In the past, LEA inspectors have had more to do with parents than HMI. But, as it works out, there will be a parents' meeting tomorrow afternoon that I will attend. We would probably have gone to that in the old days anyway.

When I asked if I could go, she said John had already asked Jane Edwards about that. But Jane had been uneasy because of the underlying tensions between the Muslim and white groups.

Later I suggested I might walk around the neighborhood to talk with people I met. I told Maggie I would describe myself as a visiting American educator who was curious about how the English felt about their schools. She thought that was a good idea. When I asked if I should check this out with John, she said with a bit of a smile, "I'd ask him afterward."

Nightcap with John

John and I settled down in the hotel lounge at the end of a long day. He began telling how he had became an HM inspector. "It started well because Nellie Learmonth was my mentor during my probationary year. My wife Lisa still teases me about how I 'Sat with Nellie.'"

Suddenly he stopped talking. I was tired and it took me longer than usual to realize that I'd fallen into another black hole. John's awkward silence indicated I was supposed to understand something I didn't. Finally, he laughed, sharing his realization:

> You have no idea what "Sitting with Nellie" means. It's an old saw from English educational history. I'll tell you about it.

During the Victorian era the new cadre of primary school teachers was mostly single women. Since schools for the poor were new and there were never enough teachers, the better older students were asked to help, sometimes with the paperwork, sometimes with teaching younger students. In order to improve their teaching skills, these pupil-teachers spent time with the teacher to learn about teaching. That was called "Sitting with Nellie."

Since many of those pupils became the next generation of teachers, John had been pleased that his HMI mentor was named Nellie. At first that was about all he had liked about the HMI induction rituals. He wasn't sure he had liked having a woman mentor. He certainly did not appreciate that Nellie hadn't taught for many years. What could she know that he didn't know better? Furthermore, because schools had changed a great deal since she had been directly involved, he wondered how she could understand the pressures school Heads and teachers were experiencing, particularly those created by the new comprehensive schools. However, he was most unhappy because he knew his work wouldn't really count until his first probationary year was over.

John confessed that his biggest difficulty had been with the idea of moderation and the necessity of reaching a corporate judgement. He had let it be known rather too quickly that he thought moderation contributed to HMI's elite narrowness. It was in the same category as other HMI customs he considered archaic, if not downright silly. He had been appalled to learn that an HM inspector shakes a fellow inspector's hand only once. "We shake hands only the first time we meet. I soon discovered that inspectors still took this custom seriously. Now I like these customs."

John soon figured out that, because he had been outspoken in his criticism of moderation, he was being assigned to tasks that involved much discussion with his new colleagues. While he had often been surprised by the depth of their understanding about schools, he felt he was spending much too much time talking with them and not nearly enough time visiting classes. He was even more frustrated when he realized that other inspectors going through probation were spending more time in schools than he was.

Nellie's concern about John's position on moderation continued into the year after his probation. One Saturday morning his supervisor rang him at home to tell him that a personal emergency had befallen the Reporting Inspector for an inspection of a primary school that was to begin the next Monday morning. Would he take charge? Confirming his gut intuition that it was unusual for a second-year inspector to serve as Reporting Inspector, Nellie assured John that, since he had progressed so well during his HMI induction and because he had had so much in-school experience before he joined HMI, she was confident he could handle it. His pride about being asked drowned out any suspicions that might have been raised when she went on to mention that it had been necessary to reassign some other members of the team as well. As if to reassure him, she told him he already knew two of them: David Thornton and Philip Jenkins, both among the most senior, the most revered HM inspectors, both known for being notoriously difficult to work with. While probationary inspectors were frequently given induction assignments with Thornton and Jenkins, John had managed to avoid them, paying them only the required deference at chance meetings.

Realizing this was an amazing opportunity, John slept restlessly. In spite of the last-minute adjustments, the inspection went well. Briefing his inspection team, managing the logistics of the inspection, and leading the early team meetings, he found his old skills served him well. Going independently about their work with great professionalism, each of the two senior colleagues went out of his way to tell John that he was impressed by the job John was doing.

The moderation discussion was scheduled for 2 hours on late Thursday afternoon to prepare for the feedback to the school's senior management team on Friday morning. John stayed up most of Wednesday night writing his judgements with supporting evidence. It had gone so well that he decided to cast it as the first draft of the report.

He began the moderation discussion by telling his team about the considerable progress he had made the night before. He suggested it would be most efficient for him to begin with what he had done. The team could build on his work by making comments or additions.

After agreeing to this procedure, Philip Jenkins, one of the senior HM inspectors, suggested that John read his whole draft first. "As a way of saving time," he had added with a funny smile.

Only occasionally writing notes, the other HM inspectors paid careful attention while John read. When John looked up from the page, Philip asked, "Are you finished?" Barely waiting for John's nod, he began:

> I disagree with your overall conclusions and many of your judgements. I think your use of evidence lacks rigor. You state that you think this is quite a good school. I think it is only adequate. I think the evidence shows that, while the students here are quite exceptional, the school in fact coasts on the quality of its students. Thus, its provision is mediocre.

The other team members reacted. David Thornton, the other senior HMI, agreed with Philip. Pauline, an inspector for only 3 years, said, "It will apparently take considerable moderation for us to reach judgements with which we can all agree."

John had had no idea this was coming. He hadn't talked with the other team members about what they were seeing and thinking. Speechless, he felt his confidence quickly leave him. He does not remember what happened next. They managed to agree on a brief statement they could make at the reporting-back session the next day and they scheduled a meeting for the following Tuesday evening for a longer discussion. The only detail he clearly remembers is how he struggled to bring that meeting to an end.

That Tuesday work session was forever engraved in John's mind:

> At that meeting, I felt the power of that particular group of inspectors working together to make sense of the particulars we had each seen in that school the week before. I began to see that it was the combination of our having been together at the school at the same time, our diverse perspectives about education, and our broad range of experience in schools that led to better, more thoughtful insights than any one of us, myself included, could have generated alone.

After that meeting he found it was much easier to prepare a draft of their conclusions than it had been to write his initial draft. After each team member carefully reviewed the draft from the Tuesday meeting, John had to work further with each one to resolve the minor difficulties each saw in the report.

John stopped suddenly to check his watch, prompting me to check mine. It was surprisingly late and we had a busy day ahead of us. John finished with a postscript to his story:

> Nellie looked pleased when I told her later that I finally understood the value of moderation. But it was 2 years before I figured out that she had orchestrated that inspection as an exercise for my benefit. I miss her.

WEDNESDAY, NOVEMBER 11, 1992—THE THIRD DAY

8:50 A.M.—Discussion of Drugs and YTS

Maggie Alexander took me directly to Mrs. Allen's Year 11 tutor's group. In most English schools a student's day begins in this group (similar to a homeroom). Each tutor, usually a member of the faculty, is responsible for the "pastoral care" and academic support of about 20 students. Rosewood's student support systems were better organized than most American high school guidance and homeroom programs. In most schools the Heads of Year have overall responsibility for the program, meeting regularly with the tutors who work with each class year. In addition to being in charge of the tutor's group for Year 11, Mrs. Rebecca Allen is a member of the history faculty.

A mixed group of students quietly entered the room, with some back-and-forth banter between minority and white students. Relaxed and polite, they seemed glad to be there. They were obviously fond of Mrs. Allen. After taking the roll and making several announcements, Mrs. Allen reminded them they would discuss yesterday's viewpoint assembly. They became very quiet.

MRS. ALLEN: Do you have any questions about drugs?
STUDENT: (After looking at me) Miss, how big a problem are drugs in America?
MRS. ALLEN: (Looking at me) Well, as you know, we have an American visitor today. Mr. Wilson, would you care to answer?

It wasn't easy for me to jump from taking notes to talking. At first the students were attentive to my rambling, but after they adapted to my accent their attention fell away. Mrs. Allen called on Charlene, who had raised her hand. (She had asked the sergeant about his power to arrest.) "Miss, that sergeant went over the top. He didn't understand my question and he answered it as if I were one of his underlings. That wasn't right."

Mrs. Allen agreed. As there was no further interest in discussing drugs, she asked if there were any questions about the Youth Training Scheme (YTS). There were none. She asked if anyone planned to sign up. There was no response. "Why not?" she asked.

My brother and some of his friends signed up. They say it's worse than an ordinary job. What's different is that you have to be interviewed many more times, the jobs are worse, and they don't pay as much.

Mrs. Allen smiled weakly. Moments before the bell sounded, she asked if they understood the schedule for the rest of the week. Everyone did. When Charlene walked past me on her way out, I heard her telling a friend, "They ought to have a YTS placement for police sergeants." Her friend laughed.

I was surprised when the student who had asked about Elvis approached me again, wanting to know what my favorite place in America was, because he wanted to live there some day. He listened politely while I talked about the Sierra Nevada and the Maine coast. Then he asked if I'd ever been to Graceland Mansion. He knew everything about Elvis, about his house and its grounds. His initial disappointment that I couldn't add anything to his store of knowledge was replaced by his joy that he could instruct me in an area where I was clearly below standard.

When I shared my observation with Maggie that Mrs. Allen hadn't come to the defense of YTS, she said:

> Teachers are in a difficult position. YTS is a Department of Employment program, not a Department of Education program. Nevertheless, teachers are expected to boost it, even if they don't think it will benefit students in their move from school to work. That's why Mrs. Allen was quiet. Teachers are much less likely to express their opinions about Government programs than they were before the reform, particularly if an inspector is around.

I told Maggie I had found the assembly depressing. As in many school events put on for the benefit of American students, the adults had demonstrated low expectations of what students could bring to it. Maggie responded with surprise:

> That's what I've been thinking. As you know, I've been shadowing Charlene. What I have learned about her in a variety of contexts has made the assembly seem even more a waste of time than usual. While I seldom write up an observation about an assembly, these events provide a look at the life of the school. And schools aren't known for respecting the intelligence of students.

9:10 A.M.—Interview with Mr. Davis, Head of Year

While we walked to Mr. Travis Davis's office, Maggie noted that all secondary schools wrestle with the tension between pastoral and academic counseling in their student support programs. On the pastoral side there is an emphasis on treating the student as a whole person in a social context, while on the academic side the emphasis is on considering the student in terms of the academic tasks and hurdles he or she is facing in the school. Maggie suspected we would find Rosewood's approach more on the pastoral side.

MAGGIE: What's your role as Head of Year (HOY) for Year 11?
MR. DAVIS: I meet and talk with students who come in.
MAGGIE: Does that take much time?
MR. DAVIS: Too much. I tell the tutors they should be the first to handle students who have created bother but they prefer to send them to me.
MAGGIE: So most of the students you see have caused bother?
MR. DAVIS: Yes.

MAGGIE: Do you encourage your tutors to be pastoral or academic in their approach to students?

MR. DAVIS: The tutors meet when there's a problem in a classroom.

MAGGIE: How many regular meetings do you have with them?

MR. DAVIS: Six in a year.

MAGGIE: How often do you meet with the other HOYs?

MR. DAVIS: Once a week.

MAGGIE: Do you have a job description for HOY?

MR. DAVIS: Mr. Stearns has it in his office. He has them for all HOYs.

MAGGIE: How well does the job description fit what you do?

MR. DAVIS: Pretty well. I wrote it.

MAGGIE: How do you see your role?

MR. DAVIS: It's both a pastoral and a disciplining role. And I organize activities, like the viewpoint assemblies.

MAGGIE: Your students seemed courteous and well behaved.

MR. DAVIS: We're working on that.

MAGGIE: Do you have a program for new students?

MR. DAVIS: Yes, we have a "settling-in program," because most students are too boisterous when they first come to Rosewood.

MAGGIE: How does a faculty member in one of the departments find out if there's a problem with a student?

MR. DAVIS: We have a liaison program.

MAGGIE: Who has the files for Year 11?

MR. DAVIS: That's part of my responsibility.

MAGGIE: If I were a teacher and I wanted to look at the files of a student, how would I do that?

MR. DAVIS: You'd ask me.

MAGGIE: Thank you very much for your time. You've been helpful.

Later when I asked Maggie if Mr. Davis was a typical HOY, she said, "Yes, he is quite typical. Although he's been here only 2 years, he's already associated with Rosewood's old guard."

11:11 A.M.—"Remembrance and Reconciliation Day"

Jane Edwards's voice was soon heard throughout the school over the loud-speakers:

Today is Remembrance and Reconciliation Day. At 11:11 everyone will stand and observe a moment of silent reflection to commemorate the end of the Great War in 1918. We should remember the men and women who gave their lives for Britain and for a better world. We should ask what we can do to be reconciled with our enemies and our past. Remember that our enemies are not only those countries that made our victory possible by their loss. Everyone please stand in silence. Thank you.

11:15 A.M.—"What Is a State?"

I hadn't spent much time with Lynn Hubert, the inspector for history. She was the youngest inspector on the team. Her tailored suits were impeccable. She always seemed fully engaged in the team's discussions, but she rarely spoke up. She asked if I would be interested in visiting an A-level history class. While walking to the class, she told me the nine students had graduated from the regular program last June and were now preparing for the A-level exams required for university admission. During their study of Nazism, this class was reading *Mein Kampf*. Mr. Gareth Alexander, the teacher, began:

MR. ALEXANDER: Last time we asked if Nazism was an ideology. You read sections of *Mein Kampf* to see what it suggested about this. One of the key questions Hitler asked was how to organize a state. In the A-level exams you'll be asked questions about concepts like: What is a state? What do you expect from a state? What makes the British British?
STUDENT: The Monarch.
MR. ALEXANDER: (He didn't hear the answer.) Is there a geographical definition?
STUDENT: Water.
MR. ALEXANDER: (Again he didn't hear the answer.) What about boundaries? Bosnia is all about boundaries. What is a state for? What does it do for you and what do you do for it?
STUDENT: The state provides services like education.
MR. ALEXANDER: Good. What do you do for the state?
STUDENT: Pay taxes.
MR. ALEXANDER: Yes, there are two sides to every coin—rights and responsibilities. What kind of state did Hitler want? Why did he want to remove the voice of the individual? (No response.)

Accepting no answer, he changed direction:

MR. ALEXANDER: Let's look at your reading. Where did you underline the text? I didn't highlight anything until page two.
(Looking at a student's book.) What did you highlight in the next paragraph? That isn't a bad line to underline, but it repeats an earlier one. How many of you dropped off while reading *Mein Kampf*?

STUDENT: I think Hitler is articulate.

MR. ALEXANDER: Is he? People often buy *Mein Kampf* but they seldom read it. Hitler was an orator who believed he should aim his message at the people with the lowest IQ.

By the end of the class only three out of the nine students had spoken. Reviewing students' essays on the Versailles Treaty, Lynn concluded they were much better than the class. Mr. Alexander did a good job commenting on what students wrote and he demanded intelligent rewrites.

When she talked briefly with him after the class, he was pleased to hear her impression of the essays. He was quite cavalier in dismissing her probes about the class, complaining that his students had a low interest level. When Lynn asked if he had difficulty hearing, he told her he planned to retire at the end of the year.

1:15 P.M.—Interview with the Head of Department for Math

Mr. David Douglas, the Head of Department for math, waited for Mike Nettles, who was a bit late because he had waited for me to return from the class with Lynn:

DAVID: Mike, you've spent a great deal of time with our department. Since my faculty has found you professional and helpful, they have asked me to invite you to the departmental meeting tomorrow to give us some feedback.

MIKE: Thank you. You know, as HM inspectors our job is to make judgements about the quality of what we see. Normally we report back to the heads of departments and they pass our findings on to their faculty. I'll consider your invitation and let you know tomorrow.

Mike asked about the support math received in the school. He asked detailed questions about the budget the school provided, the equipment, the space, the department's policy about students using calculators, computers, math software, and the assessment of students.

When Mike mentioned calculators, Mr. Douglas said he understood Mike had disagreed with the school policy that students use them only to check their answers, not to compute. Mike coldly insisted he hadn't disagreed with this policy but as head of the math department Mr. Douglas should know that the National Curriculum urged the use of calculators for all work.

Mr. Douglas was also concerned about assessment. Mike asked what teachers were expected to do during a week to assess their students and what organizational structure was in place for that:

DAVID: I'm concerned about teachers spending too much time on assessment. The National Curriculum has made us deskbound with all the assessment recording it requires. This takes away from class time.

Mr. Douglas then described the department's elaborate system of assessing, auditing, and planning for each of the attainment target levels. At Mike's request Mr. Douglas showed him those files.

Mike asked about *banding* and *setting*. These are good examples of the many concepts that teachers in England use when they talk about classrooms. Banding is placing students with different abilities in different classes (most like tracking). Setting is placing students within a class in groups that have similar abilities or tasks. Although he was against banding on principle, Mr. Douglas and the math faculty decided they had to band if they were going to deliver the National Curriculum. As if to assure Mike, Mr. Douglas said they didn't band students until the end of the ninth year and then they did it carefully. When Mike asked about the proportion of minority and white students in each band, Mr. Douglas wasn't sure. But he strongly asserted that minority membership wasn't important, particularly in math. Mike asked Mr. Douglas if he had seen the recent article in the *Times Education Supplement* that speculated that children from the section of India where Tamil is spoken are stronger in math than English children. He had not.

Mike asked how the math classes were scheduled, how students had changed over time, how the school had reacted to publishing test scores, and what he thought about his team of teachers. Shifting in tone, the interview became more like a collegial discussion:

MIKE: You have a good team, is that it?
DAVID: Yes, they are a good team. Some feel we go out front too much. Oh, we have job descriptions all prepared.
MIKE: I'll take a look at them.
DAVID: Our main problem is finding enough time.
MIKE: Yes, the time scale is always too short. And all these changes must make it more difficult.

2:00 P.M.—The "Gross National Product"

When Mr. Gurbachan Kundi began the A-levels class in economics with eight students, Lynn Hubert and I were sitting in the back of the room. The class had an air of purpose and anticipation. Mr. Kundi explained the class would analyze the videotape of a recent speech to Parliament by Mr. Lamont, Britain's Chancellor of the Exchequer. Mr. Lamont and the Government's economic policies had recently been under strong attack. The pound sterling had fallen dramatically in international markets.

Mr. Kundi first reviewed some of the key jargon they would hear, such as GDP (Gross Domestic Product) and PSBR (Public Sector Borrowing Requirement—the difference between what the Government spends and what it collects in taxes for a given period). He then reviewed the monetarist economic position advocated by Mr. Lamont. Students participated well. Stopping the videotape at key points to ask questions, Mr. Kundi urged the students to tie their specific comments with their more general ones. Only one student did not participate.

When Lynn asked him after class why he hadn't pushed a student who had failed to give a complete answer, Mr. Kundi said that the student's brother, who was in the Army, had left that morning for Northern Ireland. Lynn didn't spend much time with him other than to tell him the class was excellent. Mr. Kundi was pleased.

3:15 P.M.—Parents' Choice: An Interview with Two Parents

The school sat at the edge of large open sports fields that were soggy from the almost daily rain. On the west the fields stopped at the edge of a neighborhood of small bungalows. Rosewood's old neighborhood, Ramlot, was up the hill from these. Ruth Thornton, chair of the Governing Body, and several other school Governors lived there. To the south older detached homes and newer apartment houses finally merged into Woolseyeford's city center, where we returned each night to the Ibis Hotel and Corridors. I had not been to the run-down industrial area to the north, which I suspected was connected to the abandoned steel mills along the river. The density of industry, even a dead industry, in English cities continued to surprise me. A small, mostly white housing estate (public housing) lay to the east. The much larger, mostly Muslim estate was several blocks to the northeast.

Deciding the Muslim estate was too far for a quick trip, I started across the muddy field toward the nearest estate. I was surprised by how constrained I felt. I wondered if the inspectors thought of the neighborhood in the same way they thought of the school staff room: "Don't enter unless invited." Even the local inspectors, who worked regularly with parents, usually met formally with them on school territory.

Fortunately my wife Les and I had already learned how to break through the expectation that Americans don't wander around estates. We had discovered that the ambiance of an estate doesn't always coincide with its reputation. We had learned that people who purchased their estate homes from the Government under Lady Thatcher's privatization program often nicely painted their doors a color different from the others.

Wandering through the small estate, I met several people who were willing to talk with me about Rosewood. I was impressed by the strength and consistency in their views about the school.

They knew the school staff believed the difficulties lay in the tensions created when Muslims moved into the large estate. While they acknowledged strong feelings between Muslims and whites, they felt those came in waves. The school made little difference in these tensions. The only exception was the riot on the school grounds that they thought had been provoked by a controversy about school uniforms.

The people I questioned admitted having had high hopes for Rosewood when Michael Franklin was appointed Head. Because he was an intercultural expert, they thought he might improve the school. But he had quickly lost their confidence. At a community meeting Michael had allowed the leaders of the white community to bully him. They had wanted the school to adopt a school uniform policy requiring all students to wear uniforms. While Michael was clearly ambivalent, he told them he supported the idea and would promote it. The leaders were surprised he agreed so readily because they knew the Muslim community would feel threatened if they thought the white community had imposed the uniform policy on the school.

After learning about these complexities Michael began to vacillate at the next public meeting, a parents' meeting. Parents were upset because the students attending the meeting had seen him waver. He finally announced that the faculty must decide the issue. In their new guidelines for dress the faculty fell short of requiring uniforms, but offered encouragement to anyone who wanted to wear them. The code for uniforms wasn't as important to these parents as the quality of the Head's leadership. Because Michael had been wishy-washy, the parents ended up on the outside again, heightening the antagonism between the Muslim and white groups. Intrigued by this story, I remembered wondering why some students were wearing uniforms while others were not.

The community residents offered two new perspectives about the school:

1. Rosewood once served a white middle-class neighborhood and a white estate. This was the school's golden past the Governors remembered. Most of the Governors had supported comprehensive education, but they had not envisioned that one day that would include Muslims. Somehow the Muslim students intruded on how they had wanted it to be. Retreating to memories of the golden past, the Governors were not able to deal well with what was happening.
2. The parent representative on the school's Governing Body wasn't in the inner circle of the informal leadership structure of the community. Those leaders thought serving on the Governing Body was a waste of time. Having a weak parent representative allowed them to criticize whatever the school did without harming their position in the community.

I asked if they felt the national reform had given them greater choice about what schools their children attended:

> The Parents' Charter is only a piece of paper. We have no more choice than before. Schools want middle-class students; they don't want ours. Middle-class parents have greater choice. Middle-class children can commute to more schools than our children.

I asked about publishing school test scores in league tables:

> My husband says, if you don't understand football, you won't learn how to understand it from reading the league tables. [League tables of the standings of the football teams are printed daily and discussed at great length.] He says people who go to football games use league tables to argue about what makes a good team good. No one would ever decide what game to attend based on the league tables. You'd go where your home team was playing.
>
> It's silly for the Government to think that, if we could choose our schools, we would base our choices on league tables.

When I told Maggie about these conversations before we went to dinner, she was surprised. "They told you all that!" Maggie wasn't sure what to think about what I told her. I wasn't an inspector. I allowed that playing a dumb American had some advantages. It had never occurred to her to interview parents on the street. That I had discovered the theme of the golden past amazed her most, because she had begun to see it in the school herself.

7:30 P.M.—Dinner at Corridors: Moderation I

During dinner the team compared notes and talked about what they would say when they reported back to the departments the next day. Their judgements were modified during the discussion, sometimes by talking them through, sometimes by considering another response to a challenge or by weighing new evidence introduced by another inspector. Several times one team member helped another out of a quandary by providing a specific piece of information or a slightly different perspective. They also discussed the new *Framework* and the difficulties it was causing.

Sitting next to me, John could easily lean over and quietly explain parts of the discussion he thought I wouldn't understand.

Watching his fully engaged colleagues, he told me:

> You are indeed fortunate, for this is a good team. This is what we hope will happen with every team, but it doesn't always. This full

discussion happens only when the chemistry is right. We can't plan it. I notice it's much more likely to happen when we're visiting a school than when we're meeting in our London offices.

You should know that, since Jane Edwards sent her message to me through you about her concern about the amount of reporting back, I've talked with her several times. We've worked out a rather intricate schedule.

I try to avoid your American term *feedback*. That sounds too much like a cafeteria.

Later, while coffee was being poured, John called the group to order to announce that the restaurant had agreed to let us stay until closing-up time. He added, "I think they hope we'll drink something other than coffee!"

Telling the team what he had told me, he acknowledged the importance of their informal discussions. He went on to say that discussions like these made inspection a truly valuable enterprise that led to a deep appreciation of his colleagues. The group murmured agreement and appreciation. Then Mike spoke up: "Since we've all done it at one time or another, we know how hard it is to be a good RI [Reporting Inspector]. You're doing a smashing job, John—this time at least."

Lynn explained that a year ago, when John served as RI on an inspection, he and Mike Nettles had had a major fight. She said open contentiousness wasn't uncommon between inspectors and, in fact, she felt it contributed to the process.

JOHN: Much of our dinner discussion will be in preparation for tomorrow's reporting back to the departments. Jane Edwards is concerned about that. She and I have met two times to work out the arrangements. The final plan deviates somewhat from traditional HMI practice, but it seems to me to accommodate both the changes required by the 1992 *Framework* and Jane's requests.

Normally each inspector would meet with Jane and the heads of departments to discuss his judgements regarding the subject discipline. She asked us instead to conduct those meetings with each department head with only a member of the senior management team present. Then on Friday morning all of us will meet with Jane and the entire senior management team to review our conclusions on the subjects and to present our main findings and key issues.

Jane's main concern is the reporting back that takes place within the school. She's made no requests regarding the final reporting back to the Governing Body on November 18. She now understands our protocol for reporting back.

The schedule will require more time than usual. Consequently, as a team, we won't be able to see as many classes as we normally would. That makes me a bit uneasy in light of trying out the new *Framework*. The *Framework* appears to call for even less reporting back to the school than our previous policies and practice. But, as we've noted more than once, this inspection is a hybrid of the old and the new.

Further, I know this team believes inspection should help the school. Because this inspection seems to have an unusually high potential for strengthening Rosewood's efforts to improve, I've temporarily agreed with Jane's plan. You're aware that, as your Reporting Inspector, it's within my discretion to decide how our team will respond to this request. But, if any of you have strong misgivings or questions, you should discuss them with me now. It's still possible to proceed in another way. I told Jane I would seek your advice before making the plan final.

The team had questions about a few details of the plan. Although they shared John's concerns, they agreed it was the best solution for this particular inspection. George Myer's problems with the plan were of a different order:

Although I don't disagree with the plan, I find it strange that we often talk about reporting back as if it were quite separate from collecting evidence and making judgements—as if it were something we do with our findings after they have been found. I think a major purpose of reporting back is how it focuses us while we go about our work. I know the school sees the reporting back as the most important event of the inspection. That may be because we are more on the spot than they are. How we and the school consider reporting back shapes the whole enterprise. That, in turn, shapes the evidence we collect. I think we must recognize that reporting back isn't merely a coda to inspection, but one of its integrated themes.

George's statement created a wave of excitement. He had put into words what many of them were thinking. In an earlier discussion in London they had argued about the consequences of diminishing the reporting back. Most of their arguments against cuts had fallen on deaf ears. Within the old orthodoxy the main purpose of reporting back was to help the school. They had to keep reminding themselves that reporting back wasn't feedback, but none of them had been able to articulate its relationship to collecting information as clearly as George had.

Knowing the discussion could go on for hours, John interrupted:

We must accomplish three things tonight.

- We must discuss any questions you have about reporting back to the departments tomorrow.
- We must build our first conclusions on issues that are easy to agree about: resources, the building, the use of time, staffing, etc.
- We must discuss where we are with the big questions about the unevenness in the quality of teaching and the school's attitudes about student diversity.

We'll meet tomorrow afternoon to hear what you each have learned from your reporting back to the departments and to conclude our discussion on our general findings. We must be sure we are in agreement before we report to the senior management team on Friday.

After everyone agreed with this plan for the meeting, Judith Barnes began: "I now have a good enough picture of the technology department so that I feel ready for what will be a difficult reporting back."

She reviewed her conclusions and asked the others what they had learned about the use of technology throughout the school. The inspectors quickly apprised her in the areas each had come to know.

Asking if the interdisciplinary group teachers used technology differently than other faculty, Roger McPherson launched a discussion about that group, which had been an issue since the beginning. Each inspector, who had visited a class taught by an interdisciplinary group member, shared his observations. After discussion they discovered no important differences. While some of the teachers in that group were knowledgeable about technology and interested in it, two members were "Luddites"—proud of their disdain of technology. One even felt technology was responsible for the decline in student thinking and writing. The other inspectors laughed, agreeing with Maggie's conclusion: "The teachers in that group are different from the other faculty because not one of them is neutral." Roger went further:

This group plays an important role in the school. Their energy is important, especially while the school is looking for better ways to engage its diverse population. While there has been no indication their teaching is any better or that their test scores are higher, there has been no evidence that they are worse than the other faculty. This school would be weaker if they weren't working together.

They aren't even that ideological about the interdisciplinary curriculum. I have always been suspicious of teachers, or any educators for that matter, who develop a curriculum or who teach as testimony to a particular ideology, whether it is "basic skills," "performance oriented" (like the National Curriculum), focused on the concept of the "whole child," or "interdisciplinary based." During my 12 years as an inspector, I've been trying to understand what makes some classes good and some bad. I've rarely seen a case that supports the conclusion that ideology is important. In fact, the ideological teachers are often blind to what matters most. Ideology often attracts attention because it's the stuff of tension and conflict within faculties. It fans the fire that causes the heat that shapes national educational policy.

Judith laughed, teasing Roger: "Would you say you have a no-ideology ideology?"

Responding with quick determination, he said, "Yes, I would!"

Directing their attention back to the interdisciplinary teachers, John discovered consensus about their importance in the school, as Roger had summarized. Maggie suggested they discuss how to approach this issue in their reporting back on Thursday.

The detailed discussion about the school's use of the building resources elicited little disagreement. The only exception was their considerable confusion and disagreement about how the 1992 *Framework* defined the new and key concept of efficiency. They agreed that John should ring London to raise their questions. Mike suggested that he ask London to fax them that section from the draft inspection report on Allendale School, another pilot inspection. The Allendale inspection team had spent hours working through the efficiency section and Mike thought they might benefit from seeing the draft.

Next they turned their attention to the main issues. They agreed there were no major patterns that would explain the unevenness in the quality of teaching. Poor teachers and the good ones were quite evenly spread across faculty factions and subjects. Likewise, some departments had better leadership than others. Although the leadership in technology was bad, they saw no clear structural condition that explained the unevenness.

Roger noted Rosewood, as quite an average school, faced a not-so-average context in which being average wasn't enough. John suggested they mull over this conclusion until the next meeting and also consider its implications for suggesting "points of action."

Moving on to consider how the school responds to its student diversity, Maggie said:

Student diversity isn't the issue here. That's a condition of the school. I've been in many schools as diverse as Rosewood, where diversity didn't matter. The issue is how Rosewood has responded to its diversity. I think that's an issue.

Everyone felt there was a fairly deep-seated attitude that something was wrong with Rosewood because it served Muslim students. They noted how the school's consciousness of the issue had first masked its importance from them. They had assumed, because the school was aware of the problem, that it wasn't a major problem. Other schools, serving significant numbers of Muslim students, had many more problems.

The inspectors noted how the school's self-perception was damaging. As the locus of the perceived problem, it was no wonder that the Muslim students felt they were going to an inferior school. Their elders shrugged, "Of course. The British always send us to the worst schools, even if they have to make over good ones to do it." Because they were at Rosewood, instead of a better school, the majority students wondered what was wrong with them. The teachers excused lazy teaching that would be unacceptable in a good school, arguing that the students weren't able to learn. Even the special courses were defined to meet these student needs, rather than defined with an eye to excellence and rigor.

Maggie added that she thought many of the longest-serving members on the Governing Body believed Rosewood had fallen from its golden past when it had to take in the Muslim students.

Although unusually quiet, Lynn Hubert spoke up:

> I'm surprised to hear you talking like this, not because I disagree with what you're saying, but because it hasn't been in our conversations before. It's been central to my thoughts ever since I walked in the door on Monday morning.
>
> The first school I taught in was a comprehensive school like Rosewood. I left after 5 grueling years. I loved that school but I could no longer work there. It was tearing itself apart with this same attitude. A good school always begins with an unconditional belief in its students. I've been quiet because I felt my personal experience was so deep that it was warping what I saw.
>
> When I compare Rosewood with my school, I see one important difference. Many schools that have never experienced change in their student bodies are now feeling unsure and despondent because of the reform. Everyone is talking about a golden past. We know the past wasn't that golden. That's what's so insidious about this national reform. It requires schools to look to central authority for the answers. Because those answers are insufficient, the schools see they must move forward on their own, almost in opposition to policy, if they're going to move at all. The very reform that was supposed to make schools better undermines their confidence to do better. I would guess Rosewood has placed its uncertainty about the reform

with its uncertainty about the Muslim children and lumped it all on the children and the Muslim community.

The other crucial point is that—unlike my school—Rosewood is trying to build something to replace its sense of inferiority. That will be difficult, maybe even impossible. But at least Jane Edwards and many others in this school are trying. I deeply hope this inspection helps them.

Lynn's statement had major impact. John spoke for the group. "Lynn, I'm glad you spoke up. I know how difficult it is to bring an intense experience from the past and make it work in a new context without distorting the power of its origins. When it happens, it's powerful stuff. You just did that."

They ended the discussion by asking how the reporting back could help. Mike wondered out loud if inspection could productively contribute to moving a school forward.

Before anyone could respond, the owner of Corridors reminded them that closing-up time was 10 minutes away. Two of us took advantage of the last call. The conversation shifted to the football games played last weekend.

THURSDAY, NOVEMBER 12, 1992—THE FOURTH DAY

9:10 A.M.—Physical Education: The Trampoline and the Pictures on the Wall

While walking to the gym, Maggie and I recognized students we'd seen in various classes. Some smiled or waved when we passed. Maggie said it was my informal American style that attracted attention; it was unusual for adults to exchange greetings with students in the halls. I sensed an increase in tension when groups of white students passed groups of Muslim students. Yet some groups were quite mixed. This wasn't the same experience as walking in the halls of an integrated American school, but I couldn't figure out what was different.

I asked Maggie how she went about her work.

I begin by looking at the school as if I were looking through a kaleidoscope. So much is going on all the time. I try to find the patterns that will best describe it. It's a convoluted process. The more you know the school the easier it is to see the patterns, until seeing the patterns is what you come to know. Once you know the school, it's easier to make judgements because you feel your feet are at least on solid ground. Judgements are better than simple descriptions for telling others what you think a school is about.

After we finished watching badminton, aerobics, and trampoline classes in the gym, I asked Maggie, "What do you specifically look for when
you go into a class?"

> First, I look for safety. Second, I look at whether the instructor knows
> the rules, the skills, and the techniques of the particular game or
> activity. Third, I look for how well the instructor uses good teaching
> strategies, such as finding different approaches for different stu-
> dents, mixing talking with modeling, giving students the opportuni-
> ty to practice and perform, and coaching the student performances.

"What's different about how you work and how inspectors who inspect
academic subjects work?" I asked.

> That's something I often ponder. At times it has seemed different and
> at other times it has seemed very much the same. At the end of the day
> I think the academic/PE distinction muddies the water. It seems to
> have more to do with perceived status and value than with real differ-
> ences. For example, the game is one advantage we have in PE. Students
> try out their skills in a game that has more dimensions than a written
> assignment or a test. Yet, when I arrive late at a PE class, the teacher
> often says, "It's a pity you missed the lesson because now you'll see
> only the game." Of course, it's how the game is going and how the
> teacher is relating to the students during the game that reveals all the
> rest of it—what the lesson was and how well it was taught.

We talked about the class we had just seen. Maggie felt it had been
good, but not outstanding. Because she was responsible not only for PE,
but also for equal ops (equal opportunities), she watched the grouping patterns and the treatment of students and faculty that could be based more
on class, race, or gender membership than on quality education. She asked
what I had noticed about the corridor display outside the gym that fea-
tured pictures of British athletes. Noting it looked new, I told her I suspected it had been mounted for the inspection.

> Of course. We expect that. People often put down inspection, argu-
> ing that, because the school knows we're coming, they prepare. Of
> course they prepare! What we see is how they have chosen to repre-
> sent themselves and how well they have managed it all. That tells us
> a lot about a school.
>   For example, the PE department head knew I was the team
> inspector for PE. He knows I'm deeply concerned about equal
> opportunities. I've taught HMI mini-courses on PE and equal ops. In

fact, the teacher we saw working on the trampoline attended one of my classes last year. And yet, in this department's inspection week display, only one picture out of 25 is of a British woman athlete. And, she's doing a floor exercise in a sexy leotard!

Maggie stopped suddenly and apologized.

Now that I've vented my exasperation, I want to make sure you understand how I see that display. One of the virtues of inspection is that I see the context. I'll note this rather blatant sexism in my report no matter what. But I may play it down more than I normally would. I have a hunch that this PE instructor is a bit intrigued with me, if you know what I mean. And he may be putting me on. I'll have it figured out by the end of the day. It's usually complicated.

10:20 A.M.—Stereotypes Within Stereotypes

I went with John to observe a media class taught by Ms. Joan Wright, a leader of the teachers interested in interdisciplinary courses. While the students were finding their seats, she showed us her planning book demonstrating she had based the class on a series of well-thought-out exercises developed by a group associated with the BBC. The unit had analyzed movies and television shows to see how they portrayed different groups in British society. The class had most recently finished a section on children. This was the first lesson in the section on blacks.

The English film set during the Second World War showed two white American soldiers being nasty to a black American soldier in an English shop. Coming to the aid of the black soldier, the shopkeeper kicked the white soldiers out of his shop. Ms. Wright fast forwarded to the last scene. The same characters were at a dance, where the black soldier was dancing with the shopkeeper's daughter. A white soldier tried to cut in on him. The altercation escalated until the shopkeeper joined the pushing and shoving. Triumphant in protecting the black soldier, he made it clear that Americans should leave their prejudice at home.

Much to my surprise the discussion considered American racism as it had been so banally portrayed in the movie. No one asked what the movie revealed about British stereotypes of Americans or American racism, or why the characters were so flat. The message seemed to be that prejudice, racism, and stereotypes had all been imported to the idyllic British Isles. The real racial tensions at Rosewood were beyond the veil of what the class talked about.

John felt the class was quite good. Although he listened patiently to my complaint that the content was superficial and not constructed to encourage rigorous thinking, he said that hadn't been the point. He was pleased that the issue of stereotypes had been dealt with at all. In his judgement the quality of the class was high.

11:15 A.M.—I Interview Jane

Jane offered me coffee or tea, knowing I might drink either. We settled into our chairs in her office. The sun reflected off a sculpture of a young boy holding an umbrella over a young girl who gazed tenderly at him. Jane noted the statue looked odd with the sun shining on it. Later she told me it had been done by a former student of hers who had been killed in a car accident. While making it clear that she was glad to talk with me, she allowed she had only a short time.

TOM: Jane, you're very involved in the welfare of this school. Why?

JANE: That's a strange way to begin. Well, I find Rosewood an important challenge. Because of the work Helene Beaumont and Ruth Thornton did before I came, there was some basis for hoping we could make this school better. What we're trying to do here is important for these students. Since British society is becoming more diverse, we need to find better answers. But at the end of the day the real challenge for a Head is to get through the mundane—that's what it takes. I didn't always understand that.

TOM: Why have you spent so much time and energy on this inspection, both in preparing for it and managing this week? Will it be worth it? What do you think you'll gain from it?

JANE: It has been a great deal of work. When I taught, I also directed plays. Inspection is like a performance. It will go well only if there has been much preparation.

What do I think we'll gain? Well, I think performances are good for people, especially institutions. It gives us a focus we don't usually have. We can see how good what we're doing is in the eyes of outsiders. But inspectors aren't ordinary outsiders, who look at the school from the outside. They're outsiders who look at the school from inside. As outsiders, they can be more objective than insiders are. They don't have to be as sensitive. Beyond learning what the inspectors see and what they report, I think this school will gain something that's quite important. We're beginning to see how good we are and we're realizing how good we can be. It doesn't always work out like that. Sometimes a school sees how bad it is and that's difficult. When I learned the team was coming, I decided I had to work with the inspection in such a way as to put Rosewood on the positive side of that delicate line.

Inspection provides a snapshot of how outsiders, whose opinions by and large we respect, see and judge our school. Along the way I've garnered insights about how I manage this school that have come from being directly questioned and from watching myself being watched. I think those will be helpful down the road.

TOM: What parts of inspection give you the most difficulty?

JANE: Most Heads will agree that there's an important tension about the final report. While I understand the function of the final report and the importance it has on the national scene, for us in the school its publication is primarily a matter of public relations.

After the team tells us what it thinks in the reporting-back sessions we'll have 6 months before the report is published. If the report indicates issues that the public will consider negative, we'll have to decide what to do at that time. Most schools take the approach of fixing the problem so that, when the report comes out, they can say, "Yes, we were aware of that before the report and now it's fixed." If the report is positive, we'll consider how to take advantage of it to recruit students and strengthen our position in the community.

But, as Head, I find the reporting back has the most potential to be helpful. Inspectors provide much more detail in their oral reporting than in their written report. Because of its immediacy, reporting back has an unusual power for a school faculty. Even though everyone knows we have put on a performance, we know the inspectors know a good deal about what actually happens here. We have a chance to ask questions, to talk with the inspectors about what they think. While the rules for this type of talking back are somewhat confining, we'll find a way. We respect this team a great deal, which makes us more vulnerable to what they have to say, whether it's good or bad.

So I won't know until this afternoon and tomorrow morning whether, in terms of the school's progress, this inspection will have been worth the work.

TOM: I understand you and John worked out a reporting-back plan that is different from usual HMI practice. Does it show how you think reporting back can best be done?

JANE: You're right to pick up on that. I think traditional HMI reporting back is limited. But, it's difficult, because, while I may not like it, I believe the judgements inspectors make are in themselves helpful. The inspectors' main purpose is not to give us what I think you Americans call feedback. Our local LEA inspectors are more likely to do that. They see themselves much more as advisors than HMI. It's strange. We've had some good LEA advisors working with our teachers here. But that's different. You know, I'm not sure I could make a case that anything is better than inspection as a way to help schools. There's something sloppy about trying to help a school without knowing what's really going on.

TOM: Other than the reporting back, what would you change?

JANE: Well, I think the local inspectors, more than the HM inspectors, have a better sense of the importance of the forward movement of this school. HM inspectors don't seem to see, and perhaps don't want to see, that, while this school hurls through space, it's becoming the school it will be in the future. They insist their job is to take a snapshot of where the school is this week. When I've been impatient about this inspection week, I realize it's because I'm frustrated by their inability to see the school as a moving target.

I think some HM inspectors believe I can actually manage my way to a good school by identifying and solving problems. Many local inspectors make an even stronger case that "good management makes for good education." I recently heard a senior national education official claim, "If you can describe it, you can measure it and, if you can measure it, you can manage it." What drivel. They steal ideas from business management, mush them up, and miss the point that education is not business. Much of the national reform has been built on this silly idea about education change.

This notion of problem solving has provided people outside of the school with a legitimacy for being involved in the school, whether they are inspectors or Government interventionists. After all, if a school has problems, someone has to solve them. It's more than a silly idea; it distracts the school and it is a waste of time. It is immoral to think anyone can make schools better by managing change. The only way to make schools better is to make the education students receive in them better. That isn't a usual management problem. To treat a school like a business misses that point. You know English Heads are not administrators like American principals. They are first of all teachers.

I was writing so fast I could only nod. I asked Jane what she thought about the standards behind the school reform.

Well, don't quote me—at least not here in England. But those standards were written by a bunch of bloody idiots who know nothing about learning, nothing about students, and nothing about schools. They aren't learning standards; they're consumer standards.

As if she had gotten off track by discussing politics, she stopped to check the time. Smiling coyly, her decorum fully restored, she said:

Well, the old stage manager in me is calling. It's time to move on. I've enjoyed this. It's strange to think that the inspectors are watching me and my school and you're farther outside, watching them, and now you and I are talking. It's strange indeed, but I've enjoyed it.

11:50 A.M.—Reporting Back to Math

Mike Nettles waited until the full faculty of the math department had found seats in the classroom. Brian Woodcliffe represented the senior management team.

> MIKE: Before I begin my report about my conclusions I want to thank all of you in the math department for your cooperation. I couldn't have done my work without your help. Thank you also for inviting me to extend the HMI reporting back from addressing only the Head of Department to having interaction with all of you. I appreciate Mr. Douglas's suggestion that the full math faculty attend the reporting-back session.
>
> Our task as inspectors is to come to conclusions—judgements— about the quality of teaching and learning in a school. These will then be published in an official report on the school. Thus, what I present now will *not* be the final conclusions of the inspection.
>
> Most faculties are disappointed by the final published report, and you'll more than likely be no exception. The final report of the Rosewood inspection will be much more general than what I will say now. We intend that it will contain no surprises. While it will represent a corporate team judgement, we'll have discussed this in our meetings with you long before it is published. When the report is published as an official HMI—I mean OFSTED—report, it will be set in stone with the full weight of the inspectorate behind it.
>
> At this meeting I'll be glad to answer any questions you have about what I have said. Because our goal is to be as accurate as possible, I'd appreciate learning if you think I've used any incorrect evidence. Based on good practices I've seen in other places, I'll be glad to make suggestions you might find useful. But, at the end of the day we're responsible for making judgements supported by evidence we've seen. While we want to correct faulty evidence, we won't negotiate our final judgements with a school.
>
> When I evaluate the math department, I'll use the grades from the new inspection *Framework* that I believe you've seen. They are: "very good, good, satisfactory, unsatisfactory, and poor."
>
> The first set of conclusions has to do with the context in which the math faculty works. Your accommodation (space, furniture, access to computers, use of display) is good, within the top 20%. The main problem is that some rooms are cramped. Your equipment and resources are satisfactory. While your textbooks are good, your worksheets and use of calculators are variable. Your staffing is good. This faculty has high qualifications and experience.

You provide good reference material for the math faculty, but your support of teachers is unsatisfactory. This is the area that needs the most improvement. New teachers need more fully to understand the overall school policies and the math program. Your teachers need to work more on helping each other improve their teaching. You need to give more attention to new and probationary teachers.

Turning to standards: student performance on A-levels [exams primarily for college entry] is mixed. The number of students who take A-levels is lower than average. You do better than most schools with students in the lower bands, but not very well with those in the highest band. The same is true with the GSCEs [exams all secondary school students take before the end of their last year]. Fewer students than average take the GSCEs. Those who do, perform well, particularly those at the lower end. I don't have good data about the achievement level of entering students, so it's difficult to speculate on the value-added approach that has become popular. You may want to collect better information about that and try to determine what Rosewood actually contributes to the achievement level a student brings when she enters the school.

Turning now to standards in the classroom and how well your students are achieving them: I saw 14 lessons that were across the Years and ability range. This sample is a snapshot in time, but I feel quite confident about my conclusions.

Two-thirds of the classes I saw were satisfactory or better; two were very good; none were poor. To be honest, I think the differences are primarily a function of different teaching styles.

Focusing on student learning (rather than teaching), I would say that most students make some progress in most lessons. The less able students need more focus, more diagnostic work, and better support for their own improvement within the lessons. You need to be absolutely certain that each student is able to perform the basic calculations required for his or her level of achievement.

The most able students need more care and attention. They shouldn't be left to work on their own. Unsupported, independent work isn't likely to stretch their skills or abilities. You need to challenge the good math students more fully. In the A-level classes your standards are not high enough or well developed.

I offer these action points about teaching for you to ponder: Develop more rigorous discussions about math among students in classes, among students and teachers, and among yourselves. Work toward greater linguistic precision when you talk about what math is and how to do it. Watch out for easy and worn-out mechanical explanations like, "If you do this, you'll end up with that."

Some additional conclusions about math at Rosewood will give you a fuller picture of what I saw:

Students by-and-large are well behaved. Their behavior is seldom less than good. The more able students sometimes exhibit irritation.

You seldom arouse the intellectual curiosity or imagination of your students.

The pace of teaching is by-and-large good. The classroom atmosphere is relaxed, but not casual. There's good attention to homework.

Of the 14 lessons I saw, 3 or 4 were distinctly underprepared. That's between 22% and 29%. Twenty-five percent is considered too high an average.

Sometimes a teacher's initial explanation of lessons is too brief or lacks the rigor that will enable students to move on easily with their practice.

Your system of tracking students raises a key question. How do you decide when pupils are ready to move onto the next step? I didn't see evidence that you've thoroughly thought that through among yourselves.

You're having trouble trying to shoehorn your old curriculum into the National Curriculum. Your students need to understand the attainment targets of the National Curriculum. You need more time to reflect on how to select what stays and what goes. Unless you do that, you are in danger of using the attainment targets as a checklist and narrowing the focus of your teaching to doing well on attainment–target tests.

That brings me to assessment. You've developed good systems for recording scores built around the student Record of Achievement (ROA). But, how many of your tests support learning rather than grading? Teachers argued 4 years ago that their assessment of student work was better than tests, because they know the students better. The Government conceded that issue and included teacher assessment as an important part of the total assessment strategy. Now that teacher assessment has been included, what do teachers do? They develop little tests based on their checklists of the attainment targets. These little tests are no more valid than the national tests.

A good teacher doesn't assess students simply by grading them. You should learn about student work in order to help students do better. Students must see assessment as neither mysterious nor arbitrary, but as a tool that will help them improve their work. They should know the grade is not as important as learning how to use it to assess their own progress. Organized, rigorous student self-monitoring helps. The best-designed assessment is a back-and-forth exercise between student and teacher, not a once-a-year test, even if that test has been teacher designed. The student must be trained to do a piece of work well.

That's all I want to say. Sorry it's been so condensed.

The faculty had been quite attentive. Mr. Douglas finally broke the silence by thanking Mike for giving them much to think about. A senior teacher raised a problem that Mike hadn't mentioned. "Class time is shorter than it used to be. We never have enough time to plan how to make our work better or to support new teachers."

Mike agreed that he hadn't considered the problem of time, admitting it was always a difficult factor in a department's planning.

12:30 P.M.—Reporting Back to Technology

Judith Barnes was meeting with Mr. A. F. Watson, the technology department head. Tina Foster, a school Deputy Head, represented the senior management team. When I entered the meeting, Judith had already begun:

JUDITH: In reporting back to you I'm going to use the headings we're expected to use when we write our report. I'll read from my script, because I want to be sure there'll be no surprises when the report is published. The tensions about the inspection of the technology department make this even more important. Please don't respond while I'm presenting my conclusions. I'll ask for questions and comments at the end.

First, I'll consider standards of teaching and learning.

I observed 12 full or partial lessons. Of those, three were good, five were satisfactory, one was unsatisfactory, and three were poor. That means 25% of the technology classes are poor. That percentage is too high. When we include the unsatisfactory class, that percentage is even higher.

Although the staff is experienced, they haven't had an adequate opportunity to use their experience well.

Students don't have good access to materials and tools. It would be better to separate the facilities so that wood and fabric, for example, aren't in the same room.

What students already know isn't well-enough considered. I talked with several students in the Year 7 hydraulics class who said they'd done hydraulics last year in primary school. They said they'd never been asked what they'd covered before they came to Rosewood.

You have not given yourselves adequate opportunity to work through the difficulties of implementing the National Curriculum.

Some of your planning is good. You've done a good job providing cohesion between the different elements of technology. But some of your faculty don't seem to care that you've done this well. Thus, your planning doesn't always contribute effectively to actual lessons.

It's difficult to see how a student progresses in technology over time. You focus too sharply on the discrete opportunities you offer students. You need to focus on the skills the students have achieved and on how to further them.

Some of the faculty are weak in their knowledge of the ideas and skills of modern technology. I know this is a difficult, fast-changing area and there's been confusion in the National Curriculum about it. But too often this becomes an excuse to avoid staying on top of what good technology teachers need to know.

Finally, the in-service plans for the faculty are poor. They fail to deal with what's important in improving teaching—such as sharpening technology skills.

I'm sorry this isn't a better report. Do you have any questions?

Mr. Watson looked like he'd been punched. He asked one or two questions about minor points that had been covered early in the report. Tina Foster, the Deputy Head, finally asked if Judith would be willing to talk with Mr. Watson again after he'd had time to take her report on board. Judith said she'd be glad to do that.

2:00 P.M.—Reporting Back to History

I went with Lynn Hubert for her reporting back to Mrs. Theonora Andrews, the history department head. Mrs. Andrews was one of several department heads I hadn't met. She was a bit uncertain about my being present, until Brian Woodcliffe, a Deputy Head representing the senior management team, allowed it was all right.

LYNN: My conclusions are based on the 14 lessons I saw. Eighty percent of those were satisfactory or good. One was very good. I believe the one lesson was unsatisfactory because the teacher returned to class today from his mother's funeral. There's good evidence that his teaching is usually at a much higher standard. On the whole it was a solid set of lessons—without troughs or peaks.

While my evidence base isn't as solid as I'd like, I think the major issue that needs to be considered here is that the students have a wide variety of skills and abilities. It's my strong impression that, if

Rosewood's students represented a more normal range, your faculty would have done very well.

While this is more personal than we HM inspectors are supposed to be, I was reminded of the challenge I faced as a teacher when I moved from a grammar school (a secondary school where students are selected by entrance tests) to a comprehensive school (like Rosewood). The change I faced was really about having to teach better. The grammar school students had clear education goals and did what they were supposed to do regardless of what I taught. At the comprehensive school what I did made more difference.

I found your lessons solid, but not imaginative, given the qualities of the student body. You need to find how to stretch your students, particularly the able ones. Too often the buzz is missing.

Although they planned the lessons well, the teachers relied too much on worksheets.

Students were diligent, spending a good proportion of their time on the task. They exhibited strong interest most of the time. While their interest flagged when the pace slowed, they didn't become disaffected when the lesson was boring.

Although students demonstrated good listening skills, you should develop their oral skills further.

Your assessment practices need to be strengthened to support learning. Your hard work to bring the history curriculum in line with the National Curriculum is fine.

In short, I found the teaching competent, but not exciting. You need to focus more on limiting the content to history, on making better class presentations, on encouraging students to work in smaller groups, and on using fewer worksheets.

Do you want to come back on any of that?

Acknowledging that her department had been working on the worksheet problem, Mrs. Andrews thanked Lynn for giving them a great deal to think about. Lynn then went on to report on the department's resources and accommodation.

3:45 P.M.—Concluding the Conclusions: Moderation II

John knew he and the team would be drained after completing their departmental reporting back. In fact, he'd asked the school to provide not only tea, but biscuits as well. He wasn't surprised to find high-quality chocolate biscuits. Not pushing to begin the meeting exactly on time, he began 15 minutes late.

The inspectors briefly summed up the reporting-back sessions with their departments. After each report, they briefly discussed how to find better language to present their conclusions.

John directed them to the final task of reaching agreement on the main findings. He reminded them that their agreement was important to the final reporting-back sessions the next day and to building the final report, since that should be consistent with what they reported back. He noted:

> This is always the most difficult time for me. It seems too early to make it final. We should have more time to absorb it all. I'm never sure quite how to respond to Philip's [a well-known senior HMI] argument that there's value in being forced to come to conclusions before we're ready. Up to a point, I think he's right. I'm convinced there's value in doing it before we leave the school site.
>
> It has been my experience that the time we spend now on the actual wording of the findings will be worth the time we'll save later on drafting the report.

He had reviewed the subject summary sheets and the notes they had given him about the themes of management, student support, and equal opportunities. Based on their notes and their discussions of the previous 4 days, John thought it was possible to reach tentative conclusions. If the team were willing, he would start by listing these possibilities.

Based on their discussion he would gladly draft one or two sentences on each finding for them to review and edit when they reconvened at 8:00 A.M. the next morning. The reporting back was set for 10:00 A.M. The team quickly agreed and John proposed the following possibilities:

> The school is better than satisfactory. The lessons and test results we saw placed the school in the high end of satisfactory. There were many indications that Rosewood is a good school that has significant strengths.
>
> While the school has had management difficulties in the past, the management is now good, under the leadership of a Head who brings a clear, strong, humane vision. Evidence is strong that the school is now working well.
>
> The school is mostly efficient in its use of resources.
>
> The students are a major asset of this school. While the student body is diverse, both white and minority students exhibit positive traits. They are well behaved, eager to improve, and represent the full range of abilities. They should be further challenged with greater rigor.

Teaching and learning are satisfactory. Steps can be readily taken to make teaching across the school more even and productive. The special attention given to those students who are behind in English-language achievement is to be commended. The well-developed assessment scheme should be more closely tied to student learning to ensure that the strengths of the National Curriculum are fully exploited and, perhaps more important, to raise the school's expectations of what its students are capable of learning.

The team commended John for a good start.

Lynn thought it was good that John had pointed out their judgement that the erratic patterns of achievement in the school were because a large number of students were behind in basic language skills. She noted that a larger percentage of the Muslim students were having trouble, but that students in both groups had significant problems. Thus, what was important in terms of standards of achievement was not that a student fell into a certain group, but that he was having difficulty with language. She urged the team to give the wording of this judgement their fullest, most careful attention so that what they said would focus on the issue as a teaching-learning problem and not exacerbate the school's racial tensions.

When the team was clear that these were their most important and agreed-upon conclusions, they began struggling with how to word these judgements to fit within the constraints of their public report and at the same time to communicate them in a way that would effectively help the school improve:

GEORGE: I'm concerned about our making references to a past we haven't seen. While I think we have a picture this week of an improving school, we're best off if we don't consider either the past or the future.

JUDITH: George has a good point, but I think the best way to present our view of the school on this touchy issue is to refer to the past. I think we want to say that the school has made progress, but that it has a long way to go. I don't see how we can do that without referring to the past.

This tension generated considerable discussion. Several inspectors experimented with alternative wording, which they tried out on the group. Mike suggested it might help to separate teaching and learning, as the *Framework* required. They could say that the teaching was satisfactory, but that, given the quality of the students, learning was not. They could conclude that the school needed to take care of business.

Roger McPherson said he'd once been on a team in Scotland that had faced a similar problem. After much discussion they'd begun to realize that their evidence supported the finding that there had been important positive movement. They decided to point out how the discussions about new plans they had heard about and the comments of teachers and students that things were better than before were evidence that indicated progress. Roger said:

> By focusing on the evidence in front of us, we were able to say, "We see this school is in a stage of dramatic improvement." We don't need to refer to the past to be able to make judgement about a process.

Several inspectors began to recount their conversations with teachers and students that supported Roger's point.

At 7:00 P.M. John finally called the meeting to an end: "This has been helpful. I think I see how to put words to it. I'll work on it tonight and we'll consider my draft at 8:00 A.M. tomorrow."

8:30 P.M.—Dinner at Corridors

The team had come to the end of another intense day and the end of inspection week. While we waited for a table, Maggie observed how she was always surprised inspection was such hard work. But when it worked, as she felt this one had, she felt she had done something important that made it all worthwhile. She wondered if the future would change this. At dinner the inspectors bounced back more slowly than usual from their thoughts about the day.

Buying the wine, I offered a toast of appreciation for their good humor in putting up with an American observer. Lightening up, Mike said:

> Well, now that the English have tests, maybe the Yanks will have inspection. If you do, maybe you can teach me how to talk American and I can become an American inspector.

The others protested almost in unison, "Forget it, Mike! You're awful at languages." "Besides," someone reminded him, "you lost your chance to go to the States when you stopped playing with Paul McCartney."

FRIDAY, NOVEMBER 13, 1992—THE FIFTH DAY

8:00 A.M.—The Final Shaping of the Findings

When we made our way to the base room on this last morning, the buzz of the school portrayed a different excitement. The faculty and staff could argue about the value of inspection on another day, but that wasn't what today was about. No matter what happened, today was a real event that would be important to the school. Although the air was full of anticipation, the faculty and staff were relaxed. They'd performed their parts. The success of the finale rested on how well the inspectors performed theirs.

The inspection team was nervous and preoccupied. With great care they went through the script John had prepared, each person wanting to be sure of cues and lines. They attacked the draft with relish:

> You can't say "the school has taken great strides." You can't see "a stride." And if you could, it should be "giant strides," not "great strides."
>
> I don't like the word *obsequious* where you say "the students are courteous, but not obsequious." It isn't clear what you mean.

Their frequent references to incidents in other inspections, when findings had been misinterpreted or strongly challenged by the school, made it clear to me that they were preparing for more than a performance. They wanted to ensure that their professionalism as inspectors and HMI's credibility as an institution wouldn't be called into question.

They combed John's draft, considering how every phrase might be interpreted by the Rosewood faculty, the Head, the Governing Body, the community the school served, and, most important, by HMI and its senior inspectors, who would also carefully review the report before it was published. They would have more time for this type of editing in the weeks to come. But in an hour they would make the first public presentation of the report to what most of them regarded as their most important audience. This added an electricity to their discussion. The deadline and the time constraints cut short several trivial discussions; they knew they had to finish.

At 9:50 A.M. John announced, "It's that time. We are in reasonable agreement about the wording we've worked out this morning. It's the best we can do for now. Thank you for your hard work."

10:00 A.M.—Reporting Back to the Senior Management Team

The comfortable chairs had been removed from Jane Edwards's office to make room for desk chairs that had been arranged in a semicircle around her desk. The 15 chairs were for the seven members of the senior management team, Jane's administrative assistant, and the seven inspectors. We were one chair short. Suspecting it was mine, I quietly mentioned it to Fred Jenkins, who hurriedly found another and placed it next to Jane's desk.

Tea and coffee were served from the table, now covered with a dark green table spread. There seemed to be a lot of fuss about cream and sugar. It was quite a while before everyone was seated with notebooks and cups in hand, the men inspectors in classic gray or navy suits, the women inspectors in tailored suits and low heels. The school management team was almost as well dressed. When everyone was comfortably in a proper place, all eyes shot to Jane for direction. She simply nodded to John that it was time for him to begin.

> First, we want to thank all of you and ask you to thank the faculty, staff, and students for their graciousness and help. You have made our job easier. We couldn't have done it without your cooperation. My team members and our American observer, as well, have greatly appreciated all you have done to make this a productive week. And thank you for the chocolate biscuits; they were excellent!
>
> As you know, what we present here today will not be our final report on Rosewood. That will be formally published in about 6 months' time. While it is our practice to make sure there are no surprises in the published report, you must understand that the findings we present today are tentative until that report is published. We'll provide you with more detail here than that report will include. We've organized our findings in accord with the outline of the 1992 *Framework*.
>
> Rather than keep you in suspense throughout this presentation, we thought it would be better to begin with our main findings. First, our overall conclusion.

Everyone was concentrating on John. Not a spoon clinked, not a paper rattled. Taking a breath, he looked at his paper and read: "This is a good school. It has some outstanding characteristics."

There was an audible gasp from the school people. John probably didn't hear Jane's quiet comment: "Thank you for that." At least there was no sign he'd heard.

> Students come from two diverse communities. They are able students, who share a strong interest in learning. The school's ethos of respecting all students and its goal of challenging each one as fully as possible are commendable.
>
> Although the standards students achieve in public examinations are on the whole below the national average, they show an unusual variance. The average quality of student writing, oral work, and numeracy in class are all close to national standards for comprehensive schools, but the quality varies a great deal, ranging from very good to poor. This variance, which is throughout the school, is *not* strongly related to ethnic membership.
>
> For the most part teachers are well qualified. They are appropriately deployed to make the best use of their expertise and experience.
>
> With a few exceptions the curriculum is well aligned to the National Curriculum.

The school is effectively led. Its mission is consistent with the needs of its students. It is well organized and administered. Understanding what areas require strengthening, the senior leadership has well-considered plans in place for most of them.

Many people outside the school and some inside the school believe the school has had a past that was more glorious than its present. This often distracts. It could cripple the school from continuing its commendable progress toward providing the best possible education for its students.

The important key issues for action are:

- Continue to strengthen your commendable programs in language acquisition for all students.
- Increase the challenge for all students, including those who achieve at a satisfactory level.
- Review student assessment procedures to ensure they not only record student progress on the National Curriculum attainment targets, but that they also provide teachers, parents, and students with information that will strengthen the provision of education.

John stopped at this point to tense silence. He broke the tension by noting that his team of inspectors was a difficult bunch. They had forced him to rewrite his first draft and remove "obsequious," which was one of his favorite words. Everyone visibly relaxed and he continued:

In my experience, senior management teams are often surprised by how positive the main findings are. Their expectations are based on what has been said in the department reporting-back sessions and what they have picked up during the week. It seems to happen in many inspections that, when we're pushing hard during the week to learn all we can about a school, we tend to see things more negatively than we do at the end, when we have to pull it together into a complete picture. Perhaps it has something to do with the nature of learning.

He suggested they take a quick break. Jane agreed.

During the rest of the morning each inspector reported back on the more specific findings of the individual departments.

It was a note-taking crowd. Jane's administrative assistant took notes of everything that was said. A senior-management team member had been assigned to each section, in addition to recording the conclusions on the department that he or she had covered yesterday. Each member seemed to write special notes on a separate sheet. On the inspectors' side, Maggie was taking comprehensive notes. She had copies of each inspector's notes with her; on each she recorded any discrepancies between what was written and what the inspector actually said and she recorded questions from the school people. When she was reporting, John took over her recording duties.

Jane made a brief appreciative comment at the conclusion of each section of the report. She then gave the senior-management team members time to comment. Most often nothing further was said and the inspectors would continue. If there was further comment, Jane would usually take the lead, sometimes working with another member of her team. First she asked questions to clarify what the inspector had said. Then she raised any errors in evidence. That normally led to a short, open discussion to determine what was correct. For example, Fred Jenkins thought the inspectors had mixed up some test data. It turned out they had a more up-to-date breakdown of scores than the school. After discussion, if it were apparent the evidence was in error, John thanked Jane and whoever first raised the point. Then he assured them the correction would be considered in the final review of the team's conclusions.

Although she acknowledged that the school couldn't negotiate the inspectors' conclusions, Jane noted twice that she didn't agree with them. Once she asked them to consider a different wording, as she was certain the *Woolseyeford Journal* would pick up their phrase in a way that would distort the overall report and damage the school. Several times she expressed appreciation that the inspectors had made a certain point. When John reported problems that would have been obvious to any visitor, such as the torn linoleum in the kitchen, she said the school was aware of that and was already working to resolve it.

There was a sense of ritual about this session. With few exceptions, it was carried out with wit and good humor. However, I could imagine that it could on occasion become the difficult and adversarial process that several of the inspectors had described.

3:00 P.M.—Good-Byes

Toward the end of the 4-hour session the school management team grew restless. Their questions and comments were short. Everyone was tired. When we left Jane's office, Brian Woodcliffe slipped me a small piece of paper, saying, "This might interest you." It said:

All faculty and staff are invited to the staff lounge at 2:30 P.M. to celebrate the end of the inspection of Rosewood School.

Everyone except John had to rush to catch the 3:00 P.M. train. As assistant reporting inspector, Maggie had confirmed that she'd received the subject, theme, and aspect notes from each one. After confirming the schedule for writing the report with John, the inspectors packed their large brief-cases and said good-bye.

John and I were left to check out the base room and return the key. He carefully tore up and carried away any scraps of paper left about, making sure they left nothing behind that would infringe on the inspection's con-fidentiality. He told a horror story about how an inspector had once left his notebook behind and how the school had used it to challenge the final report. He viewed this as unacceptable, unprofessional behavior.

John and Maggie planned to meet on January 21, 1993 to complete the first draft of the report. We agreed I would visit them that day. I thanked John again for allowing me to tag along. We said good-bye and he headed back to his office, leaving me behind to finish some notes.

On my way out of the school I passed the staff room by the front entrance. It was filled with sounds of a good, but subdued, Friday party after a hard week's work.

Rosewood and Woolseyeford were enshrined by the early winter twi-light of the north. I had hoped Ian would be my mini-cab driver, but he wasn't.

THURSDAY, JANUARY 21, 1993—LOOKING BACK

The Inspectors Reminisce

When he met me at the Barringham Station, John was relaxed, but hardly amused that BR was on time. He had received my letter. He felt my draft of the elements of inspection was on target and that I had covered his ear-lier concern about giving moderation enough importance. My questions about the Rosewood inspection intrigued him. He had shared my ques-tions with Jane Edwards, who would meet briefly with me in his office before we three had lunch together at the Distaff Wine Bar. Later I would visit Rosewood and talk with Jane again and with Timothy Merrill, the English teacher John and I had observed.

John and Maggie, the assistant reporting inspector on the Rosewood team, gave me a full report on their reporting back to the school's Gov-erning Body. Shorter than their reporting back to the senior management team, it had focused on their overall conclusions. They felt the Governors had been pleased with the report, pleased that the school was beyond its past leadership difficulties. They had found the report surprisingly thought-ful about the school's history and its attitudes about the diversity of its stu-dents. They decided to set up a task force to continue considering these issues. The task force would not only relate with the chosen representative to the Governing Body, but also would contact all leaders of the communities the school served. Supporting that, Jane recommended they involve the teachers as well. It was too early to know if it would be productive.

Although they also were pleased with the progress they had made in writing the report, John and Maggie were both resigned to the fact that it probably would have little effect. A senior OFSTED inspector was now reading the draft and they weren't expecting much difficulty. They wondered if the recent public concern about allowing Muslim schools to qualify as state-supported religious schools would lengthen the review time.

They had prepared a memo for OFSTED summing up their discussions about standards and the *Framework*. Since OFSTED was already preparing the first tenders (bid proposals) for the privatized inspections of secondary schools that would begin in the autumn, they expected their memo to generate little action. John had recently returned from London, where he had attended a meeting about what OFSTED would be like. He felt OFSTED was relying on privatization ideology and management schemes, not on the proven tradition of inspection. The *Framework* would be slightly revised in the spring. In the past a memo like theirs would have generated a great deal of internal discussion. But now their colleagues were self-absorbed and indifferent.

John saw through my question, when I asked, "If you were able to start from scratch, how would you construct an inspection system?"

> I know you're wondering if inspection would work in America. I can't answer that. It appears we have decided that traditional inspection no longer works here. I think we're making a bad mistake.
>
> For me the key part of inspection is how it keeps us in close touch with how learning and teaching actually happen in schools, how it stimulates collegial discussion about the value of what we see, and how it fosters the basic goodwill of teachers because they see we are more for them than against how they think and work.
>
> I would agree that we haven't done well with the element of inspection that you have aptly called "next steps," that is, what happens after the inspection. Although I think an official public report is a good thing, it needs to be in a context that will continue to consider the real life of schools. While we had that opportunity with the LEA inspectors and advisors, it never really happened. The new *Framework* actually does better on this score by requiring an action plan from the school.
>
> However, I believe schools will find the information from "privatized inspection"—as OFSTED now defines it—will be little real help in building a plan that will improve the actual quality of teaching and

learning. I predict we'll have many superficial plans that are heavy
with management solutions and management ideology. Inspection
will become a tool that pushes schools away from the issues they
should most constructively consider. It's all very depressing.

This came as we were finishing our sweets at the Distaff. I wanted Maggie and John to gain some cheer from my acknowledging a deep appreciation for what they had provided me. John concluded on a more optimistic
note, "Well, maybe there's some hope. After all, we've survived worse
things than this Tory Government. At least we know one American who
appreciates the value of sweets, who now knows they're not just desserts."
When she picked me up at the Distaff, Helene was even more discour-
aged than Maggie and John. She had learned that her LEA would cut its
inspectorate budget in half in April. The national debate about piloting the
English tests for the National Curriculum was growing. Teachers had united and she expected a major showdown with the Government in the spring.

It's most discouraging that the impetus to change has been fueled by
politics in London. The politicians seem hell-bent on damning teachers and all of us who work in schools. Even worse, they're so out of
touch with the day-to-day reality of schools and with how teaching
and learning happen that they don't even know their policies are
bad. So they interpret our questioning as being merely political.

Avoiding my questions about her future, she redirected my attention
to Rosewood, which was coming into view.

A School Head Reminisces

Jane greeted me at her office door. Although the table was back in place, there
were no chocolate biscuits next to the coffee thermos. She allowed that it had
been 2 weeks after the inspection before she felt the school was back to routine. She, too, had been thinking about the questions I had sent her:

JANE: So you want to know what impact the inspection has had on
Rosewood? Perhaps it's that we'll never return to the same routine
we had before. We are in a different place than we were before.
    Mr. Watson, head of technology, now talks with me in an almost
civil manner. Rumor has it that he was so devastated by the report,
he was thinking about leaving teaching. Lately other department
heads have supported his inquiries about doing in-service for his
department. The teachers working on the interdisciplinary plan are

now much more content. They've been finding new ways to work with their departments. The Governing Body is leading our efforts to work more productively with our diversity. They plan to make a clear decision about school uniforms at their next meeting. While I think it is coincidence, Brian Woodcliffe says he's planning to retire next year.

I'm really not sure what you mean by long-term impact. That must be an American idea. The inspection changed Rosewood and Rosewood will continue to evolve from this point. The inspection has become an event in the history of this school. I don't think that's what you mean.

Although intrigued by Jane's response, I didn't distract her with long-winded explanations. Time was short.

I think the power of inspection comes from the inspectors knowing the real life of a school. Although much determines how well they will know a school, perhaps the goodwill of the people in the school is most important. When inspectors are at our school, that mere fact means we must either deny them access to what goes on here or engage with them so they can come to an understanding of it. In either case it isn't a neutral event.

When inspectors are in the real act of knowing a school, they become a special part of its daily life for a brief time. That interaction changes that daily life. The fact that they are judging the quality of our teaching and learning increases the potential of what they offer us.

I guess in some basic way my ideas about inspection haven't changed. Inspection can lead to silliness or it can be quite profound. The difference lies in how the school team and the inspection team work together. The formal report is necessary and useful, but it doesn't represent the real power of inspection.

As I grow older, I realize more and more the power of knowledge that comes from being there, the power that comes from having something to say about the life you see when you know something real about that life.

I left Jane to meet Timothy Merrill in the staff lounge. He is the English teacher whose poetry class I had observed. In the midst of class period, the school's halls were quiet. Walking past the gym, I noticed the photo exhibit of British athletes had been taken down. However, the technology classroom mural, "What is Technology?" had become even dingier.

Timothy was eager to talk about what the inspection had meant to him:

John Turner put me off at first. You remember how he wouldn't talk about my class when we first sat down in the cafeteria? I was furious. He seemed so self-important.

I expected him to talk with me about the details of my teaching. I know he is well regarded as a teacher of English and that he's kept his hand in the teaching of poetry. I couldn't believe that all he could say was that I had to tie my intellectual life to my teaching!

I had been offended by how Mr. Watson, the technology head, criticized inspection all around the school. But after John's chat with me, I began to wonder if Watson wasn't right.

On Sunday after the inspection I woke in the middle of the night with an unusually clear mind, realizing John's comments had changed how I thought about my teaching. It was no longer important to me that he had not said what I thought he should say. What was important was that he was right. In that brief moment he forced me to deal with the most important issue of my teaching, which I had successfully avoided.

John could never have done what he did, he could never have known my teaching at that level, if he hadn't been right there in my classroom making judgements about its value as I went along.

Saying good-bye to Rosewood for the last time wasn't as difficult as I had expected. The sun had broken through what seemed like perpetual clouds. As the muddy playing fields began to soak up the warmth, the smells of early New England spring were liberated and I found myself thinking it was time to go home.

AT THE END OF THE DAY

I took the Underground from King's Cross Station to Charing Cross, where I caught BR to the Blackheath Station instead of Maze Hill, which was closer to our flat. I enjoyed the walk home from Blackheath Village across the mile-square Heath, which is open land surrounded on three sides by the crowded borough of Greenwich and on the other by Royal Greenwich Park. Some say it is called Blackheath because the Black Plague victims were buried here in the 14th century. This is where the Danes pitched camp during their 11th-century invasions. This was the site of the Peasant's Revolt in 1381. In 1450 Jack Cabe started his rebellion here. Kings were met on this high plain above London when they returned from the Continent. Here Henry VIII met the undelectable Anne of Cleves, whom he had agreed to marry, based on a painting that had distorted her homeliness. England's first golf and rugby clubs began here. In more recent times the Heath has served as a major anti-aircraft site against the German bombers and an assembly area, if London were ever to come under atomic attack. Recently All Saints Church at the edge of the Heath hosted the welcome-home celebration for Terry Waite, held hostage for many months in Iran.

Crossing the Heath after my last trip to Woolseyeford, I remembered my reaction the first time Les and I saw it. "This is rather dumb," I had said, wondering how anyone could make such a big deal out of such a monotonous stretch of land. The mile-square land just lay there, doing nothing. It wasn't a park in any true sense—like Royal Greenwich Park at its northern border. Now that is a real park enclosed by a three-mile-long, seven-foot-high brick wall, its 10 gates locked every night. Inside the Royal Park signs point toward special spots like the Royal Deer Park or the rotting Royal Oak, which in the 16th century Queen Elizabeth I was said to have danced around as a child, or the Royal Greenwich Observatory, where the Prime Meridian stands and where Greenwich Mean Time is set.

But on the Heath there are no signs or walls or stumps and no obvious plan for its use. Yet the roads that crisscross the open fields, which include the historic London-to-Dover road, make it less than a wild and open space.

I realized we had learned much about the Heath since we had lived nearby. Its different moods—the misty days hiding history, a bright sunlit Bank Holiday spreading families everywhere, and the moonlit nights pulling the past and present smoothly together. A varied place, the Heath has a wild area that is home to foxes who visited our garden during early mornings, the Prince of Wales Pond where children and adults sail model boats, the wide-open places where you can see, but not hear, the traffic. In designated spots there are special activities—like a small gypsy carnival, or the large Greenwich Festival housed in its giant tent, or fireworks on Guy Fawkes Day—and always there are the colorful kites.

The Heath had become an accepted part of our daily life. Part of that acceptance was knowing we would never be able to understand fully its secrets or grasp what it means to our English friends who have known it for much longer than we ever will.

Chapter 4

Elements

These elements that describe the method of inspection have been tugged directly from Chapter 3. This more analytical description provides an efficient handle for thinking about the nature of the inspection method and how it is different from and similar to other approaches to knowing and judging schools.

BEING THERE

The English have this peculiar belief that they can learn something about schools by visiting them. No element is more basic to inspection than *being there*—actually visiting a school while it is in session.

The importance of the physical presence of the visitor was assumed in the early history of inspection. The inspector's right to be there is established by national law. Being there is not simply sitting in the back of a class, being careful not to intrude. Being there is the prerequisite for doing a professional job that requires moving around the classroom, asking students questions, and examining student work while a class goes on. Key to inspection practice in all eras, including that advocated by the Education (Schools) Act of 1992, this element clearly differentiates inspection from American assessment.

As the prerequisite element, being there is closely tied to the other elements. Evidence is regarded as less valuable if the inspector has not seen or heard it at the school. Not immune to gossip, inspectors want evidence to come directly from their visit.

When the inspector is there in the class, she lives through a teaching event with a teacher. This common ground can be a powerful focal point when she and the teacher discuss the quality of the teacher's work.

Because both of them know that the inspector's judgements about the class have just been formed, each has a higher stake in their conversation about the class than if the judgements had been formed in hindsight. The teacher's stake is obvious. But the inspector is also vulnerable. He wonders if his perspectives and observations are accurate, if they will be helpful to the teacher; he wonders how the teacher will respond.

The sharing of their common ground can be either a powerful positive experience or a disaster that destroys the teacher's confidence or results in a legal challenge of the inspector's observations or professionalism. While these extremes seldom occur, their presence in inspection folklore raises suspense in both the teacher and the inspector about the conversation that will take place. The teacher and inspector are more vulnerable talking about a real piece of classroom life they have experienced together than they would be talking about teaching in general, or about another teacher, or if they were talking on the phone, rather than in person at the school.

Teachers in England, like the rest of us, sometimes build defensive walls against challenges to their competence or to their view of the meaning of events. Having been present in a class and a part of what happened there, an inspector can tell a teacher he saw nothing to support her explanation. The teacher must consider the real-life class that provided the evidence for the inspector's judgement, rather than more abstract principles or ideas.

Being there makes inspectors especially valuable to Government policymakers because, as Government staff, they know what actually is happening in schools.

At the turn of the century the teachers' unions soured on inspectors. Although they questioned who HM inspectors should be and what they should do when they visited schools, they never questioned the right of inspectors to be there. This statutory right did not apply to local inspectors. Yet, while school Heads and others might question the value of local inspectors more than HM inspectors, I never heard anyone challenge their right to be in a school. The statutory right that originally and specifically applied to HM inspectors has carried over to the new inspection teams established by the current reform.

The presence of inspectors in a school, sometimes 14 on a team for longer than a week at a time, creates a host of social complexities for both the school and the inspectors. What room will be the inspectors' base room? How will the inspectors fit into, or interfere with, the regular school schedule? How will the line between what is private and what is public be honored? Understanding the importance of these details, a good inspection team will carefully work them out beforehand with the school.

During preliminary discussions with the Reporting Inspector, a school will usually make stringent arrangements to limit the intrusive nature of inspection. The school can relax these later, if the inspection is going well. In contrast, if a school were dealing with outsiders whose work was not based on being there—such as regulators, researchers, or memo writers— it would be less likely to relax these limits.

As a visitor of visitors, I thought a great deal about what makes being there so important. Some inspectors believe Christian images support the importance and meaning of being there—in order to be convincing, a person of faith must have a real presence in the world. For both visitor and visited, a visit entails more work and energy than a memo, a phone call, or even a workshop. For whatever reason, someone thought it was important enough for the visitor to take the trouble to be there. For most inspectors it is a basic way to approach the world. Whether the visit is seen as an intrusion, a blessing, or a nuisance, the visited must summon the energy to deal with it.

Being there gains some of its meaning from the other elements. Inspectors come to watch the life of a school and to make judgements about its value. They don't come to bear messages, give workshops, fill out forms, or evaluate programs. Thus, the whole school is more vulnerable when they come.

Being there strengthens the power of evidence because it places a particular observation within a larger context that gives it meaning at that site. When a piece of evidence is framed by its institutional context, it is easier to see its connections to other observations and to the ideas that describe the life of that school. These connections make this evidence more useful to the practicing teacher and administrator than information that has been scrubbed clean of the messiness of context.

Inspectors seek to construct a snapshot of the school at the time of the inspection. We normally think context relates only to the present. But an inspector is able to consider both the past and future of the school. She has access to the vague currents that reveal what the school has been and what it is becoming. These currents would not be available by phone or memo. Perhaps access to information that must be sensed to be known is what leads people to say, "You had to be there to know." A wise, retired HM inspector referred to the inspection snapshot as a product of past currents. "What's happening at the school right now will shape its snapshot in the future." An LEA inspector said, "To make a valid judgement about how good a class is now, you need to know what happened before, what the teacher's intentions were, and what happened afterward. You learn about all of these when you visit."

Being there allows an inspector access to a more complex perspective about what's happening than he would have if he were working from an office. Being there exposes an inspector to more views more quickly and gives him access to the interplay between them.

Being there is different from watching a movie, a video, or even a live television broadcast of the school. The visitor's mind can have a much wider focus than a video camera. The visitor's awareness of how he makes sense of a school and how his chosen focus determines what he sees makes a more powerful understanding of the meaning of the school possible than if someone else had created the images. After the visit a photograph of what the visitor has seen and comes to understand can be more powerful than a written account.

Education policy is better when it is informed by what actually happens in schools. The argument that knowledge can be acquired well only by being there was made again as recently as 1992. Although being there has some vague attributes, it is at the heart of inspection. It has always been part of the rationale for inspection. In 1970, John Blackie, a former HMI, wrote:

> The inspectorate must not be so small that it cannot spend most of its time in school. [If the inspectorate became too small it would become] a miniature corps d'elite, experts who cerebrated, researched and preached a doctrine. [That] would, in my view, be a menace to everything that is best in English education: its informality, its friendliness, its encouragement of individual initiative, its pragmatic approach. (Blackie, 1970, pp. 71–72)

In 1916, A. H. D. Acland, vice president of the Education Council in Gladstone's Government, wrote:

> I feel no doubt at all that from the point of view of real national efficiency the weakest point about the Department was in my own time and has been ever since that the principal administrators and the principal advisers of the Minister have had relatively so very little practical experience in their own lives of the work of teaching. ...
>
> I do not hesitate to say after nearly 30 years given to attention to national education and singularly advantageous opportunities of seeing and talking to Government officials that I have learnt far more of what has been valuable to me from members of the Inspector[ate] ... than from the chiefs of the Department who have spent most of their official lives dealing with education on paper and by interview. ...
>
> I feel quite certain that it would have been more useful to the nation if (with of course now and again some rare exception) all its leading administrators had had at least five years (in some cases more) outside Whitehall as Inspectors or in other capacities. (Quoted from Lawton and Gordon, 1987, p. 124)

THE FOCUS

Once an inspector has arrived at the school, what does he think about? Contemporary inspectors ask, "What is the unit of analysis?" Since the focus on teaching and learning has been longstanding, the question becomes more particular: "What does an inspector examine or measure to judge the value of teaching and learning in a school?" Answers have varied over time.

In 1839 the focus was on the school. During Payment by Results, the focus was on student achievement with teachers bearing the consequences of that achievement. In the 1880s the focus shifted to the classroom and the subjects taught. In the early 1900s HMI began to evaluate the quality of teaching provided in the classroom in order to rebuild the respect and trust of the teachers after the Payment by Results era. Consistent with this new focus on the practice of teaching, HMI integrated a focus on the whole school, which had been practiced in secondary school inspections. The quality of teaching practice and learning has continued to be a central focus at both the national and local levels (Gordon, 1989, p. 41; Boothroyd, 1923, p. 62).

In the 1970s HMI focused more on issues across schools. The 1992 *Framework* sets the focus on schools and accentuates student performance on tests.

THE JUDGEMENT OF THE INDIVIDUAL INSPECTOR

Making judgements is the key element of inspection. An inspector goes to a school primarily to make judgements.

Although judgement always has been considered a part of inspection, it is first explicitly mentioned in the 1897 Revised Instructions to inspectors:

> Your report should be confined to a short judgement upon the general character of the school with the addition of your opinion of any special excellence or defect to which it is desirable to call attention. (Quoted in Boothroyd, 1923, p. 36)

Judgement is an element inspectors frequently discuss. Making a judgement is the most important contribution an individual inspector will make in the inspection process. While an inspector will usually express his judgements in specific terms, the underlying process of how he makes them is vague and personal. Judgement is based on the inspector's point of view, which shapes how he will make connections between the pieces of evidence and how he will clarify his point of reference for calling something good or bad. The point of view itself can and will change, depending on his experience.

Three inspectors describe what is at the heart of the individual inspector's judgement:

- AN HM INSPECTOR: Inspection requires judgement. Judgement requires considering relationships and values, considering what happens to the children. Without judgement it is no good.
- AN LEA INSPECTOR: You can't make a judgement until you know the teacher's criteria and see what the students actually do. Your framework must include what happened before, what the intentions were, and what happened afterward.
- AN LEA INSPECTOR: While participating in a program to learn more about business, I shadowed a middle-management employee of British Telecommunications. Having difficulty making sense out of the management employee's day, I reflected on my job as an inspector. Because I know the process of teaching, I know how difficult it is for a teacher to give her experience and what she knows to children in a way that's right for them in their world, which is a different world from hers. Because I know that from having been a teacher myself, I have an insight into it as an inspector. The judgements I make are based on that knowledge. The hooks I pin it on include language. Since I have taught, I have the experience and the language. That's why we can make judgements—because we have the hooks.

Most inspectors insist it is important to understand judgement as the collective judgement of the inspection team, rather than as the individual judgement of the team members. The individual judgements are the building blocks for the corporate judgements. Moderation, an element discussed later, is the alchemist between them.

The individual inspector's sense of what is good and bad about what is happening to children in a school is at the heart of her judgement. This introduces a moral sense into the inquiry.

Judging and collecting evidence happens simultaneously. Both are done on site when the inspector is face-to-face with a real and particular school or class. A judgement is formed in the heat of action and then refined. It is not an objective conclusion that is induced from information collected at the scene, taken away, grouped with other information, and then analyzed.

Because of her confidence in her ability to understand the meaning of an event or behavior in light of the school context, a good inspector will trust the insights she forms about the school on site. She does not refer to policy or other forms of external authority. Her judgement is professional. An important part of her skill and confidence comes from her past teaching and other direct school experience. Faced with, and concerned about, the constantly changing details of real life in schools, she always finds a challenge in making sense of it. It will be difficult for her to become stuck in conceptual ruts, because she continually discusses what she sees and thinks with both her inspection team colleagues and the people in the school. Because she must defend her judgements and because those judgements can shape policy, she knows they will matter. Since she must actively draw on her knowledge about subject matter, schools, teaching, learning, and policy, she realizes her experience is the most powerful touchstone for sorting through the inherent ambiguities and contradictions she finds. Because she knows her experience is valued, she doesn't think the system will undermine her or that she must look to others to learn what is correct to say.

Most inspectors question judgements that appear based on teaching theory or education ideology, rather than on the realities of classroom life. As we will see, the process of moderation serves as a check against unwarranted or unproductive use of generalized theory in making judgements.

Judgements are based on a complex set of explicit and implicit standards. Before an inspection visit inspectors often establish criteria to ensure they won't be influenced too much by the views of the school and that they won't lose the balance and usefulness of the wisdom of their consolidated experience.

Unlike the modern social science approach to gathering information, replicating a judgement is not relevant in inspection. Inspectors aren't troubled that another inspector, seeing the same class, might come to a different judgement. They ask each other what they think. They change their ideas based on what other inspectors say. An individual inspector can be more daring in making judgements in the heat of the action because he knows he will have the opportunity to scrutinize them with his colleagues, who are simultaneously making sense of the same school. Often the more daring judgements generate the best discussion. Knowing the limits of the moderation process, particularly that time is short, inspectors impose self-restraint.

Consistent with making matters specific, the 1992 *Framework* set standards for inspectors' judgements. The *Framework* insists that judgements be "reliable, in that they are consistent with the evaluation criteria in Section 2 of this *Framework*" (OFSTED, 1992, p. iii). In Chapter 3 this specificity about judgement caused John Turner's concern that much was being lost.

EVIDENCE

Constructed to support judgements, evidence must be clear, precise, and accurate. Evidence is a brief description of a small part of the actual life of the school that the inspector notices and writes down at some point. Ideally, it should be impossible, or at least difficult, to refute—particularly by a teacher or administrator from the school. Ultimately evidence should hold up in court.

Evidence became an element during the turbulent years of Payment by Results, when there was a dramatic shift to precise, apparently standardized evidence that greatly diminished the importance of the inspector's judgement. The importance of evidence in determining the size of a school's grant led to questioning: What is evidence? What is the unit of analysis? How is evidence collected? When is it objective?

Inspection evidence differs in interesting ways from that sought by a researcher, an investigator, or a Government regulator. An inspector will use evidence first to make and then to support a judgement about the quality of the action directly at hand. She will judge the quality of particular behavior that is happening in front of her, not build generalizations about principles of behavior. She will use evidence to understand what she is seeing now, not piece together what happened in the past or assign blame to the past. She will interpret a complex set of standards in forming her judgement, not use codified rules that have no regard for the particular action that created the information.

While evidence must be observed directly, there are exceptions—for instance, evidence from prime documents prepared by the school or evidence provided by a testing authority. Hearsay evidence is not valid.

When I asked the chairperson of a borough education committee, who frequently visited schools, how what she learned when she visited a school was different from what the borough inspectors learned, she said:

> I don't learn about some aspects of the school that they do. I visit a school as a layperson. I think about whether I'd send my child there. I notice the atmosphere the Head has created; how well the Head is managing the school; and what kind of relationship the school has with its Governors.
>
> An HMI can see differences in quality of student work. I can't do that. I can't judge student work against standards or make judgements about classroom organization. Those are on the technical side of education and I'm not a professional.

Finally, like wisdom based on common sense, inspection evidence is often mundane, ordinary, and even boring. Most inspection interviews for collecting information in schools are quite routine. These interviews don't try to encourage new insights, figure out a new way to think about schools, or generate thoughtful discourse. Inspectors try to make thorough, professional judgements about the value of what a school is providing its students. An LEA inspector commented: "There's too much fuss about the mystique of inspection. In fact, that's a cover-up for a common-sense job. It's one of the few jobs where someone can get by just by observing and using common sense. But, you have to be able to write well." The 19th century poet, Matthew Arnold was an HM inspector. He also complained about the repetitious and boring aspects of inspection.

The unit of analysis focuses on what evidence is collected. Focus on a specific topic, such as the implementation of the National Curriculum, shapes what evidence will be collected. Some inspectors will construct an aide-mémoir or a pro forma before an inspection visit to shape the collection of evidence. A pro forma is a checklist of what to notice. The aide-mémoir is usually a general list of topics to be addressed in the written report and/or questions or criteria about the school that emerged in team discussions prior to the visit. These tools allow the corporate view to inform the inspection process. Some inspectors see the new *Framework* as a massive pro forma.

When I asked a retired and highly respected HMI what he looked for when he went into a school, he told me:

Nothing at first. You want to see the school as if through a kaleidoscope, partly because at first the staff will be putting you on. Then you see how students move about, what teachers say when students first come into their class. Then the list gets long and you end by looking for the standard of the work students are doing.

Inspectors collect evidence by observing classes; interviewing teachers and staff; checking samples of individual student work; talking with students and watching how they perform, behave, and interact both in classrooms and around the school; reviewing records, policies, the school's test scores, development and staff plans; checking the school's accommodations and resources.

I wrote this journal entry after watching an HM inspector at work:

She's focused and precise in how she questions students and staff. She asks whether they know why they're doing what they're doing, whether they understand both the material and the design. At the same time, she's trying to identify what came before and what will come next. She looks at what students are working on now, as well as at the finished work in their folders. She asks teachers about the students, and students about the teachers.

Interviews occasionally serve purposes other than collecting evidence, such as making a key school administrator feel included in the inspection process so he will not be hostile to the report.

In short visits that are topic specific, the inspector often uses reporting-back sessions with teachers and staff for collecting evidence. For example, I observed one LEA inspector talking with the Head of Department about a teacher's class, who asked about the professional-development support the department provided that teacher and how that teacher fit into various department and school staff roles.

Both the Head and the teachers in a school control the inspectors' access to evidence. More can always be made available; for example, conversations can be more frank or more informal, confidential documents can be more available, and inspectors can be given easier access to more typical classes. After spending many days at one school, I wrote in my journal, "I now have access to more evidence because I know more"—a common belief of field researchers. But the process of inspectors at work seemed different. The more the school saw them as professionals and trusted them as professionals, the more it gave them access to information. When they entered the school, no one assumed they were dumb and presumed they would become bright after learning about that particular school.

Inspectors usually take notes during their visits. HM inspectors complete a reporting sheet on each class they visit and each interview they conduct. All evidence collected by individual inspectors that supports final team judgements will be included in a formal, written record of evidence.

When they feel they lack evidence to support a judgement well, inspectors become anxious. It is important for them to have an impressive number of observations, preferably covering more than one day.

During a week-long inspection, student work is formally reviewed by the team, usually at the end of the second day. HM inspectors don't find this formal review, as described in Chapter 3, terribly useful. They find examining student work in actual classes more valuable. In the shorter LEA inspections, it is more helpful to review student work formally, as LEA inspectors often do not have time to see it in the classroom context.

Most inspectors believe the evidence they marshal has been shaped by their individual judgements, by the unit of analysis, by the particular circumstances of that school at the time of the inspection, by the decisions made both by them and by the school about when and where to observe, and by how they collect their evidence. They don't usually regard evidence as an objective building block for their conclusions.

Most inspectors rely on their common sense for making good decisions about collecting evidence on site. For example, based on his early observation, an HM inspector became unsure about the quality of teacher support the math department provided. Deciding to observe and talk with another teacher, a new teacher who required more than usual support from the department, he changed his schedule to do that.

One LEA inspector I observed was clearly collecting evidence from a class to make a point to the teacher that she had formed prior to the visit.

She wasn't using evidence as an integral part of forming judgements about what was happening. Several HM inspectors told her, "You must know what you see, not see what you know." Many inspectors believe the more specific *Framework* for the new inspections creates a mindset for seeing what they know, or at least for seeing what the *Framework* says they should know.

One inspector with both HMI and LEA experience holds this interesting view about evidence. Good evidence is not only the observed data collected to support a judgement. An inspector must also collect and consider various perspectives within the school about the meaning of an issue or event. For this inspector, the test of objectivity comes when all the various perspectives are brought together. Information does not become objective simply by separating it from the perspectives that shape it and give it meaning.

STANDARDS

The English are more familiar than Americans with the idea of standards. *Standard* is used more often and has a richer variety of meanings. "The Standard" was a shopping area near our flat. We occasionally went to a pub named, "The Royal Standard." It is common to note if a restaurant's service is "up to standard." In Chapter 13 the provocation, *Making Standards Work*, provides more history on the general use of standards. It is not surprising that standards are important to inspection.

The standards a traditional inspector uses to arrive at judgements are rooted in:

1. The inspector's past practice as a schoolteacher and/or administrator
2. The inspector's current practice as an inspector
3. Legitimate public sources, such as the Examination Boards and current statutory codes, including the National Curriculum

Examination Board standards have influenced how academic achievement is defined. It is too early to know if the new attainment targets of the National Curriculum will exert similar influence on how people think about what students need to know.

Many inspectors believe standards ultimately rest in what is a "good deal for children."

Selecting, weighing, and applying standards to a particular school or class is the key to an individual inspector's judgement. As during Payment by Results, many inspectors believe their professional judgement is now being circumscribed by the simpler methodology of checking the school off against explicit, set standards.

The inspector's view of what makes a school good, an education good, will be central to her standards for judging the value of what goes on in classes and schools. An HM inspector explained to me that inspectors share a set of implicit standards for a good school. These shared standards are first learned through a mentoring induction. These standards are influenced by knowledge of actual schools and by the standards and expectations of the society at large. They change slowly in a common-sense way and are implicit in all inspectorate reports.

The traditional view of standards confers on many inspectors the responsibility of being a standard bearer. An inspector's visit at the school calls attention to how well the school is doing. The inspector can, and often does, explain a standard or exhort the school to do better.

Standards are not guides for making inspection judgements. They exist in the school, regardless of the formal codes. Thus the standards of the school can be judged and, most important, raised. It is accurate to say the inspector uses her intrinsic professional standards to judge whether the school is up to standard, according to what is expected of that institution.

During a moderation session, one inspector concluded that, since the students in that school were doing well, that school was up to standard. Another inspector reminded him, "We're charged first to say if the standards are good and then to say whether they're good enough."

After a session with a group of LEA inspectors, who were reviewing an early draft of this section, a bearded member of the team said he had been fascinated by my observation that inspectors are standard bearers. Alluding to the eight prophets of Israel, who had set standards that went beyond the working values of society, he noted that inspectors must go beyond the immediate and remind teachers that they, too, are professionals, not mere technicians, and that they, too, must look beyond the *how* to the *why* and to the future.

While most inspectors would not want to be compared with the prophets, they would agree they do not use standards as simple criteria for measuring student performance. In 1987 Denis Lawton and Peter Gordon, both knowledgeable observers of HMI, wrote:

> There has always been a concern, not simply to report on standards, but to change standards, both in the sense of making standards more appropriate and of improving the overall quality of the educational service. (p. 153)

The 1992 *Framework for Inspection* presents itself as the only legitimate source of standards. It seeks to limit ambiguity by specifying explicit standards in place of the complex, less clear, and more dynamic standards of an individual inspector. This would seem to simplify the inspector's role by making him a reporter on how the school is measuring up to a set of specified standards. Unfortunately the *Framework* redirects the ambiguity from the internal moral core of an individual inspector, making professional decisions while confronting a class, to an arena that invites continuous argument about what the standards mean, how they are applied, and what their value will be.

MODERATION OF INDIVIDUAL JUDGEMENTS

Moderation tests and hones the judgements of the individual inspectors into a corporate or team judgement. Viewed by many inspectors as crucial, moderation both ameliorates the negative aspects of relying on personal judgement and adds wisdom from a discussion that is greater than the sum of its parts, greater than the initial judgements of the individual inspectors.

Moderating individual judgements into a corporate judgement may have roots beyond the inspection tradition. For years it has been common practice in England for teachers to moderate the grading of important student exams. First, several teachers read the paper independently from one another. Second, they moderate their individual judgements by discussing them with the other teachers, and last, they determine the final grade together. Because of the prevalence of this practice, moderation in inspection has not been considered unusual.

Moderation develops the corporate voice for inspectors that has more power than their individual voices:

> Only gradually were the firm foundations laid upon which any inspectorate must rest: on the personal side, absolute loyalty to one's colleagues and superiors, unimpeachable integrity, constant vigilance to ensure the good name of the service; on the administrative side, uniformity of approach and procedure, and "all of one voice" in public utterances. (Edmonds, 1962, p. 29)

A senior HMI noted that:

> through discussion, both the varied views of the inspectors and the underlying assumptions and evidence on which the judgements have been made are questioned. No matter how rushed it may become, it is best done collectively. (*Journal Entry*, no. 14.6)[1]

In 1854 Matthew Arnold wrote:

> Inspection exists for the sake of finding out and reporting on the truth, and for this above all. But it is most important that all inspectors should proceed on the same principle in this respect. (1882, p. 30)

The formal moderation process calls for thorough, open, rigorous team discussion under the leadership of a Reporting Inspector. Significant discussion time is built into the school-visit schedule—usually after school and in the evening of the last 2 days of the inspection.

All judgements presented in feedback to the school and, even more important, those published as the inspectorate's corporate conclusions in the final inspection report are expected to have been subjected to moderation by the team and by at least one senior inspector, who was not present during the inspection. The moderation will continue through the review of all drafts of the report, hopefully only to refine agreed-upon judgements.

In moderation discussions the usual approach is for one inspector to present his initial judgement with his evidence. During the discussion, new insights may emerge, judgements that are similar may be combined, and basic questions might be raised. If the team agrees the judgement is valid, supporting evidence will be solicited from other team members. If the team disagrees, they will work to understand what is behind the disagreement and try to reach a new agreement.

When someone questions a judgement, the team will try to resolve the issue by considering several factors, including the context of the school, the circumstances of that inspection, and the differences in inspection experience, specialist knowledge, and temperament of the inspectors involved. If convincing evidence is not forthcoming, the team usually will decide to check out the matter further the next day in the school.

Throughout the moderation process the team works actively to build consensus. A judgement that will be made public must have team consensus and strong evidence supporting it.

During moderation discussions, the team will consider how the wording of a statement will affect the school. (This happens more often with LEA inspections.) While the inspectors give priority to ensuring the integrity of their judgements, they try to support the school, if possible. They are usually pleased when this tension has been balanced and the final wording does both.

Moderation is not easy. At its best, the team of experienced school people, who have spent time together at the same school, will dig deep into what the dynamics of the school are, what the school needs to be about, and what the inspection report should be about. Many inspectors view moderation as the most difficult and most rewarding part of their work. Since it's conducted at the site with many demands competing for each inspector's attention, it can suffer both from distraction and a shortage of time.

Much moderation takes place in informal discussions among inspectors, further accentuating the importance of the team approach.

FEEDBACK TO TEACHERS AND SCHOOLS

Some inspectors abhor the term *feedback,* considering it American organizational jargon. Feedback, as it is used here, often includes the formal reporting-back sessions and other conversations inspectors have with teachers and the school, some that provide advice not closely related to inspection judgements.

In formal reporting-back sessions the Reporting Inspector, or sometimes another team member, will give the report, most often based on notes the team has agreed on during its discussion. The presenter may read the exact written text or some of the more controversial points the team has worked through.

The history of how feedback became an element is not clear. Most inspectors consider feedback an important part of the inspection process. Its practice has varied. I was present when a school was pressuring an inspection team to provide more feedback than it thought it should. Although he probably would not like to be quoted, one of the HM inspectors said:

> Teachers shouldn't expect feedback; we don't know what to say
> because we're still thinking about it. We do our jobs as professionals,
> not to win popularity contests. (*Journal Entry,* no. 11.49)

Feedback is more valuable for inspectors who want to help schools directly, for those who want "to do good as they go." In the closer relationships between LEA inspectors and schools there are opportunities beyond the formal feedback sessions to do good, such as providing information to isolated schools or helping a school find and hire a teacher it wants. These interventions are usually judged to be more powerful than feedback. But, as the definition of inspection has become more codified and the LEAs have been weakened, the informal opportunities to do good are drying up, placing more importance on formal feedback.

There is evidence that, during the Payment by Results era, feedback to Heads became common practice, since the Head had much to gain or lose as a consequence of the inspector's report. As one inspector from that era cavalierly described:

> If the master was a good fellow and trustworthy, we looked over the few
> papers in dictation and arithmetic, marked the examination schedule, and
> showed him the results before we left. Then he calculated his percentage of
> passes, his grant, and his resulting income; and went to dinner with what
> appetite he might. But if the man was cross-grained and likely to complain
> that the exercises were too hard, the standard of marking too high, and so on,
> he would be left in merciful ignorance of the details. (Edmonds, 1962, p. 82)

Today, although formal feedback sessions are usually described as a one-way process—the inspectors report the results of the inspection to the school—they may serve an important two-way function. A feedback session is considered productive if there has been implicit agreement by both the school and the inspectorate team that each has conducted itself in a professional manner; that the conclusions are accurate and in the school's best interest at some level; and that the rest of the process, primarily the preparation and publication of the report, will be played out according to script with a reasonable amount of decorum. Because the tense period of interaction between the two groups has ended, feedback sessions frequently provide a strong catharsis.

There are several rules guiding formal feedback. The closer the person receiving the feedback is to the actual event that has been observed, the more detailed and precise the feedback will be. Nothing should be said (at least publicly) about a person or a group (for example, a subject department) at a higher level of authority than has been said to those involved at a lower level. Individual teachers and students are never identified in formal feedback.

During the feedback, the inspection team will try to discover if the school sees any problems with the evidence it has collected. If the school raised a question about the evidence, the inspectors would consider the school's position and make accepted corrections immediately. Although a school may suggest corrections of factual errors in evidence, it cannot change the judgements.

There's a strong expectation that, as soon after a class has been observed as possible, the inspector will discuss his observations with the teacher. This is expected more of LEA inspectors, who are more dependent on their ongoing relationships with local teachers. Feedback sessions are also held, depending on the school and the focus of the inspection, with heads of departments, the senior management team and the Governing Body.

Formal reporting back usually comes with formal inspections. All inspection visits will have some informal feedback elements through which the school may learn what the inspectors think. As noted earlier, informal feedback can be used not only to correct evidence but to generate new evidence.

For LEA inspectors, more often than HM inspectors, feedback has the dual function of assessing and problem solving. LEA inspectors believe their oral feedback is "what will really make the difference." LEA feedback is more varied and more closely tied to the issues of monitoring and advising, discussed further below.

How the school perceives the value of the inspection is shaped by the quality of the feedback and how it has been presented. This can influence the school's response to the inspection report and affect its follow-up response. An LEA inspector noted:

> If school people see the inspectors as willing to be more honest about what's wrong in the school than the school staff can be, given their constraints as insiders, they will respect the inspectors. Honest feedback increases what an inspector will learn by building respect.

How the inspectors perceive the capability of the teacher or the Head "to take on board" what they have to say will influence how they shape feedback, unless they consider a person hopeless. With considerable skill, both HM and LEA inspectors will go to great lengths to ensure that what they have to say will be effective and not push the targeted individual "over the top."

I watched an inspector who was critical of the weak leadership a Head was providing the inspected school. When he learned she was going through a personal crisis, he made extra allowances for her. His feedback was mild and supportive. Afterward he told me, "It wouldn't have done any good to have given her a hard feedback. The situation wasn't bad enough to warrant her leaving."

THE INSPECTION REPORT

Reports have been expected from inspectors since the first inspection. What the formal inspection report represents, how it is compiled, who sees it, and when it will be seen and by whom have received much attention over the years.

Mr. H. S. Tremenheere, the second HM inspector hired in 1839, frequently commented in his reports on social conditions surrounding the schools. This generated a debate that Robert Lowe muted in 1862 by insisting that from then on reports should confine themselves to schools and not include general problems. During Lowe's term, Parliament became alarmed by rumors that Department politicians and civil servants were altering inspectors' reports, thus compromising their integrity. At the very time Lowe was arguing before Parliament that no reports had been altered, a copy of an altered report was circulating through the House. The Government was defeated on the vote. Although he was unaware of any alterations, in the tradition of a good British civil servant, Lowe resigned. This historical precedent for the integrity of inspectors' reports survives today (Lawton and Gordon, 1987, pp. 11–12).

Since 1983 all HMI reports have been published as public documents, available to anyone who requests them. Currently the published report of a school inspection is accepted as an authoritative and final statement about the quality of that school at the time of the inspection. Conclusions cannot be modified. The published inspection report has the full weight of HMI (or the LEA inspectorate) behind it. HMI has taken this view seriously, assuring the inspectors that in the end this protects them in making their judgements. Moderation has taken on further importance because the published reports represent the position of all HM inspectors. There are no minority reports. The report deliberately protects the anonymity of the inspection team members, who conducted the school visit and who wrote it. Viewing the anonymity positively, HM inspectors have appreciated the protection it provides. Knowing that the report will represent the corporate, official HMI view, they take additional care writing it.

The Reporting Inspector's responsibility for the report includes writing general sections, compiling team members' sections, and managing the reviews of several drafts. The Reporting Inspectors are not elevated superiors within an inspectorate. Any inspector may be chosen to lead a team. Most HM inspectors have at one time or another served as Reporting Inspectors. Thus, all HM inspectors have team leadership capabilities. Most inspectors like to write and have good writing skills.

The report writer must be more concerned about an audience of writers than an audience of readers. This audience includes the voices of the different team members, the inspectorate leaders, and the tradition of the inspectorate. The challenge is to find the balance between these voices. This dynamic affects the substance and tone of all inspection reports, and may account for the solid, moderated, somewhat wooden rhetoric for which they are known. After all, a school report isn't meant to stir action but to be a public record stating the value of the school.

When the team has agreed to the final draft of the report, it is forwarded to the Chief Inspector, who will forward it to the Secretary of Education. The new *Framework* has required all school parents to receive a free report summary; full reports are now available at cost.

The HMI style is established. There are jokes about "HMI-speak." The *Times Educational Supplement* has published guides on how to decode it. The following example of report language illustrates the deliberate, moderate, confident, and reasoned style:

> Resources are readily accessible and during the inspection many
> items of equipment, including the microcomputer, were seen to be
> well used by the children and teachers.

The use of "during the inspection ... were seen" probably means: while the inspectors saw good use of computing resources during the visit, they were not certain whether this was normal school practice or whether it was in place only because of their visit. Lacking good evidence to support their suspicion, they handled this ambiguity accurately by limiting the judgement.

Although they expend much serious effort preparing reports, inspectors often question their value. An LEA inspector, who takes writing seriously, commented:

> I don't think our published documents are all that clear about shortcomings. They are coded and cautious. I'm not sure that kind of dialogue is necessary, but it is part of the culture of this authority. I don't see critical comment as something negative.

In response to my asking how helpful he found HMI reports, a national education reporter said:

> The standards language is not very helpful, if the purpose is to support improvement or radical change. While the judgement is included, it's often vague and points to no action. The language appears to be shaped by its comfort or discomfort value.

SCHOOL FOLLOW-UP

During a full inspection, the Head of the school told me: "If inspection was all that happened, I would be disappointed."

Follow-up is what a school does with feedback. HMI sees follow-up by the school as being the responsibility of the LEA and the school. The inspection process provides a thoughtful basis for fixing or improving a school. Many HM inspectors believe that a lack of specific follow-up at the school has been a major weakness in traditional inspection. Follow-up differs dramatically between LEA and HMI inspections.

LEA inspectors, as LEA staff, have ongoing responsibilities for a school. They frequently see inspection as the first step in a longer process to improve the school. How follow-up is carried out and what role the LEA inspector will play varies among LEAs.

What the school will do with the inspection results depends largely on how it has judged the quality of the inspection and how it has regarded the inspection team. For example, the Governors of a school near Leeds had a high regard for the Reporting Inspector. Having helped design the inspection that was in process, they had reasonable confidence in it. Believing the Governing Body had been an important part of the school's difficulties, the Reporting Inspector attended several of their meetings and interviewed many of them, which he reported went well. At the feedback meeting I attended, he brought a stiff message to the school. He ended by telling them:

> Too many people at this school, including the Governors, justify the school's poor performance by arguing that the students come from poor families of new immigrants.

Quietly accepting this major criticism, the Governors scheduled a meeting to discuss how they should consider this perspective. One member commented, "Your report woke up our ideas." It was more difficult for them to dismiss the conclusion of the report because they respected the inspector.

The new *Framework* requires the Governors of an inspected school to prepare an action report to show how they will respond to the inspection report. With the demise of the LEA inspectorates and teacher advisors, the school will be on its own in making improvements.

INFORMING GOVERNMENT POLICY

Reporting to the central Government about what it learns so that the bureaucrats and politicians can make better policy has always been a central HMI purpose. Over time this has become a complex matter, as it has evolved to include providing advice on policy, not merely reporting. A senior education official, now retired, noted in his comments about the old HMI:

> To those who make the policy decisions, inspection should provide an informed voice—not with certainty, but with goodwill. Without good knowledge of what is actually happening in the schools, one is at the mercy of the voices of the time. HMI should spot what Government policy should be in the future and thus consider issues that will be important 2 years from now. Tests don't tell us what to do. Inspection information can do that because it can describe good practice so others can replicate it.

HMI has provided advice to the Government through several mechanisms: the *Chief Inspector's Annual Report on the State of English Education*, which is based on all school reports for that year; reports on issues of special Government interest (for example, educating students with special needs, implementing the National Curriculum, and using technology in schools); and participation by invitation in policy work groups.

More than likely the informal relationships between HMI and Department policymakers have been more important than these reports. Due to the Official Secrets Act there are only scraps of evidence available to demonstrate that the relationship between HMI and the Department has always been dynamic, and at times torturous.

HMI saw its independence from the Department as crucial to its effectiveness in advising central Government. Its argument was obvious: If it were to give high-quality advice, it had to be independent from Government politicians. This allowed inspectors to be trusted in the schools and HMI to take a longer view than politicians in defining the issues. Glimpses of HMI's relationship to the Government suggest a fascinating and important story. That story is not about the method of inspection; it is about its organizational history and context. We turn now to consider inspection's history and tensions.

Chapter 5

History

Tracing the origins of many ideas that shaped inspection methodology during the last 150 years, this history will show how the institution of inspection fared as a tradition of accountability.

A GOOD BEGINNING FOR AN OLD TRADITION (1839–1857)

On August 26, 1839, Sir James Kay-Shuttleworth became the first Secretary of Education for Britain. On September 24, 1839, the Committee of the Council on Education formally established Government inspection of schools. In December 1839 Sir James hired Reverend J. Allen and Mr. H. S. Tremenheere, a clergyman and a lawyer, respectively, as the first HM inspectors, the first Government inspectors of schools.

Where did the idea of inspection originate? What was happening in England in 1839 that led to this dramatic beginning?

Government inspection was built on an older tradition of inspection. One historian has traced it back to St. Paul and the "visitorial tradition" of the Christian Church. This tradition was important when church leaders visited the abbey schools, England's earliest schools. The description of this ancient practice resonates with current practice:

> A "primal sympathy" linked visitor and visited who were all of one family. … It sought to persuade rather than threaten, to encourage rather than dismay, to endorse the good whilst eradicating the bad. Above all, it was no sinecure for the Visitor himself, who needed to combine physical toughness with his saintliness and scholarship, if he were to survive the long, even perilous, journeys. (Edmonds, 1962, p. 1)

Inspection had also appeared in the ideas of Britain's social philosophers. In 1786 Jeremy Bentham, a founder of the philosophical approach called Utilitarianism, considered the role of public inspectors in his rather frightening designs for prisons. Later in writing about the public good and education he saw inspectors as a major instrument of Government policy, as enforcers of what needed to be done for the common good (Curtis and Boultwood, 1966, pp. 401–406).

It isn't clear whether the fact that the Irish had hired Government school inspectors in 1820 was an incentive or a disincentive for Sir James (Ball, 1963, p. 8). Probably the most powerful explanations for the beginning of inspection rest in why the office of Secretary of Education was created and why Sir James was appointed.

By 1839 most of the great private schools for children of the English aristocracy were well established. Early in the 19th century the Industrial Revolution swept through the Kingdom with an intensity that made its American progress seem mild. At that time national interest in educating the large numbers of poor children rose sharply.

For many years voluntary societies, associated with the churches, had provided some form of education for the poor. Forty years after it was founded in 1699, the Society for the Propagation of Christian Knowledge (SPCK) provided 2,044 schools for 51,161 children. In the early 1800s the National Society for Promoting the Education of the Poor in the Principles of the Established Church (usually referred to as the National Society; the established church was the Church of England) and the British and Foreign School Society (the nonconformists) sought to establish schools for all poor children. In 1815 The National Society schools served 200,000 children.

The societies energetically viewed the moral and practical education of poor children as their responsibility. But there were too many to enfold into their domain without greater financial resources. As the need for more money became clear, the Government had no choice but to become involved. It had never considered giving its money to the societies without strings attached.

The religious societies were using inspectors, visitors, organizers, and traveling agents to establish new schools, to learn what was happening in existing ones, and to help improve all of them. For example, Dr. Andrew Bell, secretary of the National Society from 1812 to 1819 and an early guru in English education, professed a specified "correct method for instruction." He employed inspectors to ensure that teachers in the societies' schools were doing what they were supposed to be doing (Edmonds, 1962, pp. 16–19).[1]

The 1802 and 1833 Factory Acts required mill owners to provide their apprentices with daily instruction in reading, writing, and arithmetic under a "discreet and proper person ... in some room ... set aside for that purpose" (Edmonds, 1962, pp. 25–26). There was no intent to provide public support for other school rooms. These Acts called for inspectors to ensure that mill owners complied with them, including the sections on education.

In 1833 the Privy Council, providing a way around the opposition of the House of Lords, established the first national grant of £20,000 "for the education of the children of the poorer classes in Great Britain" (Lawton and Gordon, 1987, p. 7). This grant was not to start public schools, but to help the societies establish new schools and improve their existing ones. Passage of this grant and concern about how it would be spent led to the creation of the office of Secretary of Education.

Sir James was asked to be Secretary because he was seen as a moral man with a vision about public education of the poor and someone who would work well with the religious societies:

> [While a man of unusual vision,] ... he did not achieve a tenth part of his dreams for universal education, embracing all classes of society and administered by "local" authorities, although aided by Government grants. (Edmonds, 1962, p. 46)

On September 24, 1839, the Committee of the Council on Education formally established Government inspection of schools. Sir James probably wrote the minutes of that meeting:

> The right of inspection will be required by the Committee in all cases; inspectors, authorized by Her Majesty in Council, will be appointed from time to time to visit schools to be henceforth aided by public money: the inspectors will not interfere with religious instruction, or discipline, or management of the school, it being their object to collect facts and information and to report the results of the inspections to the Committee of the Council. (Edmonds, 1962, p. 31)

Construed in a way that was responsive to the political realities of the time, Government school inspection began as the central education agency's practical solution to the problems of accountability and school support.

Sir James saw inspection as a way to "do good." Inspection was also a way to answer two practical, classic questions:

Are the schools spending public money well?
How can the central office help the schools become better?

Hiring men to visit the schools was neither extraordinary nor innovative. It was plain common sense. There was no such thing as program evaluation or standardized testing. At that time people, not machines, provided information. Even though Victoria had been Queen for two years, no one ever would have thought of sending a woman. Further, the relationship between Government and the religious societies was delicate. Government questions about funding schools were piddling compared to the societies' questions about Government meddling in their affairs.

When the first two inspectors were appointed, "a new principle of administration, with very far-reaching consequences, was established; namely, the principle that, if the State spends money, it has a right to see that it is spent in a manner in which it approves" (Boothroyd, 1923, p. 4). However, the schools were not Government schools, but religious societies' schools. Sir James made this clear in his first well-known instructions to his two new inspectors:

> [I]t is of the utmost consequence that you should bear in mind that this inspection is not intended as a means of exercising control, but of affording assistance: that it is not to be regarded as operating for the restraint of local efforts, but for their encouragement. (Cited from Gordon, 1989, p. 32)

In 1846 Sir James further elaborated on this:

> The inspector will act under instructions restraining him from all interference with the discipline and management of the school. He will have no authority to direct, and will not be permitted even to advise, unless invited to do so by the school committee. With these precautions against the exactions of authority, he will not fail to be useful to all schools which he may visit, by skillfully planning under the light of a searching examination, conducted in the presence of the managers, the actual condition of the school. The results of his experience will be available for their instruction and guidance. (Edmonds, 1962, p. 49)

In 1897, more than 50 years later, Fitch, an HM inspector, summed this up rather well:

> [The inspector's] first duty is to verify the conditions on which public aid is offered to schools, and to assure the Department that the nation is obtaining a good equivalent for its outlay. But this is not the whole. He is called upon to visit from day to day schools of very different types, to observe carefully the merits and demerits of each, to recognize with impartiality very various forms of good work, to place himself in sympathy with teachers and their difficulties, to convey to each of them kindly suggestions as to methods of discipline and instruction he has observed elsewhere, and to leave behind him at every school he inspects some stimulus to improvement, some useful counsel to managers, and some encouragement to teachers and children to do their best. There are few posts in the public service which offer larger scope for the beneficial exercise of intellectual and moral power, or which bring the holder into personal and influential relations

with a larger number of people. It will be an unfortunate day for the Civil Service if ever the time comes when an office of this kind is regarded as one of inferior rank, or is thought unworthy of the acceptance of men of high scholarship and intellectual gifts. (Fitch, 1897, p. 169)

Sir James had built "a working compromise from which something could grow" (Edmonds, 1962, p. 50). This compromise defined the tension between monitoring schools and providing support for their improvement, a tension that exists today.

From this historical vantage point it would be tempting to conclude that all the talk about advice, influence, and support for changing schools had been merely to sugarcoat government inspection for the societies. The historical record clearly indicates that, when the government began to invest in schools, it did all it could within practical political terms to monitor, regulate, and enforce its views on them.

However, it would be too simple to dismiss the soft side of inspection—its support for the schools—as grease for political compromise. It is inherent in democracy that a government must support the schools that educate its children. It would be simpler for a government to try only to control its schools, but that would distort the real tension that exists between monitoring and supporting them. English history defines this tension with greater clarity than ours.

By 1860 inspection was off to a good start. The number of inspectors had increased to 48 (Lawton and Gordon, 1987, p. 163). All men, half clergy, most graduates of Oxford and Cambridge, none had taught in an elementary school. HMI memoirs from this period stressed the importance of inspectors coming from the same social class as the school administrators (Gordon, 1989, p. 31).

The inspectors quickly earned the respect of most of those who counted:

The [Department], in fact, was beginning to realize how much it depended on its "eyes and ears"—the inspectors. One of the very rare compliments ever made to "Civil Servants" in any age was paid to them in 1852: "The inspectors' reports constitute the foundation of the whole system of education." (Edmonds, 1962, p. 51)

MAKING IT PRECISE—PAYMENT BY RESULTS (1858–1897)

During Payment by Results, the second era of inspection history, the Government ignored the tension of the "working compromise" between monitoring and support that Sir James had so carefully constructed. It used inspection only to extend its central control over schools. This brought about grave difficulties.

The rapid increase in public spending to educate the poor raised new questions about "efficiency." In 1860 the Newcastle Commission reported:

> There is only one way of securing this result (i.e., efficiency in the teaching of every scholar) which is to institute a searching examination by competent authority of every child in every school to which grants are to be paid, with a view to ascertaining whether the indispensable elements of knowledge are thoroughly acquired and to make the prospects and position of the teacher dependent to a considerable extent on the results of this examination. (Cited in Edmonds, 1962, p. 73)

It is easy to see how this led to the following conclusion in the Department's 1871 report:

> If a teacher produces nothing, he gets no pay. ... The object of the State is to have results; the machinery for producing them is immaterial. (Cited in Edmonds, 1962, p. 130)

With considerable competence and vigor, Robert Lowe, the Secretary of Education, set up the Revised Code of 1862. From the beginning it was clear that HM inspectors would be the "competent authorities" who would examine the students. This Code, revised because of the furor it created when it was introduced, was a more radical change in national education assessment policy than the 1988–1992 reform, because it was the first time the Government had tried to use such precision.[2]

Defining a new standard for student achievement, the Revised Code became the basis for Payment by Results. The code required schools to group students by their achievement levels. Each group was called "a standard." (This brings an interesting connotation to the still-used phrase, "That student is not up to standard.") The important subjects were reading, writing, and arithmetic, and needlework for girls. Although schools could continue teaching other subjects, those would not be counted when the Government set grant amounts (Gordon, 1989, p. 34).

While this clearly was the beginning of the "three Rs," the historical record is silent on why it was not called the "three R's and the one N." The tortuous history of women in HMI began with the conclusion that, if there were needlework classes, women had to inspect them. HMI did not hire the first women inspectors; they were hired by local school boards at the end of the 19th century (Bailey, 1986). HMI first used women to provide advice to HM inspectors about needlepoint.

During Payment by Results, annual attendance and student exam results, precisely calculated by HM inspectors, determined the size of each school's grant. The grant provided 4 shillings for student attendance, based on the average number in attendance for the year. (The grant was 2 shillings and 6 pence for evening schools.) Every student, who had attended over 200 meetings during the year, was examined in the basic subjects at his standard. If a student were more than 6 years old and had passed all the exams, the school received an additional 8 shillings, provided an inspector had determined he was up to standard in each of the basic subjects. The school was docked 2 shillings and 6 pence for each subject in which a child was not up to standard. The inspector's examination determined up to two-thirds of a school's grant. The inspector could decide that the school should receive no grant at all if certain standards of provision were not met, for example, if the school did not have an adequate building, a certified school Head (principal), instruction in needlework for girls, or registers of student attendance "kept with sufficient accuracy to warrant confidence" (Edmonds, 1962, pp. 73–74).

Payment by Results not only raised questions about what the unit of analysis for inspection should be, since it had abruptly changed from the performance of the school to the performance of the individual student, but it also raised questions about how to measure student achievement.

Early instructions on how to carry out the examinations tried to reassure the inspectors that not much had changed:

> You will judge every school by the same standard that you have hitherto used, as regards its religious, moral and intellectual merits. … It does not exclude the inspection of each school by a highly educated public officer, but it fortifies this general test by individual examination. (Cited in Edmonds, 1962, p. 75)

When the Department of Education issued the 1871 Revised Instructions, specifying how inspectors could speed through the examination drill, it was clear that inspection had changed. The instructions (paraphrased below) told inspectors:

> Line up the children according to their standards. Each child is to carry only his slate on which he has already done his sums and transcriptions. As each child passes the inspector he hands his slate to the inspector, who in turn gives him the book for his reading, pointing to the passage he is to read. While listening to the reading, the inspector can mark the arithmetic and writing on the form. Then the inspector rapidly turns over a few pages of the book, and the child reads again. The child gives the book back to the inspector, takes his slate and goes to his place. The next child comes up, gives the inspector his slate and is dealt with in the same manner. (Cited in Boothroyd, 1923, pp. 29–30)

Inspectors, paying flying visits to schools, often came upon a dress rehearsal in which the children marched rapidly, slates in hand, before the master's desk. One HM inspector estimated he had tested 46,000 students in a year (Boothroyd, 1923, pp. 29–30).

While an inspector had the power to determine a school's grant, his job was dull and routine. But, because a school's survival was in his hands, school Heads paid much more attention to the inspection process. The high stakes made them much more likely to follow the inspector, while he was in the school, and to take seriously the summing up at the end of the visit.

Because school grants were based on individual student achievement as determined by the inspectors, the evaluation of teacher performance and teacher pay began to be based on how well one's students performed. Thus, it is not surprising that the relationships between inspectors and teachers deteriorated rapidly.

In response to the Code, one school placed an inscription over its door that warned, "Learn or Leave" (Gordon, 1989, p. 35).

Payment by Results altered the relationship between the inspectors and the Department of Education. With formal authority to withhold grants, the inspectors had more power, but they were no longer resources for advice. Even if they had been asked what they knew about schools, they no longer knew schools in a way that would be useful to those either in the Department or in the schools. Edmonds summed up the main advantage of Payment by Results: "Above all it was easy to understand" (1962, p. 130).

At first many inspectors and parents believed Payment by Results would work by forcing the schools to focus on teaching the essentials. By the time it was dropped in 1897, the Revised Code had no support. Yet no one can deny its impact on English education and inspection. Payment by Results partially defined the practice of inspection by clarifying what it was not.

In his attack on the new system, which he saw as an abomination, Sir James Kay-Shuttleworth clarified the distinction between an inspector's influence and his power, essentially the same as the distinction between monitoring and supporting that is discussed to this day:

> [The inspector] has hitherto exercised greater influence on the improvement of the schools by his experience and conciliation of co-operative effort, than by his power to recommend the withdrawal of the grants to the teachers and pupil-teachers for neglect and consequent unsatisfactory results, either in organization, instruction or discipline. His time, under the Revised Code, would be consumed in a mechanical drudgery which would necessarily withdraw his attention from the religious and general instruction, and from the moral features of the school. (Blackie, 1970, p. 16)

Matthew Arnold, probably the best-known inspector, was at work when Payment by Results began. He found the new scheme so deplorable he left England. He thought good inspection was old inspection:

The whole school felt, under the old system, that the prime aim and object of the inspector's visit was, after ensuring the fulfillment of certain sanitary and disciplinary conditions, to test and quicken the intellectual life of the school. The scholar's thoughts were directed to this object, the teachers' thoughts were directed to it, the inspector's thoughts were directed to it. (Cited in Edmonds, 1962, p. 80)

Edmonds, the best historian of inspection of that era, summed up his review of the inspection reports:

All too frequently, emphasis is laid on the wrong things: the fact that a child was too cold in school to be able to hold his pen is of less importance than the fact that he was accidentally marked present in the register on a day on which he happened to be absent; lack of light, ventilation and sanitary facilities in schools would seem to weigh less with inspectors than the performance of children on examination day. Within a very short time after the institution of the Revised Code, education may have been cheaper, but it was certainly poorer than before, and the quality of inspection was poorer, too. (1962, p. 79)

In 1878, at the end of the Payment by Results era, Lord George Hamilton recounted what Lowe had told him about why he had established the code:

What happened was this: when I was at the Education Department, as my eyes hurt me a good deal, whenever I went into the country I used to send to the National School to ask them to let me have one or two boys and girls who could read well, and they used to come up to me and read in the evening. I found that few, if any, of these boys and girls could really read. They got over words of three syllables, but five syllables completely stumped them. I therefore came to the conclusion that, as regards reading, writing and arithmetic, which are three subjects which can be definitely tested, each child should either read or write a passage, or do some simple sum of arithmetic, and the idiots who succeeded me have piled up on the top of the three R's a mass of class and specific subjects which they propose to test in the same way. (Boothroyd, 1923, pp. 20–21)

By this time teachers were an important force. They had increased in number; they were better trained, more independent and, most importantly, well organized. Unhappy with the HM inspectors, they made it known that inspection, limited to the examination of individual students for Payment by Results, harmed their schools and lowered the value of education.

In 1888 Frank Silverlock, a teacher, and Mr. Dibben, an HM inspector, tragically dramatized this position. Dibben had determined that renewing Silverlock's certificate for teaching (his "parchment") should be deferred because there was evidence that, during the parchment lesson, some boys in his class had asked questions, thereby showing a lack of discipline. Two months later the management committee of the local board demanded Silverlock's resignation. "That evening shortly before six o'clock, carrying two letters, one to his fiancée and the other to his parents, Frank Silverlock committed suicide, run down by a train at Highbury station." In the letter to his parents, Silverlock wrote, "I hope my act will be forgiven, and I shall go to where there are no dull stupid boys, and no inspectors" (Betts, 1986, pp. 18–19).

This dramatic event became a focal point for growing teacher unhappiness with both Payment by Results and inspection, prompting the following in the *Schoolmaster*, a newspaper for teachers:

> The letters … are painful reading, but they are the embodiment of sentiments and anxieties which are at the present hour only too familiar to thousands of teachers of the United Kingdom. Once more we ask, why should the teacher's life be more miserable than that of other men? … The ceaseless worry which falls to the teacher's lot … will grow and not diminish until the advent of the better times when Payment by Results, shall in the present mode of administration, be swept away as an evil for which there is not the slightest justification. (Cited in Betts, 1986, p. 20)

At this time the Cross Commission, examining elementary education, inquired about the legal basis of inspection. In May 1888 the *Schoolmaster* commented on the teachers' testimony before the commission:

> The Inspectors of schools were the subjects of many hard sayings, and the men, who under a system founded on common sense, would be deemed the ornaments of [at the peak of] the profession, are derided for their unfitness and irregularity. To be a university man is a good thing, but it by no means invariably implies the presence of a gentleman, and without long experience of the practical work of a teacher it as invariably implies a man unqualified for the work. … The pets of patronage have had their day. (Cited in Betts, 1986, p. 21)

Although the Cross Commission noted many complaints about inspectors, its report concluded that "on the whole the country has been well served" (cited in Betts, p. 21, nn.20–21). The commission recommended that elementary schoolteachers be included in the inspector ranks.

In 1894 the newly formed National Union of Teachers (NUT) submitted the following memo to a commission that was considering secondary-school inspection:

> An inspector of schools should not only be just, cautious, and accurate in his habit of mind; he should also be sympathetic, genial, courteous, and a lover of children. Above all, he should possess practical knowledge of teaching and should have had experience of the difficulties alike of teacher and taught. (Cited in Edmonds, 1962, pp. 120–121)

This memo pointed out in firm language that HM inspectors lacked the qualities and experience of local school board inspectors, who had been "generally helpful" to the schools. Thus, the unions argued, local boards, not the central department, should handle secondary-school inspection. This foreshadowed the struggles of the next era to set in place a working compromise between national and local control.

WHAT LOCAL AUTHORITY HAS TO DO WITH IT (1898–1940)

At the end of the 19th century, Payment by Results petered out and other issues came to the fore. Only 40% of England's poor children were in school. The voluntary efforts of the religious societies had not met their goal of universal education. The Government clearly had to provide more resources. Its most important response to this challenge was establishing local government agencies.

The Education Act of 1870 created local school boards that had the power to raise local taxes and the responsibility for establishing new schools. Allowing HMI to organize on a territorial basis and eliminating the inspection of classes in religion, this Act signaled the end of the era of the religious societies. In 1872 the London School Board appointed the first local government inspector (Edmonds, 1962, p. 91). The local school boards, serving small geographic areas, grew in profusion until there were 2,214 autonomous boards, each having its own procedures for inspection. Most asked their own members to inspect schools on a voluntary basis.

The Act of 1902 reorganized the governance of both education and inspection. Eliminating the school boards, it established the Local Education Authorities (LEAs), giving each power over all schools in its geographic territory. Despite ups and downs in their power and effectiveness, LEAs remained substantially in place until the 1988 Education Reform Act. Two-thirds of the members of the LEA Governing Committee are appointed by and are members of the local council, elected by the people who live within its geographic jurisdiction. The LEA Council appoints the remaining third of the Education Committee's membership from local citizens with education interests (Lawton and Gordon, 1987, pp. 17–18).

The Act of 1902 reorganized HMI into three divisions: elementary, secondary, and technical. The secondary branch, established in 1892, was originally independent of HMI (Lawton and Gordon, 1987, pp. 14–18). HMI incorporated into its inspection practice the secondary branch's notion of a full school inspection, which had evolved from the need for inspectors to consider the many academic departments in the secondary schools.

In 1905 the Women Inspectorate was created—with 14 inspectors at first. That separate inspectorate made clear that women inspectors were a breed apart and could not become HMI. This passion for administrative clarity was partly the result of the career of Katharine Bathurst, who joined HMI in 1899 as the third woman subinspector. She was appalled by the rote learning and drill that characterized the infant schools (ages 3–5) for poor children. She was outspoken about the lack of opportunities for girls, compared to boys, in the schools. But she was not circumspect. She had the ear of a member of the House of Commons. Bathurst was transferred several times to different HMI districts, but she couldn't be contained. In 1906 she was asked to resign. There was little question that a separate and unequal inspectorate for women would be easier to manage. Many of the changes for infant schools advocated by Bathurst were adopted, although the use of rote in infant school education continued (Gordon, 1988).

With considerable ill ease, everyone adjusted to the new century. Part of HMI's task was to woo the respect of teachers, who no longer trusted HM inspectors. The era of good relationships between inspectors and teachers was 50 years in the past. HMI knew it must reestablish the goodwill of teachers if inspection were to have value for schools, the new local agencies, and the central Government.

In its deliberations with the unions HMI declared that an inspector would never again judge the performance of an individual teacher, but would confine his judgement to the quality of teaching and learning practiced in the school. In 1905, to further demonstrate that HM inspectors were helpful, HMI issued the first of a long-lived and well-received series entitled the *Handbook of Suggestions for Teachers,* "which offered guidance to teachers 'and even more to encourage careful reflection on the practice of their profession'" (Gordon, 1988, p. 42).

All LEAs faced the problem of how to relate to their schools. Inspection, as a known tradition, was a possibility from the beginning. Because there were no guidelines for organizing inspection at the local level, it evolved in a great variety of ways since the authority to decide how to use inspection rested locally.

The 1902 Act marked the beginning of the ragged relationships between local and central authority, which included those between local and HM inspectors. That story focuses on two issues: Were LEA activities under the purview of the national inspectors? Should HM and LEA inspectors work together as the national and local branches of a coordinated effort?

In 1912 Sir Lewis Amherst Selby-Bigge, then Permanent Secretary, the highest civil service office in the national Department of Education, told the Royal Commission on the Civil Service:

> The inspector in fact is, I think, one of the most effective instruments of decentralisation and in leaving a great deal of discretion to the inspector we feel we are leaving a great deal to the discretion of the local education authority. (Cited in Edmonds, 1962, p. 140)

Not everyone will agree about the accuracy of Sir Lewis Amherst's observation. Nevertheless, given the complexity and tension in the relationships between the LEAs and the Department, there was consistent agreement that HM inspectors—by then mostly former teachers—had been successful in reestablishing a positive reputation and relationship among the nation's teachers.

NATIONAL POLICYMAKING AND INSPECTION (1941–1991)

From the beginning of World War II, Britain had anticipated the formidable task of rebuilding the Kingdom. Whereas the United States changed more during the war, Britain saw many changes after the war ended. As part of its rebuilding, Britain wanted to move beyond the constrictions that its rigid class system had imposed. Central Government was to engineer this directly by providing increased social services to ensure a productive national life.

The 1944 Education Act, the most important education act since 1902, provided the design for shaping education in postwar Britain. It provided universal secondary education, abolished fees for students attending public schools, and reduced differences between the support provided for elementary and secondary education.

Although the 1944 Act decreased the number of HM inspectors, it reaffirmed their right to inspect, but with a different tone:

> It shall be the duty of the Minister to cause inspections to be made of every educational establishment at such intervals as appear to him to be appropriate, and to cause a special inspection of any such establishment to be made whenever he considers such an inspection desirable. (Lawton and Gordon, 1987, pp. 22–23)

This national attention to rebuilding stimulated a quantum leap in the importance of Government planning—both to guide the reconstruction and to provide new comprehensive health, housing, transportation, and education services. Government planners called upon modern social science and management methods for collecting, analyzing, and using information to define problems and evaluate results.

Increased politicization of educational issues accompanied the increased importance of policy and planning. Policy debate intensified and positions on issues became identified with the political parties.

Creating and implementing education policy took a special twist because of the LEAs. While the national Government could make policy, the LEAs had direct administrative control of the schools. The patterns of response between local agencies and central Government became more complex, as elaborate games of influence and compliance were devised.

These shifts—the active role of Government, the emphasis on planning, the politicization of educational issues, and the role of the LEAs—all provided new challenges for national inspection. The increased importance of national policy and public opinion raised questions about how inspection would contribute and how HMI should proceed. The tensions between the local authorities and central Government were always present.

These changes brought greater complexity to national inspection. School people viewed HM inspectors with new suspicion. Teachers and school staff, seeing HM inspectors as having a pipeline to department decision makers, were careful about how they responded when HM inspectors were around. Few opportunities were present for productive working relationships between LEA and HM inspectors.

HMI's relationship to this new form of policymaking was neither consistent nor certain. In 1941 four senior HMI officials sat in on the discussions for preparing the confidential Green Book, *Education After the War.* Their influence was slight. Most HM inspectors knew little about these discussions (Lawton and Gordon, 1987, pp. 22–23).

In the major debates about the merits of comprehensive schools there is evidence that HM inspectors joined other civil servants at the Department of Education in opposing the new arrangement (Lawton and Gordon, 1987, p. 24). Later HMI followed the Labour Government's support of comprehensive schools, although some HM inspectors were ambivalent.

In the "great debate" on standards launched in 1976, HMI played different roles. (The "great debate" is discussed below.) HMI collected important data for the Plowden Commission by devising a nine-level rating scheme for comparing the quality of elementary schools and then collecting data on 20,000 schools (Lawton and Gordon, 1987, p. 40). HMI has usually played no role or only a background role in most public edcational debates. Likewise, HMI has seldom been their target. For example, in the debate on national standards HMI presented itself as a source of professional knowledge about the inner workings of schools that would assist the Department, not as an advocate for a position.

In the 1970s HMI issued several national reports on elementary and secondary schools and the curriculum. HMI became a strong supporter of the idea that a National Curriculum would increase rigor in the schools and establish consistency across them.

Two factors explain the great variety in HMI's influence in these public policy debates. First, HMI was trying to shape a role that was independent of politics. Second, HM inspectors, like school practitioners, believed the important focus was what happened inside schools. They saw the public debate as part of national politics, not connected to their professional concern about schools.

In this age of Government planning, HMI and local inspectorates were subjected to numerous reviews and investigations, some conducted by Parliament committees, others by task forces of lay experts. Highlights of the key studies that follow provide glimpses of inspection and the issues of this era.

1943—The Norwood Report

A commission led by Sir Cyril Norwood was charged to consider exams and curriculum matters. At the same time there were informal discussions about the future of HMI. In the process of meeting his charge, Sir Cyril learned a good deal about HM inspectors. What he saw so impressed him that he included HMI in his report, which helped stabilize HMI's future:

> There must be a guarantee to the nation in any real democratic system that the business of the schools is education, and that it is being carried out in freedom according to the ideals and methods which are proper to it. They [the Inspectorate] must therefore themselves be recognised as men and women who in important problems are expected to exercise an independent judgement and to be free to say what they think. Just in order to emphasize this claim and this responsibility we feel that the Inspectorate should continue to be known as His Majesty's Service. (Gordon, 1989, pp. 49–50)

> [It is the duty of HMI to advise the Ministers of Education] and educational administration in matters that concern them, of helping schools with counsel and advice, and of guaranteeing to the nation at large that the schools are doing their duty by the children. In this way we shall not intensify what is called bureaucratic control in education, but shall be taking a long step towards rendering it impossible for such external and impersonal control ever to develop into a serious danger. (Cited in Gordon, 1989, p. 52, n.76)

1944—The Roseveare Report

This report called for a large increase in HM inspectors and for eliminating their distinctions of rank. HMI implemented many of the recommended changes, which remained its basic structure until 1992 (Gordon, 1989, pp. 50–52).

1967–68—The Select Committee (Parliament)

While critical of HMI, this report was even more critical of the Department of Education. Noting the myth that HMI was independent from the Department, the committee felt the Department did not make good use of HMI expertise. It recommended ending full-scale inspections and placed an emphasis on consulting rather than inspection (Lawton and Gordon, 1987, p. 25;

Taylor, 1989, p. 64). A former HM inspector, J. Blackie, wrote one of the few published accounts of HMI history, seemingly to defend HMI against the charges of this report (1970). The full published testimony before the Select Committee provides an unusual record of a public discussion of inspection.

1969–70—Fulton Committee Memo

A committee chaired by HMI's Senior Chief Inspector considered the implications for HMI of the Fulton Committee's report on the reform of the Civil Service. The first of eight internal reviews of HMI during the 1970s, this memo

> ... emphasized the primary function of the inspectorate as being the provision of independent advice to the Office, a function which in future would require not only data based on individual institutions, but "extensive use of survey techniques and – vertical studies concerned with continuity or related questions of teacher training and supply." According to the [memo], HMI would have less time for the exercise of their "pastoral role" in relation to individual schools. A move toward a more specialist Inspectorate was seen as inevitable. (Taylor, 1989, pp. 65–66)

1976—Yellow Book

This internal report, formally titled *School Education in England: Problems and Initiatives*, was prepared by the Secretary of Education at the request of Prime Minister James Callaghan, who had just made a famous speech at Ruskin College arguing for higher standards in education and a focus on basic subjects. This speech helped launch the "great debate" on standards, which did not engage the public in a substantive way and which further polarized the educational progressives and traditionalists.

Leaked to the press, the confidential *Yellow Book* argued for a more rigorous curriculum and for a larger centralized planning role for the Department (Lawton and Gordon, 1987, p. 27). The report argued that HMI was important and that its independence should be assured:

> HM Inspectorate is without doubt the most powerful single agency to influence what goes on in schools, both in kind and standard.
> ... if the Inspectorate is to maintain the respect and confidence it has built up, it may have to say things in its reports which will not be wholly palatable to the Government of the day; second, it will have to be staffed to perform its functions in an efficient and adequate manner; and finally, we must find ways to make the general public (i.e., parents) and teachers aware of its attitudes and findings. (As cited in Taylor, 1989, pp. 67–68, n.24)

1983—The Rayner Report

As Prime Minister, Margaret Thatcher asked Sir Derek Rayner, a respected corporate CEO, to conduct a series of reviews of Government efficiency. HMI was one target. The rumor was that Thatcher felt HMI was overstaffed and did not spend enough time in the field inspecting. Placed under the closest scrutiny, HMI emerged with a mostly favorable account:

> … a relatively small but highly regarded group of well qualified professional people in an established position of long-standing which largely pervades the educational service.
>
> … fundamental changes in the role and structure of HM Inspectorate would require very powerful arguments indeed and even then would require careful consideration and handling if the fragile balance of HM Inspectorate's relationship with the education system were not to be disturbed. (Lawton and Gordon, 1987, pp. 141–149)

Summarizing these reports, several important points stand out:

- On the whole, HMI came through the reviews well, often better than expected. Once the examiners understood how HMI worked and saw the caliber of the inspectors firsthand, they saw HMI in a different and positive light.
- The relationship between HMI and the Department of Education has always been a consideration. Often these reports concluded that the inspectorate added an important dimension to the Department and that HMI's independence from the bureaucrats and politicians was crucial to its role.
- Most studies since 1944 have recommended that HMI use more modern methodologies for collecting and analyzing information. No one ever analyzed the pluses and minuses of HMI's traditional inspection methodologies. It was always assumed that newer methods would be more objective and that they would improve inspection, whether they were sampling or survey techniques, public reporting, or aggregating generalized conclusions.

These conclusions provide a base for understanding why the Education (Schools) Act of 1992 came about. We will consider the radical changes in the organization and practice of inspection mandated by that Act after we catch up with the history of LEA inspection.

Between World War II and 1992 LEA inspection was on the rise. The lack of a centralized plan generated great variety in the quality of LEA inspection and increased the opportunities for exploring different inspection methodologies and organizational arrangements (Audit Commission, 1989, pp. 1–2).

The story of the Inner London Education Authority (ILEA) is a dramatic example. Created in 1963, ILEA had LEA responsibilities for all London schools. It was the only agency in England under the control of an elected board that was responsible only for education. Many educators, both in England and abroad, saw ILEA as the most dynamic and progressive public educational agency in England and as one of the best in the world. Viewing ILEA as a Labour stronghold, the Tories aimed a major attack on it. In 1979 a Tory select committee proposed that ILEA be disbanded. HMI and others successfully opposed this notion. The 1988 Education Reform Act ordered ILEA to "cease to exist." Its "abolition date" was "1st April 1990" (Parliament, 1988, Section 162). New ideas about inspection worked out by ILEA for its large inspectorate included the better use of survey and test score data, as well as consistent training and support for its inspectors.

ILEA was replaced by 13 new London LEAs, each tied to a borough council. The LEAs provided another opportunity to build new inspection organizations. At this same time the LEAs and HMI were charged to help implement the National Curriculum in the schools. This challenge strengthened LEA inspection and spurred LEAs to rethink and reorganize it. The borough where I was attached deliberately attempted to meld inspection and advice. Another borough sought to strengthen local inspection by following short annual inspections with a major one every 4 years. Unfortunately these new attempts were practically stillborn with the arrival of the radical reform of inspection in 1992.

THE GREAT DEBATE

The postwar forces set the stage for the "great debate" about falling standards, which paved the way for the 1988 reform that mandated the transformation of inspection in 1992.

A generous visitor might note that at the heart of this debate the important issue was whether a teacher should start with the child or with what needed to be taught. In face of the polemics, such questions had tough going. The Government and the press attacked teachers, educationists (those with a stake in the existing educational system), and their apologists as being soft-headed communists and permissive pied pipers, who were leading the nation's youth to indulgence and the nation to ruin.

The debate on standards was launched in 1967 by the Plowden Report, soon followed by the Black Papers. Named for Lady Plowden, who chaired a commission for the Central Advisory Councils for Education on all aspects of elementary education, the Plowden Report concluded that parental attitudes regarding the learning of their children were important; it advocated that teaching should start with the child; it recommended abolishing corporal punishment in elementary schools and developing closer ties between elementary schools and the communities they served.

A series of polemic papers, such as "an open letter to members of Parliament" written by several academics—Sir Cyril Burt and Brian Cox, among them—the Black Papers argued that standards in England's schools had been failing for years because of the soft-headed ideas of incompetent educators, the best example being those who defended the comprehensive schools. They offered test data to support their claims.

In the late 1970s the great debate about falling standards became even more political. Discontent about the state of the nation's schools grew on all sides, but the debate involved only the political parties, not the public. Coming to power in 1979, Mrs. Thatcher was not only England's first woman Prime Minister but the world's first national leader who had served as a Secretary of Education. It is reported that she was greatly frustrated in her attempts to improve schools from a weak central Department. She was critical of the Department and its civil servants, believing they were not "of us," not interested in conservative reform. In 1982 school reform was a major objective on the Conservative Party's domestic agenda.

Education replaced housing as the hot media issue. Standards, their erosion, and how to raise them became a Conservative rallying cry. The debate generated the political will for reform. The teachers agreed that the nation's schools must improve. The reform plans were based on the Tory ideology of privatization.

In 1986 the Government locked horns with the teacher unions about pay. This followed legislation that curbed union power after the Government's significant victory over the coal miners. Compared to the coal miners, the teachers' unions were a pushover. Dividing the two major unions, the Government broke the power of teachers and destroyed their morale as well (*Journal Entry*, no. 1.27–28). Teachers were publicly blamed for the deplorable state of British education.

The Conservative Party's strategy for reform provided a simple focus for what needed to be done. Because the Labour Party has not seriously challenged this strategy, one might conclude that the serious difficulties the reform has encountered are inherent in the strategy itself. These difficulties cannot be attributed to effective political opposition on the national level.

THE PRIVATE ENTERPRISE SOLUTION (1992—)

The most radical transformation of English public education in history, and perhaps the most systemic restructuring of a democratic nation's school system anywhere, was set in place by law by the 1988 Education Reform Act (ERA), followed by three other reform acts that Parliament passed between 1989 and 1993.

The central strategy of the reform is to raise the standards of student achievement so Britain can maintain its place in the world. Precise standards set by the National Curriculum spell out what each child is expected to know in each of 11 subject areas, plus religious education. The school will "deliver the curriculum." Each child will be tested four times during her school years. All test results will be made public, allowing parents to see how well schools are doing so they can "choose" the best schools. Money will follow children. This market concept will be a constant decentralizing force for improving schools; the worst schools will close down. This approach requires systemic change in all aspects of the education system.

The National Curriculum has generated the greatest American interest. Prior to the 1988 Act, when the National Curriculum Council was beginning to prepare the new curriculum, most teachers and many citizens supported the council. They believed a curriculum would bring greater and healthier order across schools and a framework that would sharpen what was taught in the classroom.

After considerable debate about whether to use an interdisciplinary or subject-based approach, the council chose to base the National Curriculum on subjects to strengthen academic rigor. Eleven "foundation subjects" were defined, including four designated core subjects: mathematics, science, English, and Welsh (for schools in Wales).

The 1988 Act mandated the Curriculum for all schools receiving public funds:

> The school will provide for religious education.
>
> The school will provide the National Curriculum, which is comprised of the eleven named foundation and core subjects. (Parliament, 1988, Section 2)

The National Curriculum will:

> Specify "attainment targets" of "the knowledge, skills and understanding which pupils … are expected to have"
>
> Specify "programmes of study" that set out "the matters, skills and processes" which are required to be taught
>
> Specify the "assessment arrangements" for ascertaining student achievement "in relation to the attainment targets"

For added measure, there are several "strands," 10 "Levels of Attainment," and 5 "cross-curricula themes" (for example, citizenship). (National Curriculum Council, 1992)

Required by law, a massive new testing system was designed to ensure that these standards are met. A student passing through 11 years of compulsory schooling (age 5 to age 16) will be tested four times to determine if he has reached the appropriate "level of achievement" for each "key stage." New tests, first called SATs (Standard Achievement Tasks), are being built to be used nationwide. The SATs will clearly test each attainment target. An 11-year-old will prepare for national tests on 147 attainment targets. Test results for each school will be made public in league tables. (British league tables for soccer teams are similar to league standings for baseball teams in the United States.)[3]

After digesting the conceptual underpinning of the Curriculum, American observers are amazed that this is a matter of national law. As an Act of Parliament, ERA emphatically states that "It shall be the duty of ... [the Secretary of Education], ... of every local authority ... and of every governing body or head teacher ... to exercise their functions ... with a view to securing that the curriculum for the school satisfies the requirements of this [Act]" (Parliament, 1988, p. 1). This is called "delivering the National Curriculum."

The National Curriculum is only one part of the Government statutory reform that includes mandated management and standardized accounting procedures to ensure local management of schools (LMS), budgets delegated directly to local schools from the national office, increased responsibilities for each school's Governing Body, a national system of teacher appraisal, and a standardized procedure requiring each school to produce and maintain a "school development plan." Finally, but of great interest, the reform radically recasts the national and local systems of inspection.

The LEAs presented a number of problems for the reformers. Before 1988 each LEA exerted administrative control of the local schools in its district, including control of hiring and budgeting. Even so, English schools were more autonomous in curriculum matters than American schools.

During the course of the great debate, the Tories attacked the LEAs for their arrogance and inefficiency, which had prevented frustrated parents from securing the best education for their children. Local Councils were at this point dominated by the Labour Party. Roughly half the Local Council budget was for education. Consistent with British politics, the councils were fair game for the Tories, who saw their task as weakening Labour wherever they could. The Tory's scheme called for increased national control of schools and less Local Council control, thereby weakening the powers of the Local Councils. Talk about nonpartisan cooperation in education is rare in England.

At first the Tories tried to sap the power of the LEAs by making systemic changes that greatly weakened their control of schools. This was possible partly because 70% of public school support was national. Before 1988 the local Governing Body of each school had primarily advisory powers. The Tories increased the power of these boards to include overall management, personnel decisions, and budget control within national guidelines. National money that had previously gone through the LEAs began to go directly to the local schools. The Tory Government gave schools the opportunity to "opt out" of LEA administrative control and to become "grant maintained"—that is, to receive their funding support directly from the central Government. Portraying the LEAs as inefficient, partisan, bureaucratic, and corrupt, the Government provided parents with incentives that supported opting out. The disbanding of the Labour-infested ILEA was a dramatic indication of Tory policy. The Education Act of 1993 greatly strengthened the Government's control of education at the expense of the LEAs.

Many argue that the Tories intended steadily to increase central control of education. Others noted that more central control of schools was logical, as difficulties in implementing the reform emerged. In any case, there is no question that there has been an extraordinary and historic shift in the control of schools. Before the reform, each school, the faculty in particular, was virtually autonomous in its teaching and curriculum decisions. From 1902 to 1988 the control of funding, management, and policy matters seesawed between local and central Government.

ERA took curriculum control away from the schools, giving them greater management control. ERA gave the Secretary of Education power to work with several national committees to design and implement the National Curriculum.

The Education Act of 1993, probably the most significant building block of the reform, is one of the longest (200 pages), most detailed and complex acts in the nation's history. While abstruse in detail, the Act clearly gives the central Government complete control over funding, curriculum, policy, assessment, and accountability. This Act gives the Secretary of Education unprecedented powers, including the power to dissolve the LEAs when enough schools have opted out to receive funding directly from central Government. The *London Times* was not alone in characterizing the Education Act of 1993 as nationalization. On July 29, 1992, the *Times* main headline read, "The State Knows Best." The leading article starts:

> The Government is dismayed at Britain's poor education record and has responded as governments always respond. It has blamed everybody but itself and decided to nationalize the schools.

The Government claims that the greatly increased autonomy of local schools will improve education. But most schools perceive their new autonomy as a distraction. Since national statute now defines the educational purpose and program for each local school, a school can no longer make the educational decisions that are at the core of its purpose. As a result, the schools have become fully absorbed in trying to implement a complex maze of required concepts and regulations. Many schools have reached the realization that, if they are successful at fine-tuning these concepts and guidelines, their students will achieve higher test scores. Not many believe this is good education.

In February 1992 Parliament passed the third of four national reform acts. Devoted almost exclusively to inspection, the Education (Schools) Act of 1992 dramatically changed inspection (Parliament, 1992). On July 1, 1992, the traditional HMI disappeared. Her Majesty's Chief Inspector (HMCI) will now head OFSTED (Office for Standards in Education), a nonministerial agency. This is roughly analogous to an American federal agency that stands apart from the mainstream hierarchy of federal departments.

This Act and the plans to implement it have changed traditional inspection in the following ways.

A Major Increase in Inspection

The Act has required each Government-supported school to be inspected once every 4 years. HMI never sought to examine all the nation's schools, but to focus on a few selected representative schools. LEAs usually reviewed all schools in their geographical jurisdiction, but only a few conducted full inspections. Some estimate this Act, if fully implemented, will increase the volume of school inspection ten-fold.

The Purpose of Inspection

Inspection no longer will contain the historic tension between monitoring and supporting schools. The Government will monitor schools and provide parents with conclusions on school quality so they can choose the best possible schools. Harking back to the Payment by Results era, student achievement has again become the ultimate measure for inspection. Inspection will no longer be about supporting schools. OFSTED will now identify which schools are failing so the Government can intervene. The Chief Inspector will advise the Secretary of Education in a prescribed manner.

To better inform parents, the Act established that the leader of a school inspection team must meet with parents before the inspection and that every parent will receive a copy of a summary of the final inspection report.

The Methods of Inspection

To implement the Act OFSTED has issued a new *Framework of Inspection* that standardizes, rationalizes, and makes public the methods of inspection.[4] Data collection will be systematically restrained by guidelines and forms. Inferences will be drawn from the data. Based on identified problems and needs, strategic plans for efficient action will be drawn up.

One experienced HM inspector noted, "At heart, inspection was an oral method, based on trust and tradition. It is becoming something else again."

The Organization of an Inspection

A team of independent inspectors will carry out a particular school inspection after they have won the tender (contract) for inspecting that school. Although the inspection team leader will still be called the RI, that no longer means Reporting Inspector. The RI will now be a registered inspector, trained, tested, and registered by OFSTED. Inspection team members must comply with OFSTED guidelines, the most important being that they must be OFSTED trained and certified. Although the original Education (Schools) Act of 1992 made each school responsible for selecting its inspection team, the House of Lords amended that, giving OFSTED that power.

The Shrinking of LEA Inspection

Because every school is required to be inspected, because the Government is closing in on the LEAs from all sides, and because the greatly increased national inspection will be funded by what formally were LEA inspection funds, LEA inspectorates have begun to shrink and to redefine their roles.

A New Relationship Between the Inspectorate and the Department of Education

To ensure both HMI's independence, as well as its ability to influence the Department meaningfully, HMI and the Department of Education always have established and reshaped their working relationship by convention and negotiation. While Her Majesty's Chief Inspector will continue to be responsible to the Secretary of Education, the Education (Schools) Act of 1992 has clearly defined those responsibilities (Parliament, 1992). The old, informal, rather continuous negotiations between HMI and the rest of the Department will now be specified by formal contractual service agreements. OFSTED may well continue to carry out HMI functions for the Department, but only when the Department has purchased these by contract—such as conducting policy studies, etc.

The Department of Education planners, who wrote the Act, believed this reform would improve the inspection process and resolve age-old tensions (*Journal Entry*, no. 15.7). In 1993 many observers believed the changes would neuter inspection and make OFSTED more vulnerable in the political fracas.

During this shakedown period, a shrinking number of HM inspectors will comprise the OFSTED staff. But, as OFSTED grows, the new tasks will require different experience, skills, and values than those of the tradition-al HM inspector. The new staff will follow the tradition of modern civil ser-vants, who are skilled in planning and managing national programs from a central Government office.

As views have changed about what the correct role of government in schools should be and what information is valuable, the history of inspec-tion has changed. As we will discuss more fully later, the tension between supporting and controlling schools has been central throughout inspec-tion's history. The Government's perception of how much certainty it requires in knowing what schools are doing has defined the balance at any given time. The current Government believes it must be so certain that students' achievement will increase along specified lines that it must direct its reform with regulations and assessment tools. The similarities between this and the disastrous Payment by Results period bode poorly for the outcome of this approach.

This history makes manifest the changes, disagreements, and imper-fection in inspection that have created the important tensions we will con-sider next.

■ ■ ■ ■ ■ Chapter **6**

Tensions

Inspection is an accountability process carried out by an organization. Thus, we must see it in its organizational context to understand it.

The tensions that are inherent in an institution help define it. Tensions result from attempting to make contentious answers lie down together. Contentious answers don't do that without rubbing against each other, provoking attention and discussion. Institutional tensions come from several sources: inherent contradictions in an institution's purpose, encrusted divisions between groups of people within an established tradition, and changes of practice that make the old and new chafe against each other. Chapters 3 and 5 introduced several important tensions that we will now explore.

The defining function of inspection is what Government agencies have in mind when they hire inspectors and establish inspectorates—that inspectors will visit schools and report what is happening there. This is what the first inspectors were hired to do. HMI inspections and the current OFSTED inspections are driven by preparing formal written reports to the Government. Even though the mechanisms are more varied and often less explicit in LEA inspections, reporting has been no less important.

This basic function of reporting becomes more complicated when it encounters issues that create tensions. Four of these are:

What is the relationship between a school and the Government funding agency? What is the inspector's role, monitoring or advising?
What is legitimate knowledge? How is it best acquired? Does the inspector use traditional inspection methodology or educational evaluation?
How does the inspector influence policymakers? Is she autonomous or does she comply?

How does an inspector contribute to the national discourse? Is he a public advocate or a Government informer?

MONITORING OR ADVISING: THE INSPECTOR'S ROLE

In his set of instructions to the first school inspectors in 1839, Sir James Kay-Shuttleworth flagged the tension between monitoring and advising:

> It is of the utmost consequence that you should bear in mind that this inspection is not intended as a means of exercising control, but of affording assistance: that it is not to be regarded as operating for the restraint of local efforts, but for their encouragement; and that its chief objects will not be attained without the co-operation of the school committees—the Inspector having no power to interfere, and not being instructed to offer any advice, or information excepting where it is invited. (Quoted from Select Committee on Education and Science, 1968, p. v)

The chafing between monitoring and assistance has pervaded inspection more thoroughly than any other tension. The overlapping and shifting configurations of the inspector's role will provide some clarity about how this tension has been played out in the inspection tradition. To delineate this tension, we will first consider the roles of inspectors as monitors, then as advisors. Then we will examine several resulting hybrid roles that lie in between: inspectors as Government officers, as problem solvers, and as portrait photographers.

Inspectors as Monitors

Inspectors usually have served partly as monitors, checking to see if regulations are followed—much like American health and safety inspectors. England has inspectors who monitor a number of different areas, such as the feared inspectors who ride buses solely to assure that everyone has paid the proper fare. Monitoring inspectors collect data that have been carefully prescribed, often by a simple checklist that requires them to exercise a limited amount of judgement.

Most school inspectors fully accept the responsibility of watching for violations of reasonable regulations pertaining to the safety of children and the integrity of a school's leadership. However, when their focus shifts to teaching and learning, most will vigorously reject a definition of their role as only monitoring. That would encroach on the value of inspection for schools and limit access to information, thus decreasing their effectiveness in informing policy.

History supports this concern. During the Payment by Results era, inspectors became monitors of teaching and learning, examining how well schools met precise Government regulations of what should be taught and learned. For most of the 20th century the role of inspector as monitor has been confined to matters that can be easily regulated, such as safety, building codes, finance, and school leadership. The Education (Schools) Act of 1992 greatly increased the role of inspection in monitoring teaching and learning.

School people, as well as most practicing inspectors, will agree that monitoring is not a useful role in issues of teaching and learning. In the inspector as monitor they see a potentially dangerous intruder, whose job is to collect information without regard for the welfare of the school. As such, the inspector will see only what the school is required to show him. School people can subvert his efforts, if they choose. Since the information he is collecting will be trivial to its purpose but vital to its welfare, the school can justify making up figures or creating a false impression. The school will feel little compunction about tricking the inspector, as the inspection visit will be carried out with little care for its regard.

When inspectors are monitors in this sense, harmful illusions are created. Because its approach is precise, the Government may believe it is collecting valuable information or, even worse, that it is at last having an impact on teaching and learning. Furthermore, this approach will provide misleading clarity about an inspector's role. In the past these illusions of certainty have not paid off, either in terms of good policy or in productive relations between the schools and the Government.

Inspectors as Advisors

The notion of inspector as monitor is in direct contrast to the notion of inspector as advisor. In the latter role the inspector's main job is to advise teachers and staff of a local school about how to do their jobs better, usually in response to a request for their assistance. The role of inspectors as advisors has antecedents 155 years ago, when the early religious-society inspectors inspected the first schools:

> The sole object of a diocesan inspector is to improve the school which he is visiting. He will, therefore, not be content with pointing out defects; he will offer advice as to the best way of supplying them. (Edmonds, 1962, p. 56)

> ... the benefits may be estimated as great. It will tend at once to raise the character and quicken the zeal of the teachers, to stimulate the energies of the scholars, and by these means to improve the general quality of parochial education. (Edmonds, 1962, p. 53)

In the late 1960s, during the heyday of this view in its simplest form, teachers had an unusually strong influence on national education policy.

Under LEA auspices, teacher centers were established to provide materials, workshops, and teacher advisors to help teachers in areas they defined. When LEAs strengthened the importance of teacher advisors, they decreased the importance of inspectors. The National Union of Teachers (NUT) called for a Ministry of Education Advisory Service, arguing that inspection as monitoring had become irrelevant, that the inspector title should be dropped entirely, and that all HM inspectors should become advisors. The Select Committee of Parliament considered changing HM inspectors to HM advisors (Lawton and Gordon, 1987, p. 105).

In 1854 the Diocesan Board of Bath and Wells identified the most important difficulty with confining the inspection role to advising:

> Could the diocesan inspection, in fact, become feeble because it was friendly? (Edmonds, 1962, p. 54; cited from the 1854 Report of the Diocesan Board of Bath and Wells)

In 1992 an LEA inspector worried about the same problem:

> I think we end up colluding with indifferent practice in the interest of supporting relationships. I would argue that we should be stronger. (*Journal Entry*, no. 2.37)

Another LEA inspector worried about the problem of boundaries for responsive service:

> To be only responsive to schools has dangers. Good responsive service does require setting boundaries. We need to have boundaries and to be responsive to them. We need and should seek political support for whatever boundaries we come up with. Without that, the boundaries are too easy to cross—making it all a muddle. (*Journal Entry*, no. 1.9)

Since 1854 political support for the advisor role has been crucial. Advising is often associated with "liberal" political views. In the hard world of policymakers, that is often suspect. Considered diffuse or indulgent, advising is an easy target when there are budget cuts.

In recent years several national studies have examined LEA advising (Stillman and Grant, 1989). Documenting confusion about LEA inspection and the diffusion of LEA advice, they offer evidence that advice is suspect and that LEAs are a frustrating waste of public money.

It is worth considering the legitimate, but usually ineffective, argument of teachers that curtailing the advisor role demonstrates that policymakers don't understand the nature of either schools or teaching. This will be given fuller consideration later in Chapter 12.

To eradicate advice as a Government function, as the current reform has done, is ineffective. The trick is to maintain the tension between monitoring and advice that Sir James Kay-Shuttleworth described in his first instructions to inspectors in 1839. Throughout the history of inspection the effort to balance this tension has resulted in four different concepts of what the inspector's role might best be. Inspectors have been defined variously as Government officers, subject specialists, problem solvers, and portrait photographers.

BALANCING ROLES

Inspectors as Government Officers

Because HMI has been independent from the Department of Education, HM inspectors have not been Government officers. However, LEA inspectors frequently have been Government officers, that is, officers of *local* Government. It is easy to condemn this practice as corrupting inspection. HM inspectors, who view LEA inspection as inferior, believe direct involvement in administrative affairs compromises the quality and utility of inspection. Although the role of inspectors as officers may be easy to dismiss, it is prudent to consider it more fully.

As an LEA officer, the local inspector represented the LEA to the school. As LEA officers, inspectors controlled local funds that could be spent by the school (for example, staff development funds). They had considerable influence on LEA decisions that directly affected the school, for example, hiring and promoting school personnel, providing opportunities for in-service training, awarding special grant moneys, increasing budgets, and protecting against unreasonable regulations and procedures.

By and large, schools have understood and accepted this role. Since the LEA had financial control over them, schools accepted that there would be someone on the LEA staff who knew the schools and who would serve as their LEA liaison.

As a local officer who visited a school frequently, the LEA inspector became a known quantity to the school, unlike the more distant HM inspectors. School people had greater cause either to cooperate with the local inspector or to subvert and manipulate her to the school's ends. These instances provide explanations for why schools would cooperate with an inspector as officer:

- Fear of what might happen if they did not cooperate. The possible negative consequences ranged from being held in low opinion by the LEA to having the LEA appoint another inspector whom they would dislike even more.

- Making the best of it—bartering cooperation for more perks.
- Trust and appreciation of the individual inspector. It takes time for a school to confer appreciation on an inspector. After she has won a school's trust, her work will take on the powerful and useful dimensions of advisor, confidante, and knowledgeable helper.

LEAs that take inspection seriously have tried to define the roles of their inspectors carefully and exclude them as much as possible from the role of LEA officer. It has been difficult to accomplish this in practice.

What happens to inspection when the inspector is a Government officer? Since the quality of what an inspector knows about a school is dependent on his relationship with that school, it is possible for inspection to work well for the school, the Government agency, and the inspector. It is also possible for this tripartite relationship to become a contentious muddle.

Even if an actual inspection process has worked well, the role of local officer often imposes perceived limitations on the inspection function. The underlying dynamics of these relationships are variable and often idiosyncratic, making it difficult for the inspectorate to aggregate information collected by individual inspectors attached to different schools, even though those schools are within the same LEA. Information collected by an inspector as Government officer can be suspect because the inspector has a stake in what happens.

The information collected by a Government officer is seldom trusted outside of the local context. The irony is that the inspector's access to information will depend somewhat on how cozy her relationship is with a school.

Inspectors as Subject Specialists

The role of subject specialist is important in English inspection. Good curriculum design and good teaching require sophisticated knowledge of the relevant disciplines. Good inspection requires specific knowledge about the teaching of those disciplines. Most inspectors believe subject specialization helps them make judgements about the quality of teaching.

While this may sound familiar to the American educator, in the tradition of inspection it works in a different way. American curriculum specialists in government bureaucracies have been a major support group for schools; in some state systems they are the group most closely related to schools, performing some of the same functions as local inspectors in England.

However, the English inspector is more respectful than an American educator of the knowledge disciplines that have emanated from the university. The American places more stock on the possibility that teaching and learning are not discipline specific. The English are more convinced that subjects are the correct and best way to consider human knowledge and that they provide the key to academic rigor.

Some argue that inspectors should be subject specialists. Most inspectors would consider subject specialization an essential part of their job, not their only one. An LEA inspector said:

> The inspector's most important focus is on the subject matter and on forwarding the school's ability to teach subjects rigorously. You can't inspect teaching, not at the secondary level at least, without subject specialization because you wouldn't know the proper progression a student must make. The concern with management and administration steals from the subject discipline. When inspectors do not set their agenda based on their subject specialization, they delete their prime focus. (*Journal Entry*, no. 2.23–24)

The issue of specialties has creaked through the history of inspection. The subject-based approach of the National Curriculum has increased the logistical difficulties for inspection, since an inspector must "have the specialty" in order to inspect it. The large number of subjects required by the National Curriculum has complicated recruiting and assigning inspectors to inspections.

Inspectors as Problem Solvers

This newer view of inspection has been influenced by contemporary ideas about organizational development—what the English call the "developmental view." Based on the idea that institutional improvement requires intervention, it sees schools as being caught up in bad habits they can't overcome by themselves. The school is improved through a process of analysis that begins with the school. Moving through several phases of American reform, from organizational development through problem solving to strategic planning, some of its features are now seen in the notions of total quality management.

The problem solver comes with a set of beliefs and practices about how organizational problems are solved. Her first commitment is to help a school work on problems that have been defined by the school or its staff. Based on her knowledge of problem solving, her outside perspective, and the trust she has built with the school staff, the inspector will help the school solve particular problems, such as how to deal with a difficult student; a teacher who resists implementing the National Curriculum or who puzzles about how to implement the Curriculum; special education staff who are struggling to develop and implement a policy on how to work in classrooms with children who have learning disabilities, etc.

This approach is consistent with the inspector's notion of "doing good as you go." It is more in line with advice than monitoring. To characterize it as a good attempt to shore up the advice side of the tension would not be far off the mark. It has provided more conceptual and organizational structure than the simpler notion of what teacher advisors do. It has been strengthened by management theories about how organizations function and how they should be helped.

Inspectors as Portrait Photographers

The inspector and her team will build a coherent portrait of the school and of teaching and learning at a school. That will then become the basis for reporting and advising. The portrait will be built from knowledge considered valuable, because it has been shaped by professional judgement. That knowledge is more independent of Government influence than simple description, more independent of ideologies than an objective report. The inspection team, relying on its collective wisdom, past experience, and skills, builds a picture of the school that is legitimate through its veracity.

This probably best represents the view held by most inspectors, particularly HM inspectors, about what inspection should be. This was John Turner's view in Chapter 3.

Because the school and the Government both value the resulting portrait, this view has worked most successfully through the tensions between monitoring and advice. Even so, the inspector as portrait maker has not escaped the pulls and shoves of the tension between monitoring and advising that is at the crux of the ongoing debate about "sharp" and "soft" inspection.

The sharp inspector insists on taking a formal portrait of the school, whereas the soft inspector believes in taking candid shots with a Polaroid and a smile, talking with teachers all the while. It is easy to side with the soft inspector. But, the fact that she is nice may not mean she is right.

The sharp inspector believes the school will benefit most from receiving a definitive statement about its quality at a particular time. Inspection will acquire an in-depth view of what actually goes on in the school. The sharp picture will have value and strength because its makers are outside the life of the school. While they must report back to the school to ensure their picture is sharp, sharp inspectors will not provide further intervention. In fact, they believe that would defuse the hard judgements that are essential in inspection.

Sharp inspectors argue that an objective, fair statement of what the school has accomplished and how well it is performing now will more likely produce good results than a report bent to the interests of the school. This is analogous to the argument that test scores prod laggard schools to action. Sharp inspectors argue that trying to bend a report to a school's interest makes it impossible for them to ferret out what is real and what has been added to accommodate the school. Thus, sharp inspection is less patronizing, less subject to collusion, less controlling of local affairs and, thus, more effective in the final analysis.

Most inspectors support a softer view of inspection.[1] They believe that judgements of quality are valuable to a school and that this value can be extended, if judgements are made carefully within the context of understanding how the school will receive them. They believe, if their knowledge of the school shapes, not determines, their picture of the school, the school will be more likely to respond positively to the report.

Those who support this softer approach are more likely to support flexibility in inspection methods, consideration of how the school defines its goals and problems, emphasis on the use of feedback, and concern about a school's inspection follow-up.

Trying to Resolve the Tension

The Education (Schools) Act of 1992 attempted to resolve the tension between monitoring and advising by legislating it away. Intending to limit inspection to a monitoring function, the Act makes it clear that no one will inspect a particular school if he has had a prior interest, or has a future interest, in that school, and that inspectors will not provide advice. As a consequence, LEA inspectors and advisors are quickly becoming extinct.

It is not completely clear how what has been a very messy issue for 155 years will work out in current practice. Many believe OFSTED inspection has changed inspection, changed it into something that must again be endured by the school.

In 1970 former HMI J. Blackie suggested it was better to work with this tension rather than to resolve it:

> ... their first task was to visit schools, and that what they did when they got there must be for each individual to decide. Their first aim would be to look into what was happening, the work being done, the human relationships, the appropriateness and use of the building and equipment, everything in fact, with the further aims of helping the teachers in any way in which they needed help and of satisfying themselves that the children were receiving as good an education as possible. They would not separate in their minds the functions of inspection and advice, consultation and discussion, and would feel that to advise without first of all having inspected, or to set up as consultants without free discussion first, would be intolerably arrogant. (1970, p. 48)

It does not seem the tension between monitoring and advising can be resolved, but rather that it must be accepted as part of the turf. We will consider later the value of accepting real tensions, rather than trying to resolve them.

TRADITION OR MODERN EVALUATION: HOW AN INSPECTOR KNOWS

British education researchers have attacked inspection for not using scientific methods and, on occasion, British politicians and Government bureaucrats have attacked it for not being objective. Brian Wilcox (1992), a former LEA advisor who is now a university researcher in education, has thoughtfully taken inspection to task for being outside the social science tradition.

Knowledgeable researchers in England have said:

The tradition of HMI and its impeccable reputation is what gives it authority. Inspectors are inducted by mentors. They are secretive. Their method for taking notes is inconsistent. HMI methods are too traditional, idiosyncratic and elite. (*Journal Entry*, no. 1.22)

Inspectors' naive assumptions about research will pull inspection down. HMI's use of evidence is the Achilles heel of inspection.

Even in a week-long inspection, it is impossible to obtain a *real* view of a whole school. You must find what is important and describe that objectively. A circus tent is held up by three poles; therefore, you can configure the whole tent if you know about the poles.

The American research establishment will never be convinced that inspection is of value. They believe numbers are the only reliable evidence. (*Journal Entry*, no. 8.117–120)

HM inspectors have returned the disdain of researchers, agreeing fully that they are not researchers and noting that university researchers know very little about real schools and real classrooms. British education researchers have much less clout than their American counterparts. There has never been a raging public debate about inspection methodology. HMI has never responded publicly to attacks of any kind. The English public would probably believe that citing HMI for not being scientific would be more endorsement than attack. It is difficult for an American to know.

When HMI was confronted with newer ideas from social science, in particular those from education evaluation that were saturating the American landscape, it gave little serious consideration to the strengths and weaknesses of its traditional inspection methods. Although HMI has received much support as an institution, there has been little support of inspection as a traditional methodology. In recent years the new evaluation methodologies have greatly influenced inspection. This includes raising consciousness that inspection is a method, increasing public concern about how it is done, defining public standards or criteria for inspection judgement, providing easier public access to inspection reports, introducing sampling techniques and issue-centered reports to inspection, and increasing inspectors' reliance on the use of numbers and probability methodologies to collect, verify, and analyze data.

In 1969 the Fulton Group conducted an internal review of HMI:

> The Fulton Group's report re-emphasized the primary function of the inspectorate as being the provision of independent advice to the Office [the Department of Education], a function which in future would require not only data based on individual institutions, but "extensive use of survey techniques and ... vertical studies concerned with continuity or related questions of teacher training and supply." According to the Fulton Group, HMI would have less time for the exercise of their "pastoral role" in relation to individual schools. A move toward a more specialist Inspectorate was seen as inevitable. (Taylor, 1989, p. 66)

The changing habits and expectations of Government bureaucrats, resulting from accepting the methods of social science as the best way to collect and analyze information to shape Government policy, were probably the major cause for this shift of focus in the inspection method.

Part of the attraction of educational evaluation is its modern sheen. As newcomers in the field, these methods had the right attributes for the time: they were objective; they were scientific; they were American; they promised to make sense out of a messy situation. Their guaranteed objectivity promised that existing problems could be solved and that Government service would be advanced. Any skepticism about the value of this influence must be leavened by the fact that, when considered individually, many of the new techniques often made good sense.

Unfortunately HMI neither explained nor defended its different, traditional approach, but hid behind the cloak of its tradition, as if to say, "We are Her Majesty's inspectors. How we do what we do is not your concern." We will see later why HMI assumed this defensive posture. HMI's failure to present the methods of inspection as being worthy of consideration was a major drawback. Due to political necessity, it adapted inspection to the new methods in a haphazard way.

As an American observer, I regretted that neither HMI, nor its inspectors, nor its friendly advocates, stood up and defended inspection as a worthwhile tradition of assessment. No one argued, "Inspection is like teaching. We can always learn how to do it better, but we must begin by clearly understanding its purposes and its relationship to schools and Government, and we must build from its historical strengths." I realize my pique is idealistic.

In any case, the Education (Schools) Act of 1992 conclusively made inspection more acceptable to the bureaucrats by making it more scientific, more objective. That Act, and the subsequent *Framework for Inspection*, stipulated methods more closely related to education evaluation and management planning than to an oral tradition of practitioners.

A former HMI official described the shift in the new *Framework*:

Inspectors no longer go to a school to think about what they see; they go to see if things are in the right place. For that you don't need to think; you need only checklists. By requiring checklists, the Government is giving the new inspectors the freedom to be sloppy. (*Journal Entry*, no. 5.21)

AUTONOMY OR COMPLICITY: HOW THE INSPECTOR INFLUENCES THE GOVERNMENT POLICYMAKER

Introducing the Twin Bodies

In 1923 H. E. Boothroyd, HMI, concluded his brief history of inspection:

No sketch of the Inspectorate would be complete which did not make special mention of the cordial relations which have always existed between the Office [Department of Education] and the Inspectorate.

Whatever success may have attended the efforts of the Board [Department of Education] is due in no small degree, to the sympathetic co-operation between the twin Bodies which together constitute the Board of Education [Department of Education].

... In 1918 we inspectors stood upon the mountain-top, looking down into the Promised Land which we expected, shortly to enter: our old men dreamed dreams and our young men saw visions. Now however we must sojourn for a while longer in the wilderness; and, for some of us there will be no entry into the Promised Land. While waiting in the Land of Hope Deferred until the moment is propitious for advance, let us recapture, even and anon, the visions of 1918. (pp. 110–111)

As it turns out, because of serious problems in the relationship between HMI and the Department, Boothroyd and his colleagues had been stuck in the "Land of Hope Deferred."

How British Government policymakers and inspection have connected and failed to connect raises some interesting questions. Established when public funding of education began in England, HMI and the Department of Education grew up together. Chapter 5 reveals a fascinating story of the relationships between the politicians, the bureaucrats, and the inspectors.

The Politicians, the Bureaucrats, and the Inspectors

The story of these key relationships could focus, as many extant histories do, on a history of titles and formal positions. British Civil Service titles are more interesting than our Civil Service titles. The same title—Under-secretary, for example—has a different meaning in different situations, a meaning always subject to change. To understand a title one must know its particular history. I have escaped to a brief, but adequate, introduction of the three groups that made up the Department of Education prior to the Education (Schools) Act of 1992: the politicians, the bureaucrats, and the inspectors.

Ministers bear the serious responsibility for the Government. Although most Ministers are elected members of the House of Commons, some are appointed members of the House of Lords. Appointed to their Government posts by the Prime Minister, Ministers serve at his pleasure.

The current top position in the Department of Education is the Secretary of Education who, as a Secretary of State, serves on the Prime Minister's cabinet. (Each time the Prime Minister forms a Government, he designates which Ministers will be in the Cabinet.) Recent Secretaries of Education have been Members of Parliament (elected to the House of Commons). In 1992 the Secretary of Education was assisted by three other Ministers: two from Parliament, one from the House of Lords.

There are two key dynamics that differ between the English and the American systems: individual English politicians can more quickly make radical changes in policy than their American counterparts; they can disappear from the scene much more quickly.

Because there is no separation of powers between the people who make laws and those who execute them, English politicians have greater influence than Americans. The legislators and the Department executives are one and the same. Thus, the Secretary of Education writes a reform bill, takes it to Parliament, and asks his colleagues to make it law. While in office, English politicians are not constrained by public opinion as much as American government officials. The notion of "ministerial responsibility" creates stronger shared expectations that both politicians and civil servants will support the policy and practice of the Government that is in power, particularly if the policy has become law.

Regularly scheduled elections create a stable, monotonous dynamic in the American system. We may not feel elections make much difference, but at least we know when they will happen. British elections may be called at any time. (If one has not been called in 5 years, one must be called.) If there is a shift in support in the House of Commons votes, the Government can be brought down overnight, causing the acting Ministers to be replaced instantly by the Ministers of the opposition party. In addition, the Prime

Minister can reshuffle ministerial assignments any time, contributing to the high drama of British politics. A Secretary of Education will be appointed for political reasons, rather than for his interest, past performance, or qualifications related to education. As in the United States, England's Department of Education is not a prestigious department and the Secretary of Education is not a coveted appointment.

Two thousand five hundred civil servants work in the Department of Education. Their leader is the Permanent Secretary, who reports to the appointed Secretary of Education. Three Deputy Secretaries, all civil servants who head the administrative divisions of the Department, work with the Permanent Secretary.

The British Civil Service is a proud institution. Membership bestows considerable prestige on a person and exacts clear compliance in a number of matters relating to political activity, public comment, and loyalty to the Government in power. The possibility of swift and radical change in political leadership increases the importance of the protection and security that the Civil Service bestows. That Department bureaucrats represent the education community's interests is a foreign concept. The civil servant's job is to carry out the business of the Government, as it happens to relate to a department, such as education. During the course of a Civil Service career, a civil servant is expected to have worked in several departments.

While the politicians and the bureaucrats seem to be two separate bodies, they form only one of Boothroyd's twins. HMI is the other. While other departments use inspectors, those inspectors do not function independently from their departments. Prior to the Education (Schools) Act of 1992, the relationship between the Department of Education and HMI was unique.

HMI is headed by the Senior Chief Inspector, who does not report to, but has direct access to, the Secretary of Education. Although the Senior Chief Inspector and all HM inspectors are civil servants, they have been appointed by the Queen (or King, as the case may be) in Council under procedures that go back to the Statute of Proclamations of 1539. This Statute gave an order of the Sovereign, issued with the advice of the majority of his or her Council, the same legitimacy as an act of Parliament. In 1923 only a few members of the Civil Service were appointed by the Sovereign—they were the "permanent heads of certain great administrative Departments, His (or Her) Majesty's Inspectors of Schools, and certain of the more important Constabulary Officers" (Boothroyd, 1923, pp. 97–98).

Before 1992 approximately 500 of the Department of Education's 3,000 civil servants were HMI. HMI was an organization of school practitioners within the Department of Education. Since the early 1900s, each HM inspector has had 15 or more years' experience working as a teacher or as a Head of a school or college. People were appointed to HMI at the end of their school careers. Few inspectors have left HMI for other positions. HMI has created and maintained organizational structures that protect, support, and stimulate its inspectors. HMI has consciously created a nonhierarchical structure within its own organization and clear boundaries between it and its twin, the Department of Education and its politicians and bureaucrats.

Independence

During the more than 150 years that established the English system of publicly funded education, the Department of Education and HMI have built a Gordian knot between them.

HMI is dependent on the Department of Education and the Government for its very existence. Established by the first Secretary of Education, HMI has worried several times that the politicians might eliminate it. The Education (Schools) Act of 1992 demonstrated that HMI has little direct control over its right to exist, its structure, or its budget. Technically, all HM inspectors are civil servants and, with some hard-won exceptions, they are subject to the same personnel polices and expectations as all other civil servants.

HMI has strongly and consistently believed that professional independence from its twin was necessary for its work. Independence was the first of Blackie's essential features for HMI's future:

> The inalienable professional independence must be supported by the way in which the inspectorate is organized—it must be a separate corps under its own Senior Chief Inspector whose status must be such as will ensure that professional independence will be unimpaired and that inspectors will not be at the beck and call of national or regional governments. Such an organization should also make it possible for the inspectorate to preserve, indeed to foster, the individuality and even the eccentricity of its members. They should never think of themselves as officials or behave like officials, but rather as colleagues of each other and of those they inspect. (1970, p. 71)

Testifying before a Parliamentary committee in 1981, Sheila Browne, then Senior Chief Inspector, told what she thought would happen if the national inspectors were no longer distinguished by the prestigious "Her Majesty's" appointment and became regular Department of Education inspectors:

> If we were the Department's inspectors, I think that we could not have a freedom of professional judgement to recommend anything at all; and I would take it that we would have to work only within areas of defined policy. I would have thought it would have restricted the things that we could have done—and a lot of our inspection is outside the realm of specific policy. I think that we would therefore be remarkably suspect in institutions because we would no longer be neutral. (Lawton and Gordon, 1987, p. 118)

No issue unites current HM inspectors more strongly than their agreement about the importance of their professional independence. Critics claim that what HM inspectors have cared about is a leisurely pace, the freedom to set their own work program and calendar, the freedom of having no one to tell them what to do, and the benefit of other perks. But it is clear that more than customary perks has been at stake.

> No one in the office tells an inspector to do something. ... There is no written constitution in this matter and precisely how it operates has probably varied from time to time, depending to some extent upon the personalities of the heads of the office and the heads of the inspectorate at any given time.
>
> An inspector's essential independence is professional. In all educational matters he is free to hold and to express his own opinions, and no departmental control can be exercised upon them. This means that what he says to a teacher or writes in a report is what he really thinks, and is not in any way trimmed to suit government or departmental policy.
>
> There is clearly an area of operation in which the degree of inspectorial independence must be a matter of doubt. This is in the area of broad educational policy, and is that in which H.M. inspectors are dealing with Local Education Authorities, rather than with individual schools and teachers. The Department could not tolerate a situation in which one of its employees was openly and explicitly hostile to a policy which it was implementing at the behest of Parliament. At the same time an inspector is not expected to preach any particular doctrine. (Blackie, 1970, pp. 52–53)

The importance of this independence goes beyond HMI's relationship to the Department of Education. Inspectors always have believed good inspection required the respect and cooperation of teachers. If they saw inspectors as resting under the thumbs of politicians and bureaucrats, teachers would treat them formally and obstruct them from seeing the life of the school. For a school to be affected by the report of what the inspectors saw there, it must in good faith expect the report to reflect what the school is about, not what the Government is about.

Inspectors believe inspection requires judgement. The values of a school practitioner are at the heart of that judgement, not the values of a Government politician or bureaucrat. Resting with the inspectors as independent professionals, the integrity of that judgement cannot depend on the Government's policy of the moment.

Although HM inspectors and school people have given the "Her Majesty's" designation much weight, most see the title as a formality that has lost its significance over the years. HMI's independence has not been the result of the kind of entitlement that many inspectors might have wished.

In its working relationship with its twin, HMI's independence has been established both by convention and by a continual internal negotiation.

The degree of that independence has varied. While HMI's excellent reputation certainly has helped matters, the Department valued HMI as a twin because of what HMI did. In the old days that might have simply been because the inspectors did the arduous traveling that someone had to do. But both civil servants and politicians have acknowledged, often rather begrudgingly, the value of knowing schools through inspection.

Some key parts of the methodology of traditional inspection evolved to strengthen the inspectorate's independence. As more than one HM inspector noted, moderation builds the corporate view that provides political protection for individual inspectors, as well as for HMI.

While over time the shape of the conventional and negotiated relationships between HMI and the Government have changed, these have been the most important constants:

- The independence of the individual inspector must be honored.
- HMI has no executive authority in either the Government or the schools. Inspection will be persuasive in deciding administrative action because of the inherent power of inspection knowledge and because it is skillfully done.
- The HM inspector will serve the Department of Education, work in a corporate style that will form and support public policy, write publicly only within the confines of anonymous corporate reports, and will not speak against Government policies, regardless of his political persuasion.

Although inspectors have been in a good position to proclaim that the "King has no clothes," their agreed-upon discipline of conformity and self-censorship makes this unlikely. This discipline comes partly from their understanding of how good civil servants must act and partly from the difficulties inherent in their twin relationship with the Department of Education.

Boothroyd cited the 1864 testimony of Mr. Adderley, a highly-placed Department official, giving a glimpse of the dynamics of the negotiated conventions at the heart of the twin relationship between HMI and the Department of Education:

> ... he found that the Inspectors had in more than one instance got into the habit of exceeding their proper legitimate functions. For example, he found that once a year they met in a sort of Parliament in the office to discuss not only abstract questions relating to education but the conduct of the office specifically, and they adopted resolutions upon a division that might or might not be consistent with the administration of the Department in pursuance of the votes of the House. In his opinion the Inspectors not only exceeded their functions in doing so, but they established a dangerous practice. He therefore took upon himself to put a stop to it. ... Again in some of

their reports he found that the Inspectors went far beyond all responsible and proper limits, entering into philosophical disquisitions upon educational theories, writing essays rather than reports. He was the first to restrain that practice. (Boothroyd, 1923, p. 22)

Centering his focus on the limits of HMI, Adderley's testimony was generated by concern of several Members of Parliament that inspection reports were being altered by the Secretary of Education and his staff. So while the inspectors were being taken to task for exceeding their functions, the independence of their reports was being firmly and simultaneously established.

The Education (Schools) Act of 1992 separated the twins, giving them clear independence from one another. By making HMI a separate, non-ministerial agency with specified responsibilities for reporting to the Secretary of Education, the Act resolved the traditional tension in the relationship between HMI and the Department. HMI was absorbed by the Office for Standards in Education (OFSTED). The Department of Education may now negotiate contracts with OFSTED for work and advice.

The authors of the Education (Schools) Act of 1992 argued that it would strengthen inspection by moving it beyond the tradition of negotiated conventions. However, it may have the opposite effect. Perhaps the secret of HMI's contribution to English education is the messiness of the old arrangement.

PUBLIC ADVOCATE OR GOVERNMENT INFORMANT: HOW AN INSPECTOR CONTRIBUTES TO THE NATIONAL GOOD

Most inspectors, both local and HMI, wax eloquent when they explain the former essence of inspection:

One of the glories of inspection is you see good things make a difference in the deal that kids get from schools. (*Journal Entry*, no. 1.28)

What we are trying to do is make life better for the children. (*Journal Entry*, no. 1.33–34)

The ultimate question for most traditional inspectors is: "Does this school provide a good deal for our children?" Several times I saw this question end arcane discussions by uncovering a clear, underlying, shared standard, and by cutting through convoluted arguments, Government definitions, or guidelines. Inspectors, particularly HMI, believe that supporting Government policies is not as important as their public responsibility to ensure that the schools are providing "a good deal for England's children."

To an American this might sound like something a child advocate would say, questioning Government programs, rather than Government employees. But this stance is consistent with the tradition of the British Civil Service. Although civil servants are expected to comply with Government policies of the day, their more basic responsibility is to do what is right for England. Exactly what that is depends on their individual judgements. If a civil servant believes current Government positions are too removed from his judgements, then the honorable action is for him to resign.

This idea that inspectors have a national mission that goes beyond the narrow interests of the Department of Education appeared in the 1943 Norwood Report:

> There must be a guarantee to the nation in any real democratic system that the business of the schools is education, and that it is being carried out in freedom according to the ideals and methods which are proper to it. They [the Inspectorate] must therefore themselves be recognized as men and women who in important problems are expected to exercise an independent judgement and to be free to say what they think. Just in order to emphasize this claim and this responsibility we feel that the Inspectorate should continue to be known as His Majesty's Service. (p. 51; quoted from Gordon, 1989, pp. 49–50)

> [It is the duty of HMI to advise the Ministers of Education] and educational administration in matters that concern them, of helping schools with counsel and advice, and of guaranteeing to the nation at large that the schools are doing their duty by the children. In this way we shall not intensify what is called bureaucratic control in education, but shall be taking a long step towards rendering it impossible for such external and impersonal control ever to develop into a serious danger. (p. 54; quoted from Gordon, 1989, p. 52)

In 1970 this link between inspection and democracy was picked up again by Blackie, as he defined the prime function of inspection:

> ... to provide some assurance for the taxpayer that his money is being properly spent. Just how this phrase "properly spent" is interpreted varies widely. In an authoritarian country it will be defined as "spent on the teaching of the curriculum precisely as laid down by the government," and even in many democracies, this definition would not be altogether inaccurate. In the United Kingdom much is left to the judgement and discretion of the Inspector. In the former case the Inspector is there to see that things are done in a particular way; in the latter to decide whether what is being done is being done well. (p. 1)

Inspection concern about the national interest does not include influencing public opinion. Inspectors are not like an American advocacy group. Although they (especially HM inspectors) have been generally well regarded by the public at large, the public admittedly has known very little about who they are, what they are doing, or what they are thinking about schools. HMI reports were not made public documents until 1983.

The press and the inspectors have shared a mutual disdain. An educational editor, telling me how useful he found HMI reports in his work, said:

> Good, but could be better. If the report is average or good, we pay it little attention. If it suggests there is a problem of some interest, we will go to the school to see what is happening. The Annual Report of the Chief Inspector is helpful.

Anonymity, professionalism, the Official Secrets Act, HMI's negotiated conventions with the Department of Education—all deterred HMI's effective participation in the national discussion, which is different in England than in the United States. Inspectors' knowledge is seen as professional; the public discussion is seen as political.

That doesn't mean inspectors, particularly in this time of drastic change, are not frustrated by their operating constraints. When a local inspectorate staff met to discuss the LEA's view of the inspectorate's new role, one member commented:

> There are different definitions of an inspector. This department defines inspection as reactive. When no one knows where an issue should go, it comes to us.
>
> We should be influencing opinion. We should be educating politicians about inspection. We have always been told, "Don't do this and don't do that." In the end we'll have nothing. (*Journal Entry,* no. 1.9–1.10)

PROFESSIONAL OR TECHNOCRAT

Inspectors describe themselves as "being professional" often enough to arouse curiosity. The English usage is different in subtle ways from the American. To the inspector professional means that he is an independent individual, who makes judgements about important matters and conducts himself in a constructive manner. It means he is a school person, not a Government technocrat.

By using professionalism to distinguish themselves from the politicians and the bureaucrats, inspectors have protected a method of inquiry that does not conform to the methods of a Government technocrat. An inspector works in his own way. Government workers can say nothing about that, because he is professional. He is not required to adopt technocratic methods, as they are not professional. Being a professional has protected the inspectors' practitioner values and practitioner skills in understanding schools.

Inspectors, no longer working as teachers, had to convince working teachers that there was cause for them to be trusted and respected. Because inspectors are seen as professionals and teachers see themselves as also being professionals, the teachers have joined the inspectors' camp, pitched against the politicians and bureaucrats.

The Education (Schools) Act of 1992 has redefined the practice of inspection so that the inspector is required to think much more like a modern Government technocrat, rather than the traditional inspector. The new inspector must be more comfortable with the habits of work of the new technocrat: planning paradigms, using numbers to infer results, ensuring the comparability of information. The inspector as new technocrat will not call upon his personal standards, skills, experience, and intuition to make sense of real life in schools.

The Education (Schools) Act of 1992 and the consequent new *Framework* abruptly sought to refashion the inspector into a technocrat:

- The Central Government specified what is to be observed. The inspector's focus has shifted from what she must figure out about a particular school to how to evaluate what she sees to fit specific applicable regulations.
- Simple explicit standards for student achievement have replaced the more complex sets of inspector's standards.
- The inspector will now record specified, standardized information on a fixed form. Requiring only narrow judgements, such forms have created the illusion of certainty by translating judgements into numbers.
- The tension between inspection and advice will no longer be a matter of individual discretion. Advice is no longer an option.
- The roles of HM inspectors will shift dramatically from doing inspections to managing them. The individual HM inspector will have much less control of his or her own schedule and work style. Although HMI is currently reducing its work force, it is not clear if new positions will become simple Civil Service positions or if more HM inspectors will be hired.
- The training of national inspectors has drastically been eroded from a long-term induction with a mentor to a one-week-long session designed to assess whether the participant is able to inspect using the new *Framework,* not to train.

An HM inspector summed it up: "More work and less thought. Now, anyone can be an inspector."

While modern Government bureaucrats, who authored the Citizen's Charter and who accepted the tenets of educational evaluation and privatization, see this as progress, it is easy to understand why others see this as having little importance.

In 1862 Sir James Kay-Shuttleworth watched Payment by Results turn inspectors into technocrats. He wrote:

> The inspector ... exercised greater influence on the improvement of the schools by his experience and conciliation of cooperative effort, than by his power to recommend the withdrawal of the grants ... for neglect and consequent unsatisfactory results, either in organization, instruction or discipline. His time ... would be consumed in a mechanical drudgery which would necessarily withdraw his attention from the ... general instruction and from the moral features of the school. (Blackie, 1970, p. 16)

Many inspectors and English observers are afraid this is happening again.

MAKING SENSE OF SCHOOLS AND TENSIONS

Americans asked how English class consciousness affects inspection. In 1970 Blackie cited an HM inspector from the working class, who was asked about the importance of class within the inspectorate:

> I think the values of the Inspectorate still have a large element of snobbery in them—houses in the country, deerstalker hats, Rolls-Royces, Jaguars and other prestige-bringing cars, expertise in wines, silver, old furniture and so on.
>
> [But] I was impressed from the beginning with the way in which men and women of the most varied backgrounds could, without strain or apparent effort, look with imaginative sympathy at the problems of primary and secondary modern schools. Any form of class consciousness would, in my view, have got short shrift at any gathering of inspectors anywhere, but I can honestly say that I have never seen any need for short shrift, or an admonition or regulator of any kind. (p. 43 ff)

Working with inspectors from a variety of backgrounds, I was impressed by the general lack of class consciousness. But, I felt they did better when discussing the reality of a school they had seen together than when talking about more abstract issues, such as the value of school reform or the future of England. Class prejudice was more likely to be present in abstract conversations.

The inspection focus on making sense of a local school influences other important issues as well. Part of inspection's freshness lies in how it handles tensions by accepting them, rather than by trying always to resolve them. Being grounded in the reality of complex school life, rather than in abstract, theoretical, or ideological renderings of that life, allows inspectors to work productively with the inevitable ambiguities that tensions imply. It is paradoxical that attempts to resolve these tensions have not resulted in progress, but have weakened not only the texture of the inspection method, but inspection as a whole.

■ ■ ■ ■ ■ Chapter 7

Contributions

WHAT INSPECTION HAS CONTRIBUTED TO ENGLISH EDUCATION

It is even more difficult today than it was for a national commission in 1982 to reach conclusions about what inspection has contributed to English education:

> It might be argued that in the end the value of HM Inspectorate can only be judged in terms of the results achieved in maintaining and improving standards within the system. Apart from the difficulty of establishing a means of measuring progress in education, there is also the problem of sifting out and labeling the contribution of the Inspectorate in that process. Although HM Inspectorate has a unique position within the national education system, it is one based on influence, not direction. (Department of Education and Science, 1982, p. 89)

HM inspectors have not explicitly shaped policy or practice; they have informed, advised, and persuaded those who did. This makes it difficult to measure its influence.

Prior to OFSTED, no one considered it important to measure inspection's impact or to build a constituency that would defend it. In fact, most HM inspectors would most likely argue that this would have detracted from the important influence of HMI, from the power of its persuasion built on its knowledge of schools. An HM inspector said:

> A good inspectorate does not have any real defenders. (*Journal Entry*, no. 4.27)

The perceived value of inspection's contribution to English education clearly has shifted over time: in the late 1800s it had a strong and negative impact; in the 1950s it had little impact; in the late 1970s and early 1980s it had strong and positive impact.

Beyond the already mentioned 1982 commission, little existing research provides a comprehensive view of the impact of either HMI or LEA inspection.[1] The study behind this book was not designed to assess the impact of inspection, but to understand what it is and what inspectors do. Some studies of local school inspection concluded that, because of the great variety of local approaches to inspection, it was difficult to decide its overall value (Audit Commission, 1989; Wilcox et al., 1993). Even with these caveats, it is fair to conclude:

The English think inspection is worth the cost.
Inspection has made important contributions to English education
    throughout its history.

What Does It Cost?

Before 1992 HMI's total annual costs were $41.6 million (£27 million) per year (*Journal Entry*, no. 7.41). In 1993, when OFSTED analyzed the total daily cost of HM inspection to forecast the cost of the new model of privatized inspection, the estimate worked out to $770 a day, or £500.[2] The 1988 cost of inspection was about $30 per student, or 0.8% of Britain's public education expenditure.

OFSTED's 1993 projection of total costs for the new inspections during the 1992–96 transition period showed decreasing costs for its central administration. However, this projection reveals that total costs for national inspections would increase by 455% because more schools would be inspected each year by private inspection teams contracted by OFSTED (see Table 7.1).

To pay for the increase the Government would phase out its support of local inspection and advisory services. Before 1992 the estimated total LEA expenditure on inspection and advising was $215.6 million (£140 million). In 1992–93 the Government cut its allocation to the LEAs by $107.8 million (£70 million) and allocated that amount to OFSTED inspections (*Journal Entry*, no. 14.6).

The 1992 reform endorsed the value of inspection by increasing national inspection by about five times. Most knowledgeable British observers believe that, if the Government provides inspection at the rate required by the 1992 act, the actual costs would be considerably higher.

With the introduction of the national testing, required as part of the National Curriculum, some observers note that inspection could be elimi-

Table 7.1 OFSTED Estimates of Costs of New Inspection

	OFSTED Administration	Inspection Program	Totals
Pre 92			27
93–4	32.7	22.9	55.6
94–5	28.5	70.3	98.8
95–6	27.3	95.7	123.0

(Journal Entry #15.98. Figures in £ millions.)

nated as an archaic and expensive system. Many believe this was actively considered. However, it was decided to consolidate inspection activity as a national function.

Even though the amount of inspection has been significantly increased, the 1992 Act mandates inspection that is quite different from the practice of traditional inspection. The assumption of policymakers that they had improved inspection is only now being tested.

What the English Value in Inspection

The following comments from teachers and inspectors summarize what features of inspection make it valuable:

- It provides a detailed picture of how our school is functioning. It is helpful to have observations and judgements of respected outsiders.
- Inspection is valuable because it asks a school person, "Why do you do what you do in that way?" Inspection spots what the teacher or the Head should be doing in a school and gives her the chance to compare it with what is going on elsewhere. When an inspector asks a teacher, "Are you aware that you are doing what you are doing better than others across the country?" the teacher is profoundly moved in a constructive way.
- The best work is done in the schools when they are preparing for an inspection. It focuses the mind.
- The power comes from the students being there. While the teacher expects the inspector to have a background in the subject she is teaching, it is because he sees her while she is actually presenting her lesson to her students that results in a great respect for the inspectorate.
- Although schools like positive judgements, they also react well to negative ones. If the action is straightforward, the school will know what to do and will have the means to do it. The school is frustrated when

complex problems are identified as being simple, when it is not given details that will help it to understand the problem or its course of action.
- Being in the big scene, as well as in the little one, gives the inspector a valuable perspective. The wider world of the future includes how politics are shifting, how it is happening elsewhere. Seeing the little scene from the perspective of the big scene and then the big scene from the perspective of the little one is both constructive and enjoyable.
- Inspection keeps inspectors from becoming involved in ideological debates—like arguments about whether to use phonics versus whole words to teach reading. In the schools they inspect, inspectors come to see that both points of view are important, that most schools in fact use both approaches and that those are the better schools.
- Decision makers need access to an informed voice—a voice of goodwill, not a voice of certainty. Inspection provides that voice.

What Inspection Has Contributed

Most observers would agree with official studies that HMI has been a strong positive force not only in shaping policy, but also in shaping the history of English education. The nature of that impact has been complex. In 1976 the Department of Education wrote:

> HM Inspectorate is without doubt the most powerful single agency to influence what goes on in schools, both in kind and standard. (Quoted from Taylor, 1989, p. 67)

In 1989 Sir William Taylor (in his overview of HMI from 1945 to 1989) summed up HMI's influence this way:

> [Most HMI] influence has been and remains indirect. Its collective representation is the steady accumulation of evidence and the refinement of judgement that come from 500 or so knowledgeable and committed educators looking, listening, questioning, and recording—from, in other words, that key activity of inspecting, without which HMI would have nothing of value to say and no useful advice to offer. It is this aspect of the Inspectorate's role that was given greater emphasis during the 1970s, and which remains its principal rationale today. (pp. 73–74)

A national education news editor answered the question, "What good is inspection?" in this way:

> [Inspection] provides national accountability to Parliament. Schools generally respect and value HMI judgements. HMI's advisory role

to the Ministers of the Department has been useful. The *Annual Report* of the Chief Inspector is well regarded. (*Journal Entry*, no. 0.157)

Before 1983 HMI did not consider it an important goal to contribute to the public's understanding of education. Since that time it has changed its stance, making its school reports public and publishing reports on aspects of good education. While difficult to assess, I saw little evidence that these efforts had made much difference in the public discussion.

Contributions to Schools

In 1970 Blackie summed up the early contributions of school inspectors in this way:

They quickly established the practice of giving constructive advice and encouragement to teachers, and were pioneers of reform and advance. They spread abroad information about successful experiments. They advocated separate classrooms, cloakrooms and good ventilation at a time when these things were regarded as needless extravagances. They encouraged the establishment of infants' schools and mixed schools. They opposed corporal punishment, save as a last resort. They recommended the provision of good books and poetry, the abandonment of rote learning, the use of maps and even geography lessons by the side of the nearest river or pond. (pp. 9–10)

Overall, I found that HM inspectors are well regarded by school practitioners.[3] A teacher or principal was only occasionally pointedly critical:

HM inspectors are bands of roving samurai. They are attractive as individuals but it is not a good system.

Before the 1992 changes, what inspectors contributed to schools was rated highly. The following conclusions are based on direct observations, review of documents, and informants' accounts:

- Inspection is a powerful intervention in the daily life of a school—at least during the actual inspection visit. While there are many stories of schools being turned around or turning themselves around as a result of an inspection, there is also evidence that some schools forget the inspection soon after the visit.
- Most school managers highly rate the value of good feedback from inspection.
- HMI's seminars and workshops for teachers are well regarded.

Contributions to National Policy

There is good evidence of the pragmatic manner in which HMI has provided Government decision makers with information about the complex reality of schools. HMI's role has been cited frequently for contributing to better national education policy over the years, including:

1850 National support for more and better elementary schools
1895 Payment by Results
1909 The importance of infant (pre-elementary) schools
1967 The state of primary education, including the child-centered approach
1975 The comprehensive school movement
1976 The need for more centralized planning and higher curriculum standards
1980 The level of standards in national testing programs
1980s The need for a national curriculum and more rigor and specialization in subject teaching
1990 "Differentiated" teaching that matches teaching strategies more closely to pupil needs
       Knowledge of science necessary for good science teaching
       Progress and issues in the implementation of the National Curriculum
1991 Effective teaching of the new technologies

Educators and the press have praised the HM Chief Inspector's *Annual Report* on the state of English education as a useful road marker for creating good national policy.

As a national system of school accountability that has evolved over many years, inspection has made an unquestionable contribution to English education.

WHAT INSPECTION CAN OFFER AMERICAN EDUCATION

Inspection is the traditional English response to one of the basic questions facing a democratic government: How can an agency of a democratic government that is responsible for funding schools do a good job of both monitoring and supporting the schools it funds?

While the questions are similar, the basic assumptions behind inspection differ from those behind the American tradition for knowing and judging schools. Thus, it is useful to consider the ideas inspection offers American education.

1. Inspection Directly Considers What Happens in Schools and Classrooms

English educators assume that what goes on in the classroom and inside the local school are important and that knowledge about this is valuable. What happens can be observed and discussed. Quality can be judged, and the adults, who are responsible for providing it, can improve it.

Because inspectors learn about and judge a school's provision by focusing on teaching and learning, they can more directly advance the quality of what happens in schools. Provision ties inputs and outputs together. Although student performance, as the main function of the school, is the important output, it is not the only means for judging the quality of a school. A school constructs what it provides from its available inputs. Although the inputs are essential and must be considered, they are important only when seen in relationship to what the school provides, rather than when seen as simple variables that directly impact student output.

Provision implies that what adults are doing in the school matters. They are providing the education for that school's students, which they are capable of improving. Provision has a future orientation. It does not mean controlling events today, but preparing for the future. Provision fosters a continual development of an extensive language for talking about the practice of teaching.

2. Inspection Builds Upward from the Particulars of Actual School Life

Inspection gathers knowledge about schools that is based on the particulars of school and classroom life that an inspection team deliberately sees and considers as it creates a word picture that makes sense of that school. Inspection shows that it is possible to gather particular knowledge and use it directly to make judgements of quality, to support immediate improvement activities at the school, and to influence government policy. By and large, the English have accepted this type of knowledge as being both important and legitimate.

3. Inspection Trusts the Judgement of Experienced Practitioners

Inspection relies on the judgements of individual inspectors that are moderated by the inspection team. While the team may disagree about the discrete judgements inspectors make, practitioners, policymakers, and the public have trusted the value of this experienced, professional judgement as a way of knowing what is happening. Disagreements, in fact, in the process of being worked through in moderation, have often strengthened what inspection has contributed to understanding and helping schools.

4. Inspection Recognizes the Pertinence of the Local School

The importance of the local school is a tacit part of inspection. The school is the unit of analysis for generating knowledge. Inspection knowledge does not need to be applied to a school; it is inherent in the school as it is being inspected.

5. Inspection Emphasizes Implicit Standards of Learning

Inspection considers the implicit standards of provision that a school uses to make decisions that directly affect the education its individual students receive. Most inspectors believe these standards, rather than formal codified ones, are what determine a school's quality and they are the important leverage points for raising the quality of a school's provision. One of inspection's stated goals is to improve a school's implicit standards.

6. Inspection Gives Practitioners an Active Role in Policymaking

Through inspection, experienced school practitioners play a powerful and constructive role in shaping national educational policy.

7. Inspection Honors the Fact that Some Tensions Are Productive

Prior to the 1992 reform, inspection accepted and maintained the tensions that were inherent in its mission, the most important one being the tension between supporting and monitoring schools. Tensions are maintained by accepting and living with ambiguity and paradox.

8. Accountability in the Service of Control Does Not Work

The failure of the Payment by Results era raises important questions about government reform strategies based on setting explicit standards and measuring student performance against them with school support dependent on the results. Although more elaborate than Payment by Results, the current English reform is based on these same assumptions about reform. Again, it appears it is not working. Government attempts to control school reform with a narrow accountability system are not consistent with democratic values for schools and they have not proved effective. These attempts are again distracting schools, teachers, and students from learning and teaching that are the key to improvement.

PART TWO

■ ■ ■ ■ ■

Six Provocations

*The purpose of art is to lay bare
the questions which have been hidden
by the answers.*

—James Baldwin (1962)

Chapter 8

Preliminaries

The first questions to greet me upon my return to American shores illustrate the directness and pragmatism of American thinking about education and its reform:

Does inspection work?
Can it be applied to American schools?

After learning more about what inspectors do, Americans ask additional questions:

- How can inspectors be sure that what they observe in schools is typical?
- Americans are skeptical of tradition, authority, elitists, and people who think they can tell others how good their work is. Can Americans grant inspectors the credibility that is necessary for inspection to work?
- When being judged, particularly by outsiders, Americans generally become moody and difficult. How can outside judgement be useful?
- Inspectors judge the schools on the quality of what goes on inside of them, rather than on student outcomes only. Isn't inspection messier and more controlling of individual behavior than an approach that stipulates the outcomes, allowing each person to do what she thinks is best as long as the objectives are achieved?
- Many American teachers are wary of state or federal governments

knowing more about what actually happens in schools. Even if that were better than outcome-based knowledge, why would teachers support it as a more effective assessment strategy?

- Policymakers, legislators, and agency officials often do not have time to consider complicated, discursive information. They want simple facts and recommended action. Isn't inspection information too complex, too subjective, too unsure?
- Inspection is person intensive. Even if we thought it was a good idea, wouldn't the cost prohibit it?
- HMI inspection reports employ what the British call "measured language." After reading samples of these reports, an American principal noted: "We are a direct and crude people. Does inspection suit our temperament?"

If the English intended to develop and pilot a better model of assessment for American schools, these questions would be appropriate. If I were advocating inspection as a model for American schools, these questions would be appropriate. Neither is the case. If they were, we would probably reject inspection as impractical and irrelevant to our concerns.

Inspection is part of the educational history of another democratic nation wrestling with important problems that are similar to ours. It would not only be arrogant for us to reject it as a model, but that would not be in our self-interest. Inspection can serve as a looking glass in which we see new possibilities for how to go about knowing and judging schools. The ideas of inspection can provoke new thinking because they reveal that another set of assumptions is possible.

The *provocations* discussed in this part of the book do not directly answer American questions about inspection. They have been drawn against my experience in American reform. They look, sometimes playfully, toward asking new questions. They are suggestive, rather than prescriptive. They don't propose new programs. They provide grist for *new possibilities* (see Part III).

Chapter 9

Particulars

The importance of the particular is inspection's most daring challenge to how Americans know schools. Inspection challenges the American assumption that measures of generalized outcomes, including student performance, are the appropriate yardsticks by which to judge the effectiveness of instruction. In their place inspection proffers the concrete, actual, mundane, day-to-day events that comprise learning and teaching in a class in a school. This provocation explores the challenge of the particular.

The importance of the particular is not unique to inspection. Václav Havel, president of the Czech Republic and a builder of modern democratic institutions, advocates the importance of finding guidance for democratic policy in the particulars of actual life.

> The only thing that genuinely bothers me, because I think it is dangerous, is the way aspects of the reforms have become an ideology. …
>
> …Right-wing dogmatism, with its sour-faced intolerance and fanatical faith in general precepts, bothers me as much as leftwing prejudices, illusions, and utopias…because [they come] from the same mental position: that is, from the certainty that operating from theory is essentially smarter than operating from a knowledge of life. …
>
> As if a general precept were more reliable than the guidance we get, in dealing with the complexities of life from knowledge, from judgement unprejudiced and unfettered from doctrines, from a sense of moderation, and, last but not least, from our understanding of individual human beings and the moral and social sensitivity that comes from such understanding. (Havel, 1992, pp. 65–67)

While general precepts and theories may offer certainty, Havel's confrontations with ideologies and planned, top-down approaches to change have convinced him of the value of "healthy common sense and the human conscience."

Havel believes that problem solving in democratic institutions works when it is based on particulars, not on generalizations or theories about what life and democracy should be. He reminds us that a great historic strength of American democracy has been its ability to consider particular, actual life.

American education and its reform are filled with generalized notions. Like the English, we think the way to change our schools is to charge at them with concepts about what should happen. Our knowledge is general and our expression is jargon: "Our schools are failing to produce student performance at the world-class level. We must raise standards." Our thinking too often leaves out the particulars of what does or does not happen in the classroom where learning does or does not occur.

The epigrams of reform—back to basics, parental participation, child-centered education, national standards, education for work, local control and management, school choice—are all minor ideologies springing from how we think about school reform. That language is disconnected from classroom practice and hides the realities of day-to-day life in schools. Our jargon seduces us into thinking about the ideology that informs it, not about the puzzles of actual classroom life.

How we think about what our schools should be doing hangs like a gauze curtain between us and the actualities of classroom life. The presence of this curtain becomes even more remarkable when we consider that incredible resources directly relating to the central concern lie on its other side. In 1992 America's 2.4 million public school teachers taught 42.7 million students for 180 days a year. If there were opportunities to engage each student in particular learning 10 times a day (about twice an hour), that would result in 76.9 billion instances of learning happening, or not happening, during the year. This is an arena of untapped knowledge that would make a difference.

A good teacher makes thousands of decisions a day about how to stimulate, cajole, praise, discipline, inform, and challenge her students. She makes decisions about particular events shaped by the student, the subject, the classroom, and herself. Each student's mind works in a unique fashion. Each student comes from a particular family; each school and each community has a history built from the lives of individuals who defined it; each community is perpetuated and shaped by those who live there. Each discipline has its own methods and bodies of knowledge. Each classroom has a unique set of physical and human resources. Each teacher has a history that shapes how she thinks and interprets what is happening. Her success will be determined by the particular decisions she makes in the heat of the action. The more she is attuned to the particulars of the student, the subject, the immediate classroom resources, and her own knowledge and state, the better her judgements are likely to be.

Unlike medicine or law, American education has neither valued nor systematically used particular knowledge as a way to think about what is important in schools. Our tradition for knowing and judging schools does not consider that what teachers actually do in classrooms is valuable, even though our rhetoric generally extols their importance as a group.

While most of us would agree that the day-to-day life in the classroom creates the history of how a student learns and achieves, we would not consider that a valid starting point for knowing and judging schools. How we learn about schools neither supports teachers in their practice nor supports them to learn from their practice. We value the generalized knowledge that teachers' colleges teach, that teacher certification programs certify, and that professional development programs develop.

Recent observers of how we know schools thoughtfully have proposed that we consider the particulars of classrooms through narratives of what actually happens. Joe McDonald (1992) has pointed out that, as a different methodology, teacher narratives have power for gaining a better understanding of classroom particulars.[1]

We think stories, ethnographic descriptions, and teacher narratives can supplement the knowledge that matters. We believe that by identifying, measuring, and analyzing generalized inputs and outputs of schools, we will reach important findings about the reality of schools.

The particulars of school life are too ordinary to be of much interest; besides they are too numerous. Particulars are too complex for our "scientific" methodologies. To deal objectively with the complexity of a classroom an investigator needs theories and data collection instruments that limit his focus to discrete concerns. If the researcher began with the particulars of what was going on in a classroom, he would face an impossible task, even if that complexity were consistent with the complexity of life.

Inspection challenges these tenets. Beginning with the particulars of school classrooms, it raises the possibility of building a systemic approach that draws "guidance from the complexity of life," rather than from generalized concepts. Of the numerous tools inspection has invented to approach actual classroom life, the most important is trusting professional judgement.

Chapter 10

Judgement

We trust a teacher's professional judgement when it comes to giving a student a grade, constructing a lesson plan, deciding that a student should be held in detention for bad behavior. We do not trust a teacher's judgement when it comes to judging the quality of a school or how well it has produced. We certainly would not base a national system of school accountability upon a teacher's judgement.

At first I found inspection's use of professional judgement quaint, unscientific, old fashioned, elitist, and superficial. But, as I came to understand the logic and power of using experienced practitioner judgement to know and judge schools, I realized judgement was the most provocative element of all.

DESCRIPTION AND JUDGEMENT

Any nation's approach to knowing and judging schools must generate information that is considered legitimate. The American tradition assures legitimacy through objectivity, counting, rational research design, and experts. Inspection assures legitimacy through the judgement and moderation of experienced, respected practitioners.

Inspectors do not describe schools. They present their findings as judgements. The reality of schools is too important, too complex, too mundane, and too particular to be summed up in a simple description. Further, inspectors don't think teachers and Heads will find a description useful, because that would not reveal what an inspector thinks needs to be done. Descriptions often hide the important connective tissue between thought and action.

A social science researcher, preparing to describe the life at a school, usually begins by clarifying the discrete goals in the design of his exercise. Before he goes to the school to observe, he specifies the hypothesis the observations will inform and his focus when he engages the real life of classrooms. Frequently he carefully constructs a checklist for his observations. He believes that to walk into a classroom without a clear focus would create confusion. Because a class is made up of a myriad of possibilities, a myriad of perspectives is possible. He tries to guard against sloppiness and irrelevancy by tying what he sees to the a priori conceptual framework of the research.

Inspectors go to classrooms to make judgements about the quality of what they find, not to describe it. Their judgement is not simply applied at the end of a description of what they saw. Judgement is used throughout the process. Judgement begins as soon as the inspector knows she is going to inspect a school. Any documentation she reads prior to the visit will stimulate her judgements. Judgement begins in earnest when the inspector walks through the door of the school and "is there."

Judgements are not only shaped by evidence, but shape evidence. When an inspector walks into a school, her initial focus is on her judgements about that school. But, at this stage at least, the formulation of a judgement initiates, rather than concludes, the process of collecting evidence. The judgement must be checked against the reality of the school's life to ensure its accuracy.

The reciprocal interaction between evidence and judgement and between the particular and the general is similar to how a good teacher connects thought with action in her daily work in a classroom. Her judgement about how a student is doing shapes what she will look for in that student's work and behavior. In turn her judgement about that student and about what she should do next will be shaped by what that student in fact does that day.

This approach to inquiry welcomes both common sense and moral sense, rather than holding them at arm's length. The legitimacy of inquiry depends on the individual wisdom of an experienced professional.

WHY AMERICANS DON'T LIKE JUDGEMENTS AND THE ENGLISH DO

THE ENGLISH INSPECTOR AND THE AMERICAN COACH

An English school inspector in physical education visited a summer camp for American athletic coaches run by a friend of his. The American was intrigued by how inspection valued judgements about quality as a way to stimulate better work. He invited the inspector to give inspection judgement a try with the athletic coaches working at the camp. The inspector accepted the offer, confident that the same skills that had won him the reputation of working well with people at home would overcome any cultural differences.

After watching an American coach working with her class, the inspector sat down to talk with her. "Overall," he said, "how you approached your students seemed satisfactory, but your knowledge of the rules of the game is not up to standard and that detracted from what the students learned."

The coach's reaction to the inspector ended the experiment.

The inspector later observed, "It is difficult to work with American coaches. Americans don't like to be told how well they are doing. I wonder if this relates to your highly touted American individualism? You seem to think your core beliefs are yours alone, that society and other people should not impose their judgements on you. You seem to respond to being judged, as if thinking, 'This is Judgement Day,' even though you know you don't have to accept what an inspector says since he clearly is not God. Whatever it is, you are not partial to being judged."

Journal Entry, no. 12.18

Many American teachers and policymakers are put off by the idea of judgement. Teachers do not like the idea that someone would sit in on one of their classes judging, rather than describing their work. Most policymakers believe that, because knowledge built from personal judgement is not objective, it is unworthy of serious consideration.

Beyond that, the idea that someone has the right to judge him raises an almost visceral reaction in an American. ("Who gave you the right to judge me?") Sustained by images of judges in black robes making legal judgements and by a supreme figure managing the "final judgement," we come to see that judgements are made by someone in authority, whatever the hierarchy. Thus, to accept a judgement we must accept the authority of the judge. Since we believe that each of us determines for herself how good she is, we are recalcitrant to give that basic individual right to another. Some say we fought for our independence to ensure that right; some would say we are still fighting.

The teacher has additional reasons for avoiding judgement. Most regard teaching as a personal and private affair. Although a teacher accepts public concern about student performance, she thinks judgements about the quality of what she does are none of the public's business. When a teacher asks a colleague to observe her work, she usually wants positive feedback, not a judgement about quality.

As Chapter 3 made clear, the English context for judgement is different. An inspector's right to make judgements is a matter of law that is generally accepted without fuss. Inspectors do not judge character, motivation, or a teacher's deepest being. They focus on what a teacher is doing and what a teacher knows. They do not evaluate an individual teacher's performance. They use judgement as a tool to create a picture of school quality. Inspector judgements focus on what actually is happening in a class or school. Inspector judgements are neither thoughtless nor immune to rebuttal. They are supported by evidence that is usually included in the final statement of the judgement. Although inspectors expect school participants to correct any mistakes in their evidence, judgements cannot be negotiated.

Almost every inspector wants his judgements, negative as well as positive, to have a positive impact on the school. While he is trying to frame his judgement, a good inspector will consider, up to a point, the effect it will have on the people involved. Judgements are not disconnected from the life of the school.

Imagine what the English would say about our considering the possible value of judgement for knowing schools:

- Americans have opinions. In fact, they are often rather loud about them. It seems an opinion cannot be attacked—or even discussed. And opinions are egalitarian—everyone has them. I once heard an American say, "Well, you have your opinion. I have mine."
- Your opinions don't seem to matter very much to you. Public opinion is another matter. It influences American politics more than it does English politics. I knew an American who seemed to feel it was more important to figure out what public opinion was on an issue than to figure out what she thought about it herself. Public opinion seemed somehow to let her off the hook, or at least prove to her that her opinion wasn't important. You Americans are a curious lot.
- A judgement reveals where you stand. When a person tells you where he stands, he opens up his observation so you can see how he puts the world together. That's what's interesting. That's what makes good conversation.
- A judgement does not have to be perfect, or even right. It isn't the last word. As an inspector, if I were to make a judgement about what you do, I wouldn't be challenging your integrity, or even your basic competency. I would be making a statement about what you did in a small space of time, a statement more about your performance than about your character, a statement that would show you what I think is important—or how good something is.
- I have the right to make judgements about your work, because that's part of what being an inspector is all about. My judgement about what happened today in your class could certainly be wrong. If I

were to see your class next week, my judgement could be entirely different.

- It is possible to discuss judgements; they aren't final. In fact, I think the discussion about our judgements is the most important contribution inspection can make to a school as it works to improve itself.
- We aren't reluctant to commit ourselves to an idea or a view because of how it might make another person feel. It is delicate territory to be sure, but the other person can always say our judgement is wrong. Are you afraid a judgement will make you more vulnerable? Or that you might impose yourself on the person you are judging? Or that you might damage him, knowing your judgement could be wrong?

Regardless of American discomfort, there are some compelling reasons for considering judgement as a tool. Judgement allows the construction of a picture that is particular to a school, that includes a moral sense, that is consistent with the way practitioners connect what they are thinking to what they do. And, most important, judgement provides a tool for selecting and connecting details.

CONNECTING DETAILS

Lawrence Sterne (1980) began his novel, *Tristram Shandy,* with an epigram from the ancient Greek philosopher, Epictetus:

It is not things that disturb humans, but their judgements about things.

Originally published between 1759 and 1767, this novel demonstrates the problem of selecting details from real life to present on paper. The novel opens with Tristram, who in midlife has decided to tell his life story by including every important detail that has shaped his life, as well as his opinions about many matters. He begins with the moment of his conception and, nine volumes and many pages later, ends 7 years before his birth. Sterne suggests, unless we intend to go backward, that we must select details. If we try to describe every detail, we will go slower than life itself. The selection is key.

The standard, "What counts is what you can count," is often used in the American tradition for knowing schools. Although this standard makes it easy to select details, it generates information that usually does not help make schools better. Let's consider four possible ways to select particular details from the interminable array that make up the real life of a classroom:

GO FOR ALL OF THEM. This might be called the Tristram Shandy solution. This is the choice made by those who seem to go backward, as they talk on and on about what they have done. Some enthusiastic first-year teachers use this approach.

WHATEVER YOU SEE IS GOOD ENOUGH. This suggests that the observer should wander through a school and see whatever details hook onto his accustomed way of thinking. Political figures, cause advocates, and graduate students working on their theses seem to favor this approach when visiting schools. It usually supplies strongly felt sophomoric information.

USE A CONCEPTUAL FRAMEWORK OR A RESEARCH HYPOTHESIS TO DECIDE WHAT DETAILS TO CONSIDER. This is the approach favored in the American tradition for knowing schools.

USE INSPECTION JUDGEMENT. Knowing why she is at the school and what she will do to carry out the inspection, she shares diverse conceptual frameworks with other inspectors, including beliefs about what makes a good school. But, instead of relying on a fixed idea to choose the details of her focus, she uses her judgements about that school's quality, which begin the moment she enters the school and evolve throughout her visit. Moderation is an important part of their evolution.

Judgement, then, can be a powerful organizing and focusing tool for generating knowledge. In the first instance, the wisdom, knowledge, and moral sense of the individual inspector provides the focus; in the second, the collected wisdom of the inspection team moderates the focus.

The importance of moderation cannot be omitted. Chapters 3 and 4 show how inspectors use moderation to integrate their individual evidence and judgements into a corporate team judgement. This process assures that the results will not be limited, controlled, or solely defined by the wisdom, knowledge, or moral sense of any one team member.

As we saw in Chapter 3, the inspector's use of judgement increases the intensity of teacher interest in what the inspector thinks about the quality of his teaching.

Judgement provides a basis for making connections to the life of the school that other methods completely ignore or deliberately avoid. Through the standards he uses, the inspector's judgement connects the life of a school to both the encoded standards of the district or nation and the implicit standards of the school. By comparing a school with others he has visited, the inspector connects it to others in the nation.

These apparent advantages of inspection judgement compel an exploration of its difficulties, the most important being that it is not considered an objective way to connect evidence.

THE PREDICAMENT OF OBJECTIVITY

While we might tolerate personal judgement in some situations, constructing public policy is not one of them. That requires objective data. The value of objectivity is so strong that we rarely consider what *objective* means or what impact it has on how we know and judge schools.

Objectivity is considered legitimate, partly because we believe it guarantees certainty. Because the perspectives and values that shape information change, and because they rest in group identities, experience, and knowledge, we try to exclude them as much as possible from the information we gather.

Certainty of knowledge is highly valued by policymakers. They want information that extends beyond the perspectives of individuals and groups in the society. Objective information will be less subject to public scrutiny and criticism. "Our recommendation is based on objective findings." Objectivity ensures rigor and discipline in the inquiry. It also ensures expertise, since only experts have the training necessary to carry out objective inquiry.

How does information become objective? Generally, it is a matter of instilling distance between the events under study and the method used to generate information about them. Some mechanisms used to create this distance are:

IMPARTIAL RESEARCHER. The researcher neither participates in the action nor has any self-interest in the institutions or people under scrutiny. In fact, the further removed she is, the more impartial and objective she is believed to be.

PRECISE, PREDETERMINED, ACCEPTED METHODOLOGY. If the inquiry is conducted according to a preset design that meets accepted criteria, the results will more likely be considered objective. The research design is set before the data are collected, providing some protection that the data will not be shaped by the design context or by the views of the researcher. By not allowing the data or the social events encountered during the inquiry to waver from the design, the researcher helps ensure objectivity.

SMALL, PRECISE BITS OF DATA. The more information can be gathered as small, discrete bits that fit predetermined categories, the more objective we believe it is. This excludes messiness at the basic level. Examples of such data include a student's answers to a multiple-choice test, checkmarks on a list, codable answers to a questionnaire or interview. The simpler the data points, the less danger there is of confusion or distortion.

REPLICATION IS POSSIBLE. If the factors under study have not changed, someone else should be able to produce the same results.

NEUTRAL WRITING. Reports written in neutral, flat prose are more objective than those that express feeling or moral judgement or that use metaphor or other expressive literary tools.

We use objectivity to assure certainty by promoting distance from the phenomena under study. This notion originated in the methodologies of social science. It is now set squarely in the American tradition for knowing schools, where over time it has become more an ideology than a tool of inquiry.

The notion of objectivity is nourished more by the public discourse than by science. Its persistence is surprising. Often it is attacked as being too mechanistic, too disconnected, and too unscientific. Most modern scientists would agree that it is not scientific.

Modern science considers how the measurement of a phenomenon influences what is learned about it. Data do not exist in a state of certainty. Even if one removes human judgement as much as possible, the phenomenon cannot be measured with objective certainty. Because the measurement and the measure are linked, both are subject to scrutiny. While this notion represents a profound change in modern science, it is not esoteric.

It is common sense that the method we use to learn about a phenomenon will shape what we learn. The knowledge we gain about electricity by sticking a finger into a live light socket is different from what we learn if we stick a new light bulb in the same socket. Most of us do not have difficulty accepting that what we use to measure something changes what we measure—a weather vane will detect a different wind than the smoke from a smokestack. Administering a multiple-choice test to a student will influence that student and his learning in a different way than asking him to describe and discuss what he has learned.

In this light it is not surprising that school practitioners often criticize "objective" research information about their school or teaching as being tepid. From the teacher's perspective this information is not relevant, because the researchers are deliberately disconnected from the school. It is not surprising that teachers wonder how researchers can learn anything that would be very helpful. These complaints are frequently set aside with the explanation that teachers don't understand the intricacies of research or the importance of building general theory. But, when the purpose of generating knowledge is to help teachers teach better, these complaints must be considered more carefully.

Distance may lead to disconnection, not to good information. It subverts common sense and conscience. It sometimes leads to triviality. To invent better ways to know and judge schools we must abandon objectivity as an ideology.

When we abandon part of a tradition, we usually lose more than we intend. We should remember what we wanted from objectivity. While a legitimate methodology can promote integrity, persistence, rigor, insight, and discipline, these ultimately reside in the judgement of the scientist, not in her method.

JUDGEMENT, PERSPECTIVE, COMMON SENSE, AND CONSCIENCE

A judgement is not a superficial distortion of what is real. Any measurement distorts what is real. Standardized tests distort our understanding of student learning. The question is which distortions are valuable and which distract us from our purpose. Rather than see the perspective of practitioners and participants as a distortion, we should accept and understand the part they play in determining what is known, accept and understand their role as an integral part of the picture. An English inspector said:

> I know I know a school well when I understand all the points of
> view that make up the varying ways different people see that school.
> A professional and objective view of that school comes when all the
> perspectives are considered, not when they are excluded. (*Journal
> Entry*, no. 9.3)

Of all of the elements of inspection, judgement is the most provocative. It provides a basis for considering how it might be possible for a rigorous method to include common sense and conscience, not only in the final interpretation of data, but in their creation. For judgement to be accepted we would not only have to move from the ideology of objectivity, but we would have to trust practitioner knowledge.

■ ■ ■ ■ ■ Chapter **11**

The Practitioner's Way of Knowing

PRACTITIONER AS TOKEN

Kathy, a third-grade teacher, had carefully prepared her presentation for the august collection of American education policymakers. She had been told her presentation was important because the policymakers wanted to hear the voice of a teacher. She tried to develop general conclusions about her day-to-day work that would be important and objective.

Kathy started well. She graciously acknowledged her pleasure about being asked to speak and conveyed her appreciation on behalf of all teachers for having an opportunity to present their views. But, as she described her 21 general points about what she thought would improve the quality of American teaching, she realized the audience's attention was waning. She tried to regain their attention by stressing that her views were important and valid. After all, she was a classroom teacher; none of them were.

Although they found most of her presentation lacking in insight—even boring—the policymakers were polite. Finding her generalizations feeble, they felt she was uninformed about the issues they faced. Nevertheless, the chairman graciously agreed that the views of teachers are important and he thanked Kathy for taking time out of her busy schedule to talk with them. Heads nodded and everyone smiled.

In their ensuing discussion about new policies, the policymakers never once referred to any point Kathy had made.

The stereotypes had been reinforced. Kathy had found the policymakers distant, looking for their own abstract, certain answers. The policymakers concluded once again that teachers don't think well enough to make policy.

—*Journal Entry, no. 16.51–53*

In England the integral relationship between HMI and the Department of Education created tension because of the rubbing together of two different ways to think about schools. At the beginning of his term President Clinton announced his pleasure upon appointing a practicing teacher to the senior staff at the Department of Education, illustrating how little policy-makers have valued practitioner knowledge in government policymaking. Since most inspectors have been practitioners, and since inspection relies on practitioner judgement, inspection is a practitioner's way of knowing schools. This provocation explores how a practitioner knows schools.

A practitioner's approach to knowing schools is grounded in practitioner knowledge, the knowledge a practitioner *uses* in his daily teaching. A practitioner bases his decisions on this knowledge as he goes through his daily work. While it may be influenced later by study or reflection, this is knowledge for action, much of it coming directly from his experience, first as a student, then as a teacher. While most would agree that practitioner knowledge is important, it is not often recognized in our schemes for knowing and judging schools.

Practitioner knowledge includes acceptance or rejection of standards from many sources, including those from the teacher's private conscience, the teaching profession, curriculum associations, university disciplines, the particular school, the community in which the school sits, government agencies, and the nation at large.

Practitioner knowledge includes what the teacher knows about the content and methodology of the subject matter. This is not inert knowledge. It is what a teacher draws upon when answering a question, shaping a lesson plan, or responding to what a student does. It includes knowing about the use of the available resources in the classroom, school, and community. It includes knowing the life circumstances of her students, as well as knowing how specific students think and act. It includes knowing from her experience how to respond effectively to a student at a particular moment. It includes knowing about herself and how she responds in a specific situation. In sum, practitioner knowledge is what a teacher draws upon to decide what response to make to a particular student at a particular moment.

The most powerful parts of practitioner knowledge are learned directly from practice. This is not to say that reflection or the study of content or theory are trivial. But knowledge from these pursuits becomes important only when it is connected directly to practice in the practitioner's mind. Most teachers report that their most substantive learning experiences have involved sharing good practice with other teachers, visiting other classes or schools, and direct apprenticeship or mentoring relationships with other teachers.

Practitioner knowledge is unique to each teacher. How a teacher's mind works, how he was taught, how he has taught—all play an important part in shaping it. Yet, like other knowledge it is shared and modified to some extent through the collective experience of others in a school, a curriculum area, a state, and a nation. Moderation that shapes a specific teacher's knowledge is largely informal and takes place daily as part of teaching.

It is obvious then that what a teacher knows plays an important role in determining the quality of teaching and learning. Our current accountability schemes minimize the importance of this knowledge, seeing teaching as influenced by attitudes and social forces. Thus, attempts at reform seldom try to improve what teachers know but try to manipulate what they do.

Legitimizing the knowledge of practitioners would require a major shift in our concept of the teacher's role and in the professional training that supports it. If practitioner knowledge were valued, teachers would not be seen simply as being consumers of knowledge about teaching, but as being the primary generators of that knowledge. This would go some distance toward solving the dilemma of how to empower teachers, since some natural power always accrues to those who define and generate knowledge.

Those who are responsible for generating knowledge about how a profession works and how it should work control that profession. Responsibility for knowledge about teaching has been primarily in the domain of education professors, government bureaucrats, or charismatic consultants—not in the domain of practicing teachers.

Accepting the legitimacy of practitioner knowledge would give school reform a different focus. That focus would improve the depth, breadth, and quality of practitioner knowledge. It would provoke policymakers to consider how to use policy to strengthen practitioner knowledge and how to use it to strengthen policymaking. This would dramatically change the way we would go about knowing and helping schools.

Chapter 12

Helping Schools

ELASTIC FOR THE BRITCHES

John, the Reporting Inspector, rushed me toward the Head's office, where the school management team was meeting for the official feedback from the week-long inspection of their school. To my surprise he stopped and urged me to go ahead. When he arrived a bit later, I asked him if everything was all right. He replied, "You are always having to pull up your britches when the elastic is worn out."

It suddenly struck me that this was the problem with American attempts to help schools. We keep pulling up the britches of our schools when the elastic is worn out, when what we need to do is replace the elastic.

—*Journal Entry, no. 3.1*

As we saw in Chapters 3 and 5, the credo of most inspectors is, "Do good as you go. Do what you can to help schools." The notion that, while a person is collecting information and making judgements about quality, he can at the same time help a school challenges our prevailing ideas about how to help schools. This provocation considers ideas about helping.

We usually design our help to meet needs, especially when government programs are involved. Since we see schools as being inherently weak, reactive institutions, we readily conclude that they require outside help to fix them.

If nothing else, this long list of school deficiencies demonstrates the strength of our view that schools lack something:

Schools block student achievement.

Schools are behind the times.

Schools are bastions of mediocrity.

School teachers and administrators are often incompetent.

School management practices are ineffective.

Schools waste money because of poor administration.

Schools lack vision or clear values.

Schools have poor operating assumptions about the use of time, division of subjects, and the grouping of students.

Schools promote, rather than assuage, group against group "isms," for example, racism, sexism, and classism.

Schools are isolated from the real world of their students. They close their eyes to critical student problems, such as learning difficulties, abuse, violence, drugs, pregnancy, hate, negligence, and malnutrition.

Schools are isolated from the real world of adults. They do not prepare youth for jobs, work, raising families, or citizenship.

Schools are isolated from parents and their communities. They see parents as problems, not as partners.

Schools are isolated from new research on development and learning; they are isolated from good ideas about practice that is happening elsewhere.

Schools require government.

Even if everyone doesn't subscribe to all of these deficiencies, some of us see schools as boring places that we were glad to leave as students and that, as institutions, are locked into administrative and support structures that brutalize their independent functioning. They are reactive, not proactive institutions. Schools nationwide, and the people who work in them, have little prestige. They need help.

Efforts to help teachers and schools do a better job often begin by thoughtfully stating the problem and declaring how the new initiative will solve it. Framed as "technical assistance" efforts, they are based on an intervention strategy built from an analysis of needs. This is *not* "doing good as you go." It is more like coming to do good carrying excess baggage.

Technical assistance is usually part of a specific program or project, that is, funded by a short-term grant, and is marginal to the school. As the intervention strategy becomes more embroiled in the actual life of a school, the technical assistor's tasks usually grow more complex and her role becomes more difficult to explain. If it is perceived as failing, the intervention must defend itself. If it is perceived as succeeding, it must be prepared to expand. In either case the effort becomes diffuse and more vulnerable.

The need for measurable results creates a strong tendency for the assistance program and the school to make a bargain. The school will concretize a real or apparent deficiency and the program will provide assistance and resources to help meet that need. In this adverse manner the program designed to ameliorate the need begins by extending it. The negative consequences of this approach are exaggerated further by the helper's reliance on ideologies or prescriptions about change. These provide a more certain path through the ambiguities faced by the helper, but less help for the institution that is wrestling with maintaining its integrity in the course of being helped. Help too often becomes a distraction for school people, rather than a strategy of improvement.

Built on a different set of assumptions, the inspectors' notion of "doing good as you go" creates a different dynamic that may help us out of this quagmire of mutual dependencies. Inspection's approach to helping schools is based on an intimate knowledge of the particulars of each school. Since they are first seeking knowledge, rather than providing help, inspectors do not assume a school is deficient. Each school is a new opportunity for creating a portrait that captures, as well as possible, the complexity of life in that school as it relates to teaching and learning. When considering how a school might be helped, inspectors do not start with programs, strategies, or ideologies about helping. As successful practitioners, they begin with their knowledge summed up in their standards about what is good and bad about schools. Sharp inspectors insist that, when a school sees its portrait, it will see what it must do.

Inspection suggests that, if we change how we know and judge schools, we will create knowledge that will directly support the improvement of practice in a way that respects and strengthens the integrity of the school as an institution. This is the new elastic we need for the britches.

■ ■ ■ ■ ■ Chapter 13

Making Standards Work

GREENWICH MEAN TIME AND THE WRISTWATCH

When my wife, Les, and I discussed which flat to rent in London, we considered costs, layout, proximity to a British Rail station, and "power showers." After deciding on a place, we both recalled seeing a poster urging a visit to the Greenwich Observatory to experience the meridian. "The Greenwich Meridian, Longitude Zero, is the starting point for measuring time and space on Earth." The Greenwich Observatory was two blocks from our flat.

After unpacking we walked across Greenwich Park to see what the Greenwich Standard might be. The Shepherds 24-Hour Gate Clock, the 142-year-old official clock, rests in a brick wall. It was 2:32 o'clock in the afternoon, Greenwich Mean Time (actually 14:32). The official tablet assured us that this was within one-half second of the true time.

After a moment of respectful quiet, we walked through the gate to look at the bronzed meridian line drawn in the cobblestones behind the clock. There we watched a man in a brown tweed coat remove the thick back plate of the Shepherds Gate Clock and, with one hand swaddled in a thin white cotton glove, manipulate the gears, moving the clock's hand ahead a second at a time while consulting a watch on his other wrist. He was wearing a Mickey Mouse watch.

—Journal Entry

In 1884 Britain scrapped with the other nations of the world to have the meridian line set in Greenwich. The case was strong—much of the detailed technical work to establish world standards for time and space on the Earth had been accomplished by the Greenwich Royal Observatory. Finally the American railroads, whose timetables had been built on the Greenwich standard, pressured Washington to intervene, leading to agreement. Even so, Ireland refused to recognize Greenwich Mean Time and the French defined the meridian as being "so many degrees west of Paris" (Hamilton and Hamilton, 1969, pp. 60–61).

Because Britain understood the importance of world-class standards for the purpose of dominion, the scrapping was worth it. Historically more conscious of standards than Americans, the British feel that Americans are generally rather inadequate and sloppy when it comes to standards. They may be right, since our founding fathers left England to some extent to escape this sense of standards. But, now that we are obsessed by standards in education, we might learn something from the English.

The use of standards in traditional inspection challenges current American assumptions about how standards should be used in school reform, as well as in the British Government's approach to its current reform. This provocation will first present a brief history of standards and then consider how a standard could be helpful in the task of improving education.

HISTORY OF STANDARDS

In England the usage of the word *standard* has a long and fascinating history that bears on how we think about what a standard is today. Standard appeared for the first time in 1138, long after Moses and the Ten Commandments and long before arguments about standards in education. In 1138 the English and the Scots were once again fighting over the boundary between their two countries in what is known as the Battle of the Standard. The English troops were told they would know their King's ship by his standard, the royal flag on its mast. It was called a standard because of the stand the troops would take. Richard of Hexham wrote about the banner in this battle: "It was there that valour took its stand to conquer or die" (Richard, 1135–1138, p. 163).

Before the New World was discovered, when the growth of trade in the European world led the English and others to consider how to deal more efficiently with diverse ideas about determining commercial value, a standard became a *common measure* backed by the King's authority. In 1429 that changed; the actual exemplar for a specific measure became a standard—whether it was the actual stick that was a yard long or the actual vessel that held a quart of liquid or the actual stone that weighed *a stone*. The King's authority was behind each exemplar.

As these exemplar standards became accepted, the meaning of a common measure was extended to include what was being measured: for example, a yard of cloth, a quart of milk, or a pound of nails. Sometimes the term *measurement* meant what was being measured, as in "I'll have a pint." In 1992 the importance of this meaning was apparent in the legal requirement that English pubs replace their pint glasses with larger ones that would provide for an actual liquid pint. The new glasses were required to have an etched line that indicated the proper standard measure for a pint that did not include the foam.

In 1563 the meaning of standard became more abstract, relying more on the authority of general acceptance, at least by those who mattered. This understanding applied to money and overall systems of value. *The Silver Standard* and *Greenwich Mean Time* are examples.

Continuing this trend toward abstraction, standard began to be used in discussing wealth or status. These standards of attainment were what was expected or condoned by those in positions of prestige. Soon people talked about standard speech, social standards, and the standard of living. As the monarchy's authority decreased, the role of law in setting and upholding standards increased. Having stoutly resisted the standards set by any authority, law became an important resolution for Americans, who believed that legal standards would help hold a society together.

Somewhere along the way the idea emerged that standards were conceptual tools that could promote excellence in the performance of craftsmen, musicians, and athletes. While these standards were learned, they had to become ingrained in the performer to influence her work. The quality of her work was determined by the standards evident in it. These standards could always be exceeded: "Her musical direction set a new standard for the performance of choral music."

THE VICTORIAN BLUNDER: COMMON MEASURES INSTEAD OF VALOR

In 1876 standards became important in English public education when, as a common measure, they were applied to student achievement. This was part of the Payment by Results scheme, England's first attempt to make public education efficient. The reasoning is familiar. As described in Chapter 5, members of Parliament, suspecting the schools supported by public money were not doing well, forced them to measure up to acceptable standards of achievement to ensure that money was not wasted. This demand for accountability had a contentious edge. The schools of concern were not those attended by the children of members of Parliament, but those established for the nation's poorer children—who by definition already had failed to reach some of the nation's standards of value.

Having no legitimate control over these religious-society schools, the Government decided to set standards in the basic subjects (the 4 R's) and to assess student performance directly in those subjects. Once the standards were set and the students were assessed, the Government would base the amount of money a school would receive on the results. Payment by Results is an interesting precursor to our system of assessing schools.

The business of setting standards for learning was eventually given over to the experts. Stephen Gould tells the fascinating story about how common measures were applied to intelligence in the 19th century, primarily through the work of English psychologists. Using the human skull as a common measure for intelligence, scientists showed that white European male skulls were the largest, thus proving that European males were genetically superior. Gould demonstrates that this measure was never scientific and that the use of precise numbers to measure vague concepts cannot in itself produce valid results (Gould, 1981). The measurement of skulls preceded the use of tests to measure IQ and school achievement.

In Payment by Results a standard in education became analogous to the actual goods being measured. A *standard* was the group of students who performed on tests at a defined level of achievement. During this era, inspectors tested students by their standard. This usage continues to be important in English education and directly ties to more modern ideas about the advantages and dangers of tracking.

England's university-related Exam Boards came into existence during this time. The Boards set standards for academic achievement by creating the exams and the courses of work the exams would cover. These powerful Boards still carry out this function in much the same way. English educators, referring to a standard of achievement, often mean the level of work expected by the Exam Boards.

Believing they could be certain about what was adequate for a student to know, the Government opted for precise measurement and certainty to judge schools. The inspectors did not agree. Although they believed standards were important, they also believed in a different way of knowing schools than testing.

It might have been better for the inspectors, and perhaps for the rest of us as well, if the Victorian task force had based its notion on the valor branch of the standard family, rather than on the common measure branch. If they had not made this blunder, educational standards might now have these characteristics:

> Doing well would mean doing well at something difficult that is important in the eyes of the community.

Doing well at the task would heighten knowledge about an enterprise that is of interest to those who want to do well. Normative test scores do not have this attribute; a musical performance does. Thus, the means for measuring performance on the standard would support good performance against the standard.

The standard would be intrinsic to the performance and the performer would understand it.

What is possible to accomplish would be set by the performer in the performance, not by an arbitrary standard.

Standards of valor seem more consistent with learning than standards of common measure. Standards in the arts and sports are closer to standards of valor. Standards of valor are easier to grasp. They are more consistent with the idea that our schools should provide children with qualities that count, rather than qualities we can count.

TOWARD A BETTER STANDARD

There is something certain in a standard. There seems little harm in being certain. Certainty promotes an order that allows us to focus on other issues. Perhaps the comfort a standard provides rests in our memory of when we could hold a standard as a real object in our hands, knowing it was a measure fully authorized by accepted authority. It is comforting to think we can improve our schools by setting explicit standards for what we want our youth to know and be.

This simplistic use of standards may provide certainty, but it does not consider what standards we want our youth to have, how a person learns standards, or how a government can effectively support the ongoing process of generating better standards.

In response to the explicit standards set by the English and American governments, our students are expected to perform on tests at the level set by the standard. Schools are expected to deliver student performance. We want more than that from standards. Explicit standards of performance set by government will not achieve what we want.

We want our children to perform on implicit standards of excellence and learning set in their minds, habits, and work, not on explicit standards for learning. We want a student to learn how to set and raise her standards. We want a student to experience the power of her own standards in her life and work. We want a student to learn the habits that connect high standards to actual and often difficult work, the work of clarifying a standard, the persistence in practice that is necessary to achieve a standard, and the self-consciousness to assess oneself. Implanting and nourishing standards of excellence for good work is a major challenge for good teaching. To teach implicit standards adults must demonstrate them in practice. The learner must be given many opportunities to practice using them until they become habits of her thought and action. It is our students whose understanding and performance we want to increase, not our standard-setting task forces.

Standards of learning are not successfully imposed by edict. They are not minimal standards. They are not separate from performance. Excellence in art, music, sports, politics, humanitarian efforts—even in mundane matters—is open ended. Actual past performance sets new standards, not a standard-setting process. An artist defines a new standard of excellence in her own best work. An athlete breaks a world record. We do not want closed, precise standards. We do not want standards that have been watered down to the lowest common denominator. We want our youth to have the internal desire to break old standards of performance and to have the skills to do that.

Standards that make a difference in what people do and think are implicit in the social order. It is naive to believe that school performance can be improved by setting explicit performance standards. Standards, like languages, are embedded in how we think and act; they cannot be disconnected, artificially altered, and then reimposed. The implicit standards held by actual students, teachers, and the school, as an institution, will be the most salient definitions of quality for what a school provides. These are the standards that must rise for better achievement and excellence to happen.

The actual standards a teacher exhibits in his work with students, the standards he uses for judging the quality of student work in his day-to-day teaching, are what make the difference. How do we raise these intrinsic standards so that the habits of rigor, persistence, thoughtfulness, ingenuity, self-discipline, and decency increase in a school?

Inspectors see standards as an inherent part of what a school provides. They believe that one important purpose of inspection is to help raise the actual standards of a school. They believe that by making judgements about the quality of what the school is doing while they are at the school they will force the question of standards out into the open. When this happens, the school will begin to focus on improving its standards. The school will not be distracted by trying to define what an imposed standard means or by defending itself against people who don't understand what the school is or what the school's standards are all about.

Inspection suggests that, as crucial tools, standards must be directly considered as integral to the school and, as we have seen, as integral to knowing and judging schools. Standards are argued about and they change. If we follow how inspection views standards, we will lose our sense of being certain at the risk of becoming effective.

Chapter 14

Government Accountability: The Need to Be Certain

It is important for the public to know what its schools are doing and to judge whether they are doing it well. It is important to monitor schools to weed out bad practitioners, bad practice, and possibly bad schools. It is important to manage schools well. Schools, like all human institutions, require considerable daily attention to details, performance, and resources. It is important that government policy support substantial school improvement. Most politicians, bureaucrats, educational experts, and policymakers want to solve public problems. They believe their task is to find workable solutions that will win public support.

Although it might seem easy to put together a system of accountability—a way of knowing and judging schools—that serves these aims, we have not done that well. Our accountability schemes provide inappropriate information based on measures that are widely viewed as invalid. Many practitioners see our systems as controlling, not supportive. Many reformers experience them as hurdles. Many policymakers see them as trivial. Demanding government workers find them ineffective, as they make it no easier politically to take drastic remedial steps, such as closing a dysfunctional school.

In 1839 Sir James used inspection to meet the responsibility of the Government agency funding public schools. Inspection supported school improvement and at the same time monitored school quality. This provocation explores the difficulties of government accountability.

The first difficulty is control. When a government is worried that its schools are not efficiently using public resources, either because they are not performing or because they cost too much, it becomes interested in reforming them.

Because schools are embedded in the fabric of a democratic society, and because teaching and learning in a democracy is open ended by nature, schools are well sheltered from direct government control. In the early history of English education the religious societies sheltered their schools. The stress that Americans place on local control of schools shelters them in a similar way from the control of state and national governments.

The accountability system is the most effective mechanism available to the government for controlling schools. Accountability mechanisms ideally ensure that government and the schools work together to make the schools as strong as possible. When the government holds schools accountable for doing what the government thinks they need to do to be efficient, the government trips over its own feet. Payment by Results dramatically changed inspection in ways so that it became useless for school improvement. The current testing program that is part of English reform has stirred resistance of parents and teachers for similar reasons. The American increased interest in new and better testing has created similar problems.

Steven Groak in *The Idea of Building: Thought and Action in the Design and Production of Buildings* (1992)[1] writes about the quest for certainty in the building industry, which he has participated in both as an architect and a contractor. In the formal systems of knowing about buildings, it is conventionally assumed that buildings are permanent, stable, and unchanging. In reality, as he demonstrates, they are in a constant state of flux. Buildings are not stable.

The construction of a building is an exercise in solving particular problems, not in creating another example of a general theory. Using available ideas to meet today's changing needs and working with materials and construction techniques that change quickly, the building that emerges is the result of the architect and contractor solving a particular problem at a specific site at a specific time. While general principles are useful, the good builder works well with the particulars he faces, such as the slope of the land at the site, the water table level at the site, the changing public aesthetic, the history of previous construction on the site, and the materials the project budget allows. This knowledge of how to work with particulars is not available in the formal systems of knowledge about building.

After a building is finished, it is not a solid, stable entity. Even the most solid building is always changing in response to different temperatures and shifts of the earth; to different uses and occupants, who use changing technologies and whose tastes change; and to the flows of human demography that define vibrant cities as well as regions in decay.

When Groak considers the types of knowledge and social apparatus that surround the building of buildings, he notes the continual bickering between architects and construction bosses about who knows what about what is important. He concludes that the uncertainty inherent in building creates risk and that this risk is not well considered in the formal social systems. People who are required to be accountable for their work abhor risk and find ways to pass it down to others. The contract is the common device for passing risk down in the building trades. A contract to deliver certain materials and set them in place by a certain date decreases the builder's risk. He simply decides if the contractor did or did not meet the specs. The contractor must take on the actual risk of making it happen. If it does not happen, it is his fault. The builder can be blamed only for incorrectly determining whether the contractor did or did not do his job. Complexities increase when the contractor passes down the risk to a subcontractor.

The uncertainty inherent in achieving results in education makes it desirable for a government agency to pass risk down, particularly when legislatures, politicians, and the public demand results. While there have been cycles of school performance contracts in education, it is more common to use the existing accountability system to pass risk down. The government agency states publicly that its job is to ensure that standards for student performance are set (or objectives for projects), to provide funding and to measure the results. If good education is not the result, it is not the agency's fault. The blame lies elsewhere—on the schools, the teachers, the students, or the political process. The government agency is free from blame since it was not its job to help achieve the results.

Using knowledge about schools that is disconnected from the real life of schools becomes a plus when risk is being passed down. If the government protects itself from the complexities of learning by not knowing anything about them, it is easier to stay out of the fray.

Inspection shows that it is possible to build a system of accountability that is not disconnected from practitioner knowledge, that directly accepts uncertainty and confronts it. Inspection provokes us to consider that it might be possible to invent an accountability scheme that supports democratic accountability. If we had better information about the practice of teaching and learning that happens in our schools, we would more easily find ways to build systems that accept the risk of democratic education and that support its continual growth.

PART THREE

■ ■ ■ ■ ■

New Possibilities

Nearly every design task involves tens, often hundreds, sometimes thousands of different antagonistic elements, which can be forced into a functional harmony only by a person's will. This harmony cannot be achieved by other than artistic means. The individual technical and mechanical elements receive their definite value only in this manner.

—Alvar Aalto, Architect, 1955

Chapter 15

Preliminaries

Before considering the implications of inspection for American education, we will revisit the argument of this book. Assuming the public discourse about education limits the potential of school reform, and that how we talk about schools depends on what we know about them, we can conclude that the way we know and judge the quality of our schools is critical to improving them.

The demands on our traditional approaches have pushed them beyond what they can bear. Those demands come from different sources: business leaders and fiscally conservative politicians, who require schools to be much more accountable for results; many reformers and researchers, who think our current tradition poorly assesses schools and impedes reform; school people, who see accountability as an intrusion on their prime job of teaching children. These demands seriously stretch each of the following ways we now use to know and judge schools.

TESTING STUDENT PERFORMANCE

The limits of standardized testing as a way to know and judge schools have become clearer in recent years. The media frequently portray testing as unreliable or irrelevant in stories about: school districts and state departments manipulating testing to assure that schools are performing "above average"; teachers teaching to the test; a greedy and narrow industry controlling testing; businesses disregarding all measures of school performance when hiring students.

Many studies have documented the inappropriate use of tests (Mitchell, 1992; Wiggins, 1993). A strong argument has been advanced that the use of standardized tests has negative effects on teaching and learning (Madaus, 1991). Standardized multiple-choice testing is "one of the most notable accomplishments of applied psychology in the 20th century—more weight is now being placed on this technology than any human contrivance can bear" (Haney et al., 1993, p. 293).

Yet, when we want to know if our schools are working, we turn to student test scores. The inconsistency in how we value standardized test scores confuses schools and weakens the public discourse about education. Arguments about the value of testing distract us from forthright discussion about what schools are doing.

Student performance on tests is an indirect measure of teacher and administrator performance. Building an accountability system upon questionable tests to measure indirectly the performance of those who are accountable makes no sense.

EVALUATING PROJECTS AND EXPERIMENTS

The legitimate way to learn about school reform is to evaluate its intervention in schools. A classical evaluation design will measure the impact of project variables on characteristics in the school, most often student test performance, since that is the coin of the realm. As a result we learn about the project, not about the life of the school.

Evaluation has been limited to assessing the effects of discrete projects whose results can be measured in some manner. Reform, now seen through the wider lenses of systemic restructuring, stretches evaluation.

SOCIAL SCIENCE RESEARCH

Psychologists, political scientists, anthropologists, historians, and other social scientists usually work in schools to advance knowledge within their respective disciplines. While this work has contributed to what we know about schools, it has usually been framed by the precepts of these various disciplines.

The conceptual and organizational cohesion of social science knowledge comes from the discipline, not from the life of the school or the process of teaching and learning. This limits its value for teachers and reformers.

POLICY RESEARCH

Policy research relies more on analyzing how forces and factors that are mostly outside the teaching and learning process affect student achievement than on understanding how teaching and learning occur. What happens in classrooms is approached only indirectly. In professions other than education—law, medicine, business—it is easier to study the impact of policy on practice because practitioners and what they know and do is considered valuable. The avoidance of practitioner knowledge weakens the potential of policy research to improve schools.

ACCREDITATION

Accreditation and state certification provide schools with a public legitimacy. Most states certify high schools that meet specified requirements to award a high school diploma. Accreditation legitimizes the value of the diploma. While accreditation includes a visit to the school, its focus is on whether the school will make it through the hoop, not on learning about the school's practice of teaching and learning. Thus, what we learn from accreditation exercises is whether the school measures up to the set standards, not about its practice. The new demands for accountability have caused a reexamination of the value and methods of accreditation as well.

INFORMAL KNOWLEDGE

Most public knowledge about schools comes from methods that were not deliberately created for knowing schools, including the press, television, newsletters, publications of professional associations, and public opinion polls. Informal wisdom about which schools are best, which teachers are best, and what happens within a school abides in each local school community. Parents rely heavily on this when making decisions about their children's education. While informal knowledge does consider what happens in a school, its influence seems to decrease in the presence of planned reform.

NEW STRATEGIES

New strategies for knowing schools include clinical and site-based studies, videotapes of actual classrooms, narratives about schools and teaching, and descriptions of good teaching practice. Some of these strategies do indeed consider teaching and learning and provide some promising perspectives. They are seen as alternative strategies. Some were not meant to challenge the prevailing tradition. Others hope to prick the tradition. But they seldom are seen as ways to replace established practice of knowing and judging schools.

When we want legitimate knowledge to make judgements that matter about school quality, we want knowledge that is objective and precise, knowledge that is created by experts, knowledge that explains the effects of generalized concepts and discrete projects on schools. We carefully design instruments to collect data to analyze and make recommendations based on that analysis.

The assumptions of our current tradition have conspired to ensure that we neither value nor know how to learn about teaching and learning in practice. This limited view of what is possible and valuable to study in schools is a major constraint.

A comprehensive review of the American tradition is necessary to analyze this further. That is not what this book is about. This book is about the new possibilities inspection provokes. Ideas that might serve as principles for better ways to know and judge schools are presented in Chapter 16.

■ ■ ■ ■ ■ Chapter **16**

Guidelines

The following guidelines illustrate some new possibilities that inspection provokes.

1. The purpose for knowing and judging the practice of schools is to improve that practice.

The inquiry tools dedicated to improving practice are weak. Inspection shows it is possible to develop robust tools for this purpose, if we begin with different assumptions. Inspection knowledge is not designed to advance social science knowledge, even though it may do so. It is not designed to enforce top-down regulations. In fact, using it as a tool to ascertain school compliance damages it as a method of inquiry. Inspection is designed to inform policy. It is designed to point out to the school that it is not "up to standard" and from that determination to persuade the school to work within established standards and policy.

Since this purpose requires different methods than those we know, we must be careful to ensure that this purpose drives the design of new methods, rather than that the old methods reshape the purpose.

2. The focus must be squarely on teaching and learning.

There is new consensus about the importance of focusing on teaching and learning that supports our interest in inspection. This focus requires that all questions and discussion about a school begin with knowledge about what happens in its classrooms. Other issues about the school, such as student demographics, budget management, parental involvement, and teacher support, may well be considered, but they are related to teaching and learning at that school.

This focus also makes it possible to consider directly how new programs and regulations affect teaching and learning at a school. Teaching and learning must be considered together, not as two separate processes. The focus on what the school offers its students is always checked against how well its students actually learn.

Since we have never considered teaching and learning as a direct focus, we must be careful to keep this focus central. Since we have not valued the particulars of the complex life of schools, and since we have no good systemic way to make judgements about the quality of teaching and learning in a particular school or a particular class, it would be easy for us to fall back to old views, such as classroom practice is routine, simple to understand and even a bit boring; classroom practice is a private matter for teachers, not a legitimate part of public interest; because classroom practice is idiosyncratic, the study of it is beyond the pale of "objective" science. If we don't think what teachers do is interesting or important, or possible to understand, then it is easy to conclude that it is not important to know. A rigorous concentration on teaching and learning corroborates the importance of what teachers do.

3. The school is the unit of analysis.

Inspection suggests that the best unit of analysis is the school. The school provides the leverage point for improving teaching.

It is within the context of the school that the work of individual teachers is considered. While the individual teacher's classroom practice determines what learning does or does not happen, he teaches within the context of the standards, support, resources, administration, and climate of a school. Inspection comments on the quality of teaching and learning in a school and targets its recommendations for improvement of the school, as an institution. Although recommendations might include requiring some teachers to hone their skills and knowledge through professional development, that judgement is based on the quality of teaching and learning at the school.

Using the school as the unit of analysis reinforces the school's importance, increasing the likelihood that it will respond to the recommendations for change. This guideline is further developed in Chapter 17.

4. Begin with the particulars of actual school life.

The quality of the particulars of a school determines whether students learn or not. Thus, particulars of events and how they work within the context of the classroom and school need to be understood.

The first task of the inspector is to make sense out of the particular events of actual classroom life. Since the portrait of the school is built on judgements about the complexities of its life, the result provides the school with a solid basis for considering how it might improve.

Since we do not usually think about the particular in this fashion, we need some help. Consider how a teacher thinks about the particular while she is in action. She must consider how to respond to what is actually happening. She must convey her knowledge, values, and skills through the particular acts of her teaching. She must judge the quality of what she does, based on her understanding of how she constructs particular teaching events and connects them to each student's learning. Her judgement is made on the spot and directly influences what she does next.

5. Use practitioner judgement.

Welcome judgement as a tool for inquiry. It provides the tissue that connects the particular events.

To learn about the practice of teaching, we should rely on the judgement of experienced teachers. While teaching experience is a prerequisite, it does not guarantee judgement. Judgement happens when a teacher is able to use his experience as a resource, not as the measure of what is good and bad. Judgement does not say, "This is how I would have done it." An inspector considers a class as it is led by the actual teacher, not as he would lead it.

Discussion and moderation sharpen individual judgements and protect them from the subjective perspective. Methods that use judgement, including inspection, often try to circumscribe an individual's discretion with requirements of focus or criteria for judging. Such circumscriptions seriously modify how judgement is used.

6. Raise actual standards.

To improve the quality of teaching and learning at a school, one must raise the standards that actually exist at that school. It is the actual standards of a school, its teachers, and its students that define the quality of education that school provides. The standards teachers bring to their work have more bearing on student performance than standards set by outside agencies. Intrinsic standards are connected to direct experience with an issue or a skill.

A government agency setting explicit standards for student performance is an easy and ineffective way to raise the actual standards in a school. In fact, there is good evidence that this is counterproductive because it can so easily distract the school from the real task of raising its standards and raising the standards of its students. Coercing schools into enforcing excellence simply doesn't work and it never has.

As an accountability device to raise standards, inspection helps make standards explicit and judges how well the school is doing in light of them. The inspection team can make sense of the total picture of the standards of a school, including how well the school has explicated important standards, how well the school has dealt with codified standards and, most important, how well standards connect to the quality of student work. The team's recommendations about how to improve that particular school are expressed in terms of how to raise the standards.

Inspection relies on inspector judgement to ascertain how these complexities in fact play out in a particular school. If inspectors simply check to see if the school is complying with standards set outside of it, the picture of standards at that school will be quite limited.

Inspectors believe that the final criterion for judging school quality is whether the school provides a good deal for the children it serves. This standard is not based on regulations or codified standards, although these can also be considered. It is based on the inspector's personal moral sense. That sense is more complex, more rigorous, and wiser than what regulatory standards can manage. The challenge is to find ways to use standards that incorporate that sense, rather than exclude it. Inspection is one method that does that.

7. Choose how precise to be, based on what is appropriate.

This guideline replaces, "Be as precise as possible." Inspectors use precision as a tool, not a prerequisite. Even American business is not always precise when it comes to quality. Cadillac's slogan is "Creating a higher standard."

Precision is an important attribute of inquiry work, but it must be appropriately applied. Precise measurements for phenomena that are notoriously imprecise will divert attention from the phenomenon to the measurement. It can lead to unimportant information. For example, when a checklist does not include a good representation of what an observer sees, it forces her to record inaccurate responses. Similarly, an unconditional drive for precision in language can lead to operational concepts and jargon that create an illusion of certainty, rather than clarity of expression.

When only the experts can understand the precision, the public is left out of the discussion. When it is used well, precision can promote clarity, useful information, and agreement. But, it can also bring about an artificial certainty that confuses understanding, judgement, and action. To avoid this, precision should be seen as a tool, not as a requisite of inquiry.

8. Accept productive dichotomies as given in schooling.

Trying to resolve dichotomies inherent in education is a waste of time. Common sense insists it is more productive to discover how to provide both content and skills than to argue about whether one is more important than the other.

As inspection demonstrates, it is easier to manage dichotomies when the focus is the life of a school, not a concept about it. Since an inspector's work is based in schools, not in concepts about them, he is inoculated against wasting time on resolving inherent dichotomies.

9. Choose methods that spawn connections, not discontinuity.

We want our schools to promote continuity, not distance, between children and adults, the past and the present, school and work, practitioners and policymakers, categories of people, values, and knowledge. Our current methods for knowing and judging schools, in the name of objectivity, often provoke distance rather than continuity. The pursuit of discrete knowledge about the results of discrete policies or projects distances decision makers from the complexity, uncertainty, and moral ambiguity of real life.

Inspection does not value moral or social distance as a methodological principle. In fact, distance is out of place in this system of knowledge that is so deliberately woven into understanding and directly affecting social events. Inspection raises the possibility that legitimate, rigorous approaches to inquiry can build continuity, rather than promote neutrality or distance. Inspection shows that we can make choices about how we learn that contribute to building continuity between a school, its teachers, its students, and its community.

10. Ground accountability in moral responsibility.

Risk and uncertainty are an inherent part of improving schools in a democracy. If we knew the best final answers for certain, we would not need the messiness of democracy.[1] The democratic future is open ended.

It is simplistic to think we can secure a sure future by prescribing what our children must learn. This is an indication that we want our responsibility for our children to be technical, rather than moral, in nature. Educating a child is a continuous struggle in a democratic society.

Good accountability for schools is built on reasonable expectations about what is possible, but allows for what does not seem possible. Our responsibility, as adults, is to provide our children now with the best we can. This includes sharing the lessons and skills we have learned and challenging our children to be the best they can.

We cannot control what our children will become. That is beyond our power as parents and adults. Neither we, nor they, can judge now the worth of a child's future. We can make the best possible decisions at each opportunity. We must accept the ambiguity that comes from this uncertain business.

Inspectors bring a moral sense to their work, as they decide what is good and bad practice. We also must accept that we make many basic decisions about what is good and bad for our children. That acceptance doesn't make accountability less valuable; it simply requires that we admit its moral aspects.

11. Welcome wonder and ambiguity.

Wonder is the saving grace of education.[2] An unexpected insight, a maturity that has grown over time, the courage to persist in spite of failure, the experience of power associated with knowledge or a skill—all are causes for wonder. Negative events are also causes for wonder. It is certain that people who are learning, particularly young people, will do the unexpected.

How we talk about knowing and judging schools is earnest. Since we want our methods for knowing to be certain and unsentimental, it is not surprising that we exclude wonder. Since inspectors work to build a portrait about a school from what is actually happening there, they often are surprised. Wonderment dwells in the phenomena of the particular. We can consider it without becoming unglued.

■ ■ ■ ■ ■ Chapter 17

Postlude: Talk in the School Yard

Since the beginning, or at least since there was one person, someone has been learning. Since there has been more than one person, someone has been teaching. Since there have been both children and adults, someone has been helping children become adults. Schools probably came with the first communities. Since there have been democratic governments, there has been a belief that education is vital for the survival and growth of the nation.

Important and uncertain changes are rapidly taking place that have challenged and that will continue to challenge our schools. Global in nature, these changes include major shifts in how the world governs itself, how the world does its business, how the world works, how the world is building new knowledge, how the world understands the working of the human mind, and how the world judges what is of value.

The changes are real and breathtaking. They are urging us toward uncharted domains. Nevertheless, we cannot ignore at least one thread that persists, which connects us to the past. We must provide for children. In a modern democracy that means we must provide schools whose primary function is to teach students how to use their minds.

We now spend an enormous amount of time, money, and energy on education. One 1995 estimate set public spending on education (elementary through postsecondary) at $345 billion each year, which is $73 billion more than is spent on defense. The recent increase in the birth rate indicates this cost will continue to rise. Only health care receives more government funding than education.

Since the mid-1980s we have tried to reform our schools. We have tried to make them more productive, so they will turn out children who can read, write, and produce in the next century. Many educators thought the reform was based on an unspoken bargain: if they fixed the schools, government would continue to provide the needed support. This basis for reform has become more illusion than substance. Even if we were successful in reforming the schools, the pressures to reduce funding would continue. Even if the goals were met and every student in the country could read and compute at a world-class level, there would be no clear agreement that our schools had done what they needed to do. This reform will not fix our schools. Our children are neither widgets nor robots. Democracy does not survive challenges by creating a certain future on the backs of malleable children. Democracy must always make room for the unexpected.

The modern challenges require us to think again about what we want our schools to be and to reconsider how to make that happen. What schools need to do now may not be much different from what they were required to do when democracy began. A democracy has a covenant with its citizens to provide children with skills and knowledge from their heritage so they can pursue their personal interests and in return they will contribute their skills and ideas to the continual growth of the democracy.

How we make the covenant work may be quite different. The primary issue no longer is how to fix our schools, but how to renew them and transform them into vital institutions of teaching and learning. We can no longer rely on the bureaucratic mechanisms, on regulations that impose change, or on standards that force narrow definitions of achievement. Schools will change when we change how we think about them.

We don't think about schools very well. The talk often heard in schools, in district offices, in state departments, and even in teachers' colleges and universities is alarming. "I don't have time to think." "I can't make sense of all these concepts and programs of reform. I can't understand what 'they' want me to do."

When we do have time to think, what do we think about? We think about concepts of education; we ponder the reform strategies; we consider how to position ourselves for the next grant in the wave of reform now gripping us. We want new ideas that are useful, practical, that we can apply tomorrow. Since our schools are in crisis and our children are key, we must have the next answer now. And the next and the next. There is nothing wrong with wanting to have a down-to-earth and practical conversation, but conversation that is disconnected from the life of schools requires little thought or imagination about what's important.

When asking about this book, most people say, "Oh, that sounds interesting." More often than not they then ask, "What are the applications?" Now that I have had the privilege to stop and think as I worked these last 3 years on this book, I am expected to return with solid practical recommendations for action.

This book will not offer a list of applications from inspection for American schools. The reasons are important. First, plucking a piece of an institution from its social and historical context and plopping it down in an alien context is usually as disastrous as moving plants and animals from their native habitats. All that's certain is that the piece that has been plucked will behave differently than it did in its original context. Specific recommendations about what to do in American schools will come best from an analysis of American experience. That analysis can be provoked by ideas that challenge our basic assumptions, but it must be built from the American experience with schools and accountability.

Second, if I listed applications and recommendations I would be continuing the tradition of how we think about reform. I would be continuing the problem, if I identified a problem, proposed a solution, and recommended steps to implement it. Since the assumptions of inspection challenge the underlying tenets of this approach, it would be ungracious to force an English tradition into an American one.

Third, such a list would hide the major benefit that inspection offers us. This exploration of inspection provides another perspective on how a modern democracy can know, judge, and change its schools. It provides some new ideas and some new images to help us rethink what we need to do.

The image that stays with me is contained in John Turner's reflection about Jane, the Head of Rosewood School, in the early part of Chapter 3:

> Jane is unusual. ... She has neither asked hundreds of anxious questions nor has she built tense walls of protection against the real and imaginary threats of inspection. Instead she's thinking hard. I like that. So few people in schools seem to think anymore. They're caught up in attainment targets for the National Curriculum or tangled up with the management objectives of the required school development plans. Approaching schools with all these concepts about how they should manage themselves may seem easier, but it discourages thinking about how to teach children.
>
> For example, that bloody form she is required to fill out. I guess none of the information it requires is worthless, but it doesn't help the school think about its most important task, teaching its particular students.

John's team of experienced practitioners spent a week together at one school, thinking about it. They considered what that school was actually doing to educate its students, how good or bad it was, what made it a unique place, and what would make it change. They learned about what actually was happening while they were there, judged the value of what they saw, and made action points about what that school should do to improve its teaching and learning.

The way of the inspector provides a dramatic possibility for responding to the challenges we face. The different assumptions upon which inspection was built suggest a different way is possible—not an experimental pilot project but a new national tradition. The way of the inspector urges us to reconnect with the real life of our children in our schools and to break the spell of concepts and ideologies that have beguiled us. It shows us how to assert again the importance of human judgement in the education of our young, in place of our overreliance on rules and regulations. Beyond this central image of inspectors at work, there are several other ideas that may be helpful.

Throughout the book we have seen that how we know and judge schools is important in thinking about how to value them, how to change them, how to hold them accountable, and how to talk about them in the public discourse.

It appears useful to consider how we know schools as a tradition, just as we have considered inspection as a tradition. Several working assumptions of inspection challenge the assumptions behind the American tradition for knowing schools:

- Inspection focuses on teaching and learning in the classroom. Inspectors do not treat teaching and learning as inputs and outputs, but as two sides of the same process, which is the primary purpose of schools.
- Inspection starts with what actually happens when teachers teach and students learn in real schools. What practitioners in the school know and are able to do is what matters.
- Inspection utilizes the conceptual strengths of professional judgement and the thoughtfulness of moderation to come to understanding what is happening and to judge its quality and suggest what should happen.
- Inspection recognizes the local school as the institution that matters. The school does the most to support or hinder good teaching.

What is most important now is to begin with the particulars of learning and teaching that actually take place in our classrooms and build our systems of accountability, and other support systems for schools, to support the changes necessary to raise the quality of what happens. The goal for accountability is both to support the creation of a rigorous, rich, and diverse set of learning opportunities and to ensure that both students and teachers meet those opportunities for teaching and learning in the classroom, not miss them. Accountability in this guise holds a difficult, but fair, template for judging the quality of teaching and schools, because it focuses on the classroom where the action that makes the difference is under way.

Imagine the benefits of changing our tradition for knowing and judging schools in the direction suggested by inspection. A student would more likely find that a school values how he thinks. This valuing would be more matter-of-fact than sentimental, ideological, or utilitarian. The school would focus on finding the best way to ensure that each student learned, strengthening his thinking, sharpening his skills, and improving the quality of his work. The school would not see his performance as a way to complete an objective, but as the objective itself. What he did would matter more, because his success is the purpose of institutional structures tuned to how he learns.

Teachers would be affected more than any other single group. Teaching students is clearly the key work of the school. Teaching would be seen less as a practice that is defined and driven by concepts, and more as a professional practice that is defined by and develops from its growing knowledge about how to teach well. Accountability systems for the school and for the whole educational enterprise, as well, would shift from assessing student performance to assessing the quality of teaching and learning. What teachers learn about how to teach would be valued more, increasing the importance of their knowledge and skills and their ideas for the whole educational enterprise.

This increase in the value placed on what teachers do would break down the notion that teaching is a private affair, not a matter of public concern. On the contrary, what teachers do is of primary importance in the public concern. But, as it is for other professionals, the public scrutiny of their work must be based on trust, rather than enforcement. This change would turn around the institutions that support teachers, including unions, professional associations, teachers' colleges, and professional development programs. The public's concern about teachers would shift from being an unfair and unproductive intrusion on their work that they must counter to protect themselves to becoming a systemic insistence that, as responsible professionals, they must continually increase their knowledge and sharpen their craft.

Schools would become educational institutions that matter more. No longer the reactive institutions we now know, they would be proactive, solving their own problems of educating their students.

School districts would work closely with each school to find ways to help strengthen its teaching and learning. The district would also engage the local community in ongoing discussions about what should happen in schools and what students should be able to do.

The role of state departments would substantially change. State departments are caught by the tension between supporting and monitoring schools. If they accepted that this tension was inherent in their work, they could develop new ways to collect and analyze information that would provide the department, the legislature, and the public with a picture of how well teaching and learning are progressing in the state that would not only support schools in building their capacities but would also support a process for making better policy.

At the national level an agency independent of government would issue a widely distributed annual report on the state of American education. This report would focus on the quality of teaching and learning. It would consider the impact of policies of government agencies.

There would also be intense initiative at the national level to develop the new methodologies; what we have called "inspectors' knowledge" might better be called "particular school knowledge." The initiative would develop a new way of knowing schools based on understanding and improving practice. It might engage a cadre of experienced practitioners to consider how to improve the methodology of visitation, to inspect randomly chosen schools, and to offer guidance to state and district visitation efforts.

Reformers, researchers, and policymakers would find better ways to support and stimulate teaching and learning in local schools. Everyone would spend more time in schools than is customary, since that is where the action is. The value of practice-based knowledge would spill into the research community, providing new impetus for research that supports practice. The point is not to replace current research on schools and learning, but to augment it with practice-based knowledge.

Changing how we know and judge schools so that we think about what happens at each school would not only stimulate new scenarios about what is possible but would also change the questions we ask:

Can we give up the simplicity of thinking that education is a matter of inputs and outputs and begin to see teaching and learning as two sides of a coin, representing the substance of what schools provide?

Can we give up the illusion of objectivity and learn to trust professional judgement?

Can we give up reform strategies based on concepts and begin to concentrate on what actually is happening in the classrooms of the school next door?

Can we come to value teaching as a practice and see teachers and schools as proactive in generating knowledge about how teaching works best and about how it is best supported?

Can we give up our generalized theories about how teaching and learning happen and begin with the more mundane, messier, idiosyncratic way it really happens?

Can we build school systems and a tradition of thinking about schools that support the local, the particular in human events?

Can we give up trying to secure our future through our children and simply take responsibility for what we, as adults, must provide them?

Can we develop a methodology of knowing schools that is tied to action and that includes a moral sense?

Work has already begun to improve American accountability, making use of some of these possibilities. Several state departments of education are looking closely at how they approach accountability. In 1992 New York State began piloting a School Quality Review process built on several ideas from English inspection (Rothman, 1992; Olson, 1994). Chicago is considering a plan to reshape school accountability that includes visiting schools to ascertain what is happening there. What is learned from these visits will inform the city's support and monitoring functions.

We eschew theory in favor of actual life; we value institutions that rely on individual judgement, cleverness, and wisdom rather than on regulations and standards of how it ought to be. It is obvious that change is imperative. We would lose too much if schools failed. At some basic level democracy rests on its institutions. Institutions devoted to teaching and learning are essential.

The idea of starting with the particular hooks into the democratic imagination, a resource that has been often overlooked. The genius of the American revolution was the idea that common people could build deliberately social institutions to enhance the knowledge, skills, wealth, and freedom of all citizens. While these institutions have often been far from ideal, and while they have stumbled to work better, they are remarkable in their attempts to serve collective needs and to provide revolutionary opportunities for individuals to find, build, and fulfill their own destinies.

The democratic imagination thrives when the particular in the lives of its diverse citizens is honored, when it takes guidance from the complexity of life. The democratic imagination begins by accepting what we, as adults, must do. When it comes to children, our first responsibility is moral, not technical. We must begin by accepting the value of human judgement, rooted in a moral sense and tempered by experience. We must do the best we can with what we have, knowing we cannot provide everything and that we cannot control who our children will become.

As we look ahead, we can take comfort in the observation of an old English friend. Although Winston Churchill was speaking about America entering World War II in 1942, his words have relevance to educational reform today:

You can count on Americans to do what is right—after they have tried everything else.

Endnotes

Chapter One—Prelude: Ghosts in the School Yard

1. I will use this form *(1962 Journal)* for references to my unpublished documents, or accounts.

Chapter Two—Preliminaries

1. I am indebted to David Green for pressing on me the importance of "knowing" a school as the basis of inspection.

2. HMI visits in recent years have also included "short" and "survey" visits. Survey visits are to gain a picture of how a particular policy is actually working out in the nation's schools. Examples of survey issues include special education, the implementation of the National Curriculum, and the introduction of information technology. Short visits are intended to keep the inspectorate up-to-date on a greater number of schools than is possible with full visits. They usually involve one inspector. They were much more common in the earlier days, when HMI had responsibility for knowing what was happening in a region of the country, the inspector's "patch."

3. Fred Erickson first made me aware of the importance of the term *provision*. His alerting me to its importance early in my work greatly helped.

Chapter Three—Discovery: What Inspectors Do

1. Winter term is from September through December, Spring term from January through April, and Summer term from May through July. August is holidays.

2. The *Framework* was later published as part of *The Handbook for the Inspection of Schools* (OFSTED, 1992) with few revisions to this version referred to here.

3. When the English use "brilliant," they refer less to potential and more to performance than Americans.

4. Prior to 1992, inspection teams were most often appointed by a senior inspection official. How an inspectorate is structured, including the defined assignments of individual inspectors, is an important factor in selecting the team (for example,

a local inspectorate may have an ongoing link assignment to a school). When creating teams, there is major concern that team members have among them the specialized expertise in the subject areas and/or other areas (children with special needs, information technology) that are defined as the main areas for the inspection. In addition, HMI, and some of the local inspectorates as well, seeks to make assignments that will enhance the growth of individual inspectors.

Chapter Four—Elements

1. Much of my description of inspection is based on the 17 volumes of journals I used for recording interviews, observations, and commentary during the course of the study. I make specific references to them only when there might be confusion about the source of a point or a quotation. The number of the entry designates the relevant volume and page number. Dates are disguised in order to protect confidentiality.

Chapter Five—History

1. Edmonds provides a fascinating account of the history of the use of inspection by the religious societies. The origins of many current issues about inspection and reform can be seen here.

2. See Rapple (1991) for an excellent detailed description of Payment by Results, including implications for American education.

3. The "slimming" of the National Curriculum in 1994 that resulted from the Dearing Report greatly reduced the complexity presented here, including the number of attainment targets.

4. The *Handbook for the Inspection of Schools* was issued by OFSTED in 1992. It includes OFSTED's *The Framework for the Inspection of Schools* which reconstructed inspection to meet the provisions of the Education (Schools) Act of 1992. It also includes OFSTED's "guidance" as to how inspections should be done and other OFSTED procedures. Some amendments were made to both the *Framework* and the *Handbook* in May 1994.

Chapter Six—Tensions

1. Upon reading this section on "soft" inspection an HM inspector responded, "I think St. Paul was right. You can't speak truth in love unless you have a love for the truth."

Chapter Seven—Contributions

1. Brian Wilcox is one of the few researchers working on this question. See Wilcox, 1992, 1989.

2. The initial proposals for private inspection were based on a cost of $540 (£350). It was assumed that private inspectors would work for less and that their

overhead would be lower. Early in privatization the Government sought the participation of existing business accounting firms in inspections. When the accounting firms learned of this low daily rate, they let it be known that they were not interested.

3. While these are sound conclusions from the study, the reader should remember that this study was not designed to measure the impact of inspection, but to understand its practice. Thus, these conclusions must be more tentative than they would be had inspection's impact been the central focus of the study.

Chapter Nine—Particulars

1. I am indebted to Joe McDonald for his eloquent exploration of the particulars of teaching. His book helped to coalesce my thinking on what teaching is.

Chapter Fourteen—Government Accountability: The Need to Be Certain

1. Groak's book contributed more to my thinking and writing than this brief reference suggests. I was deeply impressed by the book's structure and clarity in considering the ideas behind architecture and the construction trades. It informed the structure of this book and it encouraged my belief that what I was attempting might be possible.

Chapter Sixteen—Guidelines

1. I am indebted to Debby Meier for this idea.
2. I am indebted to Ted Sizer for the idea of weighing the importance of "wonderment."

References

Aalto, A. (1955). *Art and Technology*. From "Mystery of Form," an exhibition at the Finnish Institute, London, October 1992.

Arnold, M. (1882). *Reports on Elementary Schools 1852–1882 by Matthew Arnold* (1910 ed.). London: Her Majesty's Stationery Office.

Audit Commission (1989). *Assuring Quality in Education: The Role of Local Education Authority Inspectors and Advisers*. London: Her Majesty's Stationery Office.

Bailey, K. B. (1986). "Plain and nothing fancy"—Her Majesty's inspectors and school needlework in the 1870's. *Journal of Educational Administration and History, 18*(1), 34–45.

Baldwin, J. (1962). *Creative Process*. New York: Ridge Press.

Ball, N. (1963). *Her Majesty's Inspectorate, 1839–1849*. London: Oliver and Boyd.

Betts, R. (1986). "My boys did rather badly"—the Silverlock case 1888. *Journal of Educational Administration and History, 18*(2), 17–23.

Blackie, J. (1970). *Inspecting and the Inspectorate*. London: Routledge and Kegan Paul.

Boothroyd, H. E. (1923). *A History of the Inspectorate: Being a Short Account of the Origin and Development of the Inspecting Service of the Board of Education*. London: Board of Education Inspectors' Association.

Caine, R. N., and Caine, G. (1991). *Making Connections: Teaching and the Human Brain*. Alexandria, VA: Association for Supervision and Curriculum Development.

Curtis, S. J., and Boultwood, M. E. A. (1966). *A Short History of Educational Ideas*. London: University Tutorial Press Ltd.

Department of Education and Science (1982). *Study of HMI in England and Wales. (Rayner Scrutiny)*. London: Her Majesty's Stationery Office.

Edmonds, E. L. (1962). *The School Inspector*. London: Routledge and Kegan Paul.

Erickson, F. (1986). Qualitative methods in research on teaching. In M. C. Wittrock (Ed.), *Handbook of Research in Teaching* (pp. 119–161). New York: Macmillan.

Fitch, J., Sir (1897). *Thomas and Matthew Arnold and Their Influence on English Education*. London: Heinemann.

Gordon, P. (1988). Katharine Bathurst—a controversial woman inspector. *History of Education, 17*(3), 193–207.

Gordon, P. (1989). Watchdogs and missionaries: The first hundred years. In *1839–1989. Public Education in England—150th Anniversary. To Mark the Establishment on 10 April 1839 of the Committee of the Privy Council for Education, the Linear Ancestor of the Department of Education and Science; and the Appointment of the First Two*

Inspectors of Schools on 9 December 1839 (pp. 27–56). London: Department of Education and Science.

Gould, S. J. (1981). *The Mismeasure of Man*. New York: W. W. Norton & Company.

Groak, S. (1992). *The Idea of Building; Thought and Action in the Design and Production of Buildings*. London: E & FN Spon.

Hamilton, D., MacDonald, B., King, C., Jenkins, D., and Parlett, M. (1977). Center for New Schools: Ethnographic techniques in educational research. In *Beyond the Numbers Game: A Reader in Educational Evaluation*, (p. 360). London: McCutchan Publishing Corporation.

Hamilton, N., and Hamilton, O. (1969). *Royal Greenwich*. London: The Greenwich Bookshop.

Haney, W. M., Madaus, G. F., and Lyons, R. (1993). *The Fractured Marketplace for Standardized Testing*. Boston: Kluwer Academic Publishers.

Havel, V. (1992). *Summer Mediations; On Politics, Morality and Civility in a Time of Transition* (Paul Wilson, Trans.). Prague: Odeon.

HMCI (1992). *Framework for the Inspection of Schools: Paper for Consultation* Consultation Number. Her Majesty's Chief Inspector of Schools in England; Department of Education and Science.

HMI (1988). *Inspection and Reporting: Working Notes for HMI*. London: Author.

Kobrin, D. (1992). *In There with the Kids: Teaching in Today's Classrooms*. Boston: Houghton Mifflin Company.

Lawton, D., and Gordon, P. (1987). *HMI*. London: Routledge.

Lightfoot, S. L. (1983). *The Good High School: Portraits of Character and Culture*. New York: Basic Books.

Madaus, G. F. (1991). The effects of important tests on students: Implications for a national examination system. *Kappan, 73*(3), 226–232.

McDonald, J. P. (1992). *Teaching: Making Sense of an Uncertain Craft*. New York and London: Teachers College Press.

Mitchell, R. (1992). *Testing for Learning: How New Approaches to Evaluation Can Improve American Schools*. New York: The Free Press.

National Curriculum Council (1992). *Starting Out with the National Curriculum: An Introduction to the National Curriculum and Religious Education*. London

Norwood Report (1943). *Curriculum and Examinations in Secondary Schools: Report of the Committee of the Secondary School Examinations Council*. London

OFSTED (1992). *The Handbook for the Inspection of Schools*. London: Office for Standards in Education (OFSTED).

Olson, L. (1994, May 4). Cricitical friends. *Education Week*, pp. 20–27.

Parliament (1988). *Education Reform Act 1988* (Reprinted 1989 ed.). London: Her Majesty's Stationery Office.

Parliament (1992). *Education (Schools) Act 1992*. London: Her Majesty's Stationery Office.

Parliament (1993). *Education Act 1993*. London: Her Majesty's Stationery Office.

Rapple, B. A. (1991). Payment by results (1862–1897): Ensuring a good return on governmental expenditure. *The Journal of Educational Thought, 25*(3), 183–201.

Richard Prior of Hexham (1135–1138). *Acts of King Stephen, and the Battle of the Standard* (1886 ed.). London: Her Majesty's Stationery Office.

Rothman, R. (1992, 9 September). New York embraces old idea from Britain in developing new way to evaluate schools. *Education Week*, p1.

Select Committee on Education and Science (1968). *Report from the Select Committee on Education and Science. Session 1967–68. Part I: Her Majesty's Inspectorate (England and Wales)*. London: Her Majesty's Stationery Office.

Sizer, T. R. (1992). *Horace's School: Redesigning the American High School*. Boston: Houghton Mifflin Company.

Sterne, L. (1980). *The Life and Opinions of Tristram Shandy, Gent* (A Norton Critical Edition). New York: W. W. Norton & Company.

Stillman, A., and Grant, M. (1989). *The LEA Advisor: A Changing Role*. Windsor, England: NFER–Nelson.

Taylor, W., Sir (1989). Continuity and change: HMI 1945–1989. In *1839–1989 Public Education in England. 150th Anniversary. To Mark the Establishment on 10 April 1839 of the Committee of the Privy Council for Education, the Linear Ancestor of the Department of Education and Science; and the Appointment of the First Two Inspectors of Schools on 9 December 1839* (pp. 57–80). London: Department of Education and Science.

Wiggins, G. P. (1993). *Assessing Student Performance: Exploring the Purpose and Limits of Testing*. San Francisco: Jossey-Bass.

Wilcox, B. (1989). Inspection and its contribution to practical evaluation. *Educational Research, 31*(3), 163–175.

Wilcox, B. (1992). *Time-Constrained Evaluation: A Practical Approach for LEAs and Schools*. London: Routledge.

Wilcox, B., Gray, J., and Tranmer, M. (1993). LEA frameworks for the assessment of schools: An interrupted picture. *Educational Research, 35*(3), 211–221.

Wilson, T. A. (1980). *The DTA Final Report. Vision, Action and Commitment: Some Limits in Our Assumptions About Improving Schools. Documentation and Technical Assistance in Urban Schools*. Chicago: Center for New Schools.

Wilson, T. A. (1995). Notes on the American fascination with the English tradition of school inspection. *Cambridge Journal of Education, 25*(1), 89–96.

Wood, G. S. (1991). *The Radicalism of the American Revolution*. New York: Vintage Books.

■ ■ ■ ■ ■ About the Author

Tom Wilson grew up in Rhode Island. He has lived in Richmond, Indiana; Daram, Philippines; Washington, DC; Cambridge, Massachusetts; Chicago, Illinois; and London, England. He graduated from John Howland Elementary School, Henry Barnard Junior High School, Classical High School, all in Rhode Island, and Earlham College, Howard University, and Harvard University. He has worked in schools for over thirty years. The dilemma of how we know and judge schools has been his central concern. He was a teacher in the Cardozo Pilot Project in Urban Education in Washington, DC; a founder of the Center for New Schools in Chicago, and a staff member of the Coalition of Essential Schools in Providence. He is now a Research Fellow in the Education Department at Brown University, working on a book about the American way of knowing and judging schools.